DATE DUE

BRODART, CO.   Cat. No. 23-221

The Power of Convergence

More Praise for *The Power of Convergence....*

"In the public sector, accomplishing the mission is paramount. The strategic practices in this book, if used within government, will not only significantly help achieve that goal, but also make it more effective and efficient."
—David K. (Bob) Edmonds
Brigadier General, USAF (Retired) and Former White House Fellow

"This book illustrates how to build a blueprint for business and technology management. Filled with vivid case studies, it is a must-read for those seeking to secure a position in today's competitive landscape."
—Maria P. Sendra, Esq.
Partner/Chair, Southern California Corporate & Securities Practice
Baker & McKenzie LLP

"The analytical approach in this book is very similar to the discipline applied by investment managers to portfolio management. It should be adopted by all enterprise initiatives that rely on technology for managing a business."
—Kamal Bhatia
Managing Director, Head of Alternative Investment Products
TIAA CREF Asset Management

"This book examines the extent that one can focus on business requirements and then follow through with the appropriate application of technology, leading to overall advantageous financial performance."
—Gideon Gartner
Founder of Gartner, Giga, and Soundview

"It's an age-old, and perennially puzzling problem: Why don't we get as much value as we should when we use technology in business contexts? Faisal Hoque and his coauthors suggest fresh answers. In the early years of this new century, this question and the search for its answers have never been more important."
—Robert D. Austin
CEO, CBS-SIMI Executive and Professor
Management of Creativity and Innovation, Copenhagen
Business School

The Power of Convergence

Linking Business Strategies and Technology
Decisions to Create Sustainable Success

Faisal Hoque
with Lawrence M. Walsh, Diana L. Mirakaj, and
Jeffrey Bruckner

Research Contribution: Colleagues of BTM Corporation,
Members of the BTM Institute

American Management Association
New York · Atlanta · Brussels · Chicago · Mexico City · San Francisco
Shanghai · Tokyo · Toronto · Washington, D.C.

This publication is designed to provide accurate and authoritative information in regard to the subject matter covered. It is sold with the understanding that the publisher is not engaged in rendering legal, accounting, or other professional service. If legal advice or other expert assistance is required, the services of a competent professional person should be sought.

Hoque, Faisal.
    The power of convergence : linking business strategies and technology decisions to create sustainable success / Faisal Hoque with Lawrence M. Walsh, Diana L. Mirakaj, and Jeffrey Bruckner.
        p.   cm.
    Includes bibliographical references and index.
    ISBN-13: 978-0-8144-1695-2
    ISBN-10: 0-8144-1695-0
    1. Technological innovation—Management.   2. Strategic planning.   3. Success in business.   I. Title.
    HD45.H66   2011

                                                                658.4'01—dc22

2010043519

About AMA
American Management Association (www.amanet.org) is a world leader in talent development, advancing the skills of individuals to drive business success. Our mission is to support the goals of individuals and organizations through a complete range of products and services, including classroom and virtual seminars, webcasts, webinars, podcasts, conferences, corporate and government solutions, business books and research. AMA's approach to improving performance combines experiential learning—learning through doing—with opportunities for ongoing professional growth at every step of one's career journey.

Printing number

This book is dedicated to *you,* the reader:
Inspired, patient, resourceful—ready to take charge,
adapt, and thrive.

Contents

Acknowledgments

WHEN WRITING A BOOK that is the result of a decade-long personal and professional journey—one that is made possible by years of working with colleagues, customers, partners, academics, and industry experts from around the globe—it is difficult to convey the gratitude I have for all those who have played such an integral role along the way in just a few paragraphs.

First and foremost, I offer heartfelt thanks to my colleagues and investors in BTM Corporation. It is through their hard work, support, and steadfast belief that the creation and application of Business Technology Management (BTM) has been made possible. Next, I thank the customers and partners who apply BTM for driving us to continuously improve upon the pragmatic approaches, solutions, and products we provide to solve the complex problems they face, which result in their sustainable success. I am particularly grateful to members and contributors of the BTM Institute for the ongoing value they provide by drawing from their own unique experiences and perspectives to enrich our research initiatives and knowledge programs.

Of course, this book would not be a reality without the support and dedication of my co-contributors—Lawrence M. Walsh, Diana L. Mirakaj, and Jeffrey Bruckner; acquiring editor Bob Nirkind, associate editor Michael Sivilli, and copyeditor Debbie Posner; my illustrator—Michelle Passaro; and my literary agent—John Willig.

And last, but certainly not least, I am forever indebted to my wife, son, family, and friends for the strength, encouragement, and inspiration they provide me to follow a path that has often required endurance, sacrifice, and patience, in pursuit of a journey that continues to provide adventure, continued learning, and satisfaction.

Faisal Hoque, November 2010

Introduction

T HE POWER OF CONVERGENCE is a call to arms; a mandate for enterprises to place critical importance on a set of fundamental principles, eschewing the application of technology to business for technology's sake and putting business strategy, objectives, and processes at the forefront of enterprise enablement. This in turn will make them more nimble, more agile, and better able to build differentiated, innovative, and adaptable processes that expand their reach and grow revenue even in the most challenging markets and conditions.

Technology is a part of everything we do. We tend to think of "technology" as something new and digital—state of the art. The reality is that technology has been a part of everything we have produced since the first humans turned stone into tools. Technology erected the Egyptian pyramids. Technology built the Roman aqueducts. Technology invented Chinese paper and gunpowder. Technology opened the seas to the Spanish and Portuguese for global exploration and trade. Technology gave spark to the industrial revolution in the British Midlands. Technology put the wind under the Wright brothers' wings. Technology blasted Neil Armstrong onto the moon. And technology is the engine powering the information age.

As the previous examples illustrate, technology has played a critical role throughout history. Achieving success, however, has never been about the technology itself; it has always been about the business. The result. The accomplishment of a goal set forth by a plan. Technology is only as good as the imagination of business leaders who are focused on customers, markets, business models, threats, and opportunities, and who can make technology do what they need it to do. Anyone can buy technology, but no one can go online to order a strategy or new business model.

The point of technology is not to serve technology itself, but to serve the products and processes that create benefits to the user and enterprise employing it. Technology is the means to an end, not a means to another means. Contemporary enterprises are huge producers and consumers of technology. Unfortunately, many enterprises fall short on truly capitalizing on technology because they focus too much of their resolve on the technology itself and not enough on their business objectives. Technologists (the crafter of tools) are famous for being enamored with their technology. They build systems that provide functionality, but build them from their perspective rather than that of the business, department, or user. The result is an endless list of underperforming or failed technology implementations that rob enterprises of scarce financial, human, and opportunity resources.

Failure to fully realize the potential of technology in business is not solely the fault of technologists. Their business management counterparts are equally culpable. While busily drafting plans for their next venture, product launch, or service offering, they will often turn to their technologist counterparts with vague concepts for systems to facilitate the execution of their strategies. Between the two sides is a vacuum of absent management structure, performance indicators, communication, and governance that prevents them from truly finding common ground in the development, adoption, implementation, and optimization of technology that will produce a true business benefit in the form of optimized processes, cost reduction, and new revenue opportunity.

Why does this disconnect exist? It's mostly due to assumption. Business managers, ignorant of technology functions and capabilities, *assume* technologists will appreciate their needs and fulfill their desires with systems that produce the optimal intent. Technologists, on the other hand, rarely fully appreciate the business needs of the enterprise, department, or individual. They develop systems and tools that may address the stated need, and will add—or omit—functionality that they *assume* the end user will—or won't—need or want. In other words, business managers assume that they're communicating when they're actually just dictating; technologists assume that business managers will appreciate their technology when they are often just delivering greater complexity.

This was essentially the state of technology in the enterprise more than a decade ago when I was working on my first book, *e-Enterprise: Business Models, Architecture, and Components*.[1] One of the book's fundamental arguments was that technology is meaningless if you don't know how to manage it and will certainly never produce a true return on investment if it is simply used for its intrinsic features. This realization came from working for large corporations, as well as from being an entrepreneur and having these corporations as customers. Guidance on the true value of technology in the enterprise was a genuine and unmet need, one I wanted to address. I could never have imagined how far that desire would lead. It has become a decade-long crusade.

In company after company I have witnessed the haphazard manner in which people managed technology, particularly technology spending, needlessly putting their entire organization at risk. The business principles they applied in other areas of operations were not applied to technology. They would not think of building a new plant without understanding exactly how it would benefit the business. But in many firms technology was bought and deployed on a hope and a prayer. This was the era of dot.com exuberance, of course, and there was a madness loose in the land, but I had seen this problem in earlier, quieter years as well.

The disconnect between business management and technology management is not lost on enterprises. Academics, book authors, and magazine writers frequently opine on the notion of technologists getting "a seat at the table" to influence management decisions and "learning to speak business" with their management counterparts. Over the last decade, management advocates have presented portfolio management, return on technology investment methodologies, and service-level performance as a means for bridging the gap between technology and business management. But no one has looked at the problem holistically—that is, with the understanding that whole entities—enterprises in this discussion—have an existence other than the mere sum of their parts. The term has become popular in speech, but is less frequently found in practice.

The term "alignment," too, has grown in prominence, but not many firms know how to realign their operations for optimal technology performance. Even the emergence of stringent government and industry governance and regulatory requirements has done little to remedy the disconnect. I am convinced that business and technology executives, respectively, still view each other across a chasm, even if they are now sitting at the same table. They can only succeed if, and only if, they take off their business or technology hats and work together holistically to build business.

To move beyond technology and find real business value, a new framework with concrete practices and procedures to turn the amorphous concept of alignment into reality was needed. In computing terms, a completely new set of instructions and a reboot.

In 1999, I founded BTM Corporation with the mission of researching and developing a set of unified management capabilities, value creation methods, financial indicators, operational blueprints, and software applications that create a common language for business and technology management. We called it the Business Technology Management (BTM) Framework. After several years we took on a limited number of customers to test it in practice—if it had no commercial value, then it would be nothing more than a nice theory. As it turned out, executives around the world wrestling with real-world problems greeted the Framework with enthusiasm.

The Framework was a fundamentally different proposition for them. Every management team has pretty much been creating its own approach and practices. Sometimes they worked, and sometimes they didn't. Now, with the BTM Framework, the haphazard art of managing business and technology together had a chance to become a science that would replace the grossly ineffective trial-and-error methodology that has created inefficiency and failure. The Framework aims to unify decision making from the boardroom to the project team. It provides a structured approach to such decisions that enables enterprises to align, synchronize, and converge technology and business management, thus ensuring better execution, risk control, and profitability.

Three years after the formation of BTM Corporation we published a book on Business Technology Management, *The Alignment Effect,*[2] which began to attract attention among university professors who were teaching the management science. Today more than a dozen universities use the book in their courses. Enthusiasm among professors and industry practitioners was strong enough that in 2003 we created the BTM Institute, a research think tank that could pull together the work of many academics, provide feedback from executive practitioners, and develop a research agenda to create a standard for Business Technology Management—much like Carnegie Mellon's Capability Maturity Model

(CMM), which is a standard for software engineering and process improvement.

Our book *Winning the 3-Legged Race* was the BTM Institute's first major publication in 2005, and would be the next step in gathering what we know about managing business and technology and pointing to areas for future research.[3] The book also set the research agenda for the science of Business Technology Management (BTM).

Based on academic research, *Winning the 3-Legged Race* provided explicit advice for practitioners on the job and perspectives from executives around the world, and it introduced the concept of *convergence*, the true melding of business and technology management as a unified strategic and decision-making structure. Convergence creates an environment where technology helps shape (rather than simply enable) strategic choices, leading enterprises to synchronize (rather than simply align) their business and technology decision making. In the best-managed modern enterprises, technology will converge with the business as completely as financial and sales management have done for decades.

In 2007 we created the Business Technology Convergence Index and released a groundbreaking research report by the same name,[4] which indicated that companies that converge business and technology reap greater financial benefit than those with a less mature level of convergence. The study examined Global 2000 corporations such as UPS, Wal-Mart, and Starwood across fifty industries and showed that working in the same environment as their direct competitors, enterprises with a more nearly converged business and technology management exhibited superior revenue growth and net margins relative to their industry groups. This research suggests that enterprise executives who focus on converging the business and technology management disciplines of their companies attain far more financial success than those who continue to treat them as silos. There is demonstrable economic value in advancing business technology management maturity, and the payoff is greatest for those enterprises that are approaching convergence.

Following the success of the Convergence Index, we continued examining organizations in the private and public sectors, as well as nonprofits, regarding the effect of converged management approach. We also followed through with several research output in the areas of business agility, sustained innovation, and operational efficiency. In 2009, we released a second study, the *Business Technology Convergence Index II*.[5] In 2010, we released three additional financial indexes on Business Agility, Sustained Innovation, and Operational Excellence. Each of these research projects and reports continued to demonstrate the discreet and cumulative benefits of converging business and technology management in a unified, strategic framework.

The Power of Convergence is the culmination of more than a decade of study, observation, research, and testing. It showcases the financial benefits of managing business and technology together and is a foundation for becoming a better business and technology leader, able to drive business agility, sustained innovation, and operational excellence.

This book is organized in four parts. In Part I, Business Technology Convergence, we focus on the underpinnings of Business Technology Management and convergence. In Part II, Convergence in Practice, we turn to what convergence means in three different types of organizations: large enterprises, the public sector, and small businesses. In Part III, The Impact of Convergence, we discuss the application of the core tenets that make up the convergence management approach. And finally, in Part IV, Let the Journey Begin, we explain how individuals can become better business technology leaders and convergence agents. Convergence is a journey; therefore the book is designed to take you through the process of achieving convergence in logical steps. Before jumping into the meat of the material, let's preview the chapters.

In **Chapter 1**, we explore the disconnect between business and technology that is the inhibiting factor against smart business innovation. For some time now, many companies have blindly allocated money to technology with little concern as to whether it was put to good use—or whether it supported the objectives they were trying to meet in the first place. We look at failed technology initiatives, which provide evidence that companies have faced this problem since they launched their first technology project. These examples reveal an unequivocal truth: To understand, communicate, and plan how they should utilize technology in an organization, companies need to converge the management of business and technology.

Value should be at the heart of every business initiative and technology implementation. In **Chapter 2**, we turn our attention to achieving value through convergence. This kind of convergence results in a modification of structures that establishes a set of enterprise-wide behaviors, norms, and practices. This chapter shows enterprise leaders how to build a management playbook and a collaborative decision-making process that is supported by a maturity advancement plan.

Chapter 3 focuses on the role of business/technology convergence and its effect on financial performance. We show what BTM's Convergence Index has consistently revealed: When enterprises place the business strategy and model ahead of technology and use technology as a supporting piece of the strategy, the enterprise will continue to grow faster and with healthier profit margins than competitors using the same technology.

Chapter 4 offers real-world examples and explanations as to how large enterprises are overcoming business challenges and creating new opportunities by converging business and technology and creating repeatable collaborative management practices. Organizations that effectively manage through this environment of rapid and continuous change can create serious competitive advantage, while those that cannot are in danger of significant underperformance.

In **Chapter 5**, we turn to the public sector, which historically suffers from mismanagement that's only concealed by scale and an endless supply of funding through tax dollars. We examine how the BTM Framework can help government agencies use the concept of convergence to overcome their mission challenges and create new opportunities by converging mission and technology. With a host of concerns ranging from terrorism and war to the economy and health care, our ultimate success or failure in those efforts will largely depend upon how well officials manage their mission and technology together.

In **Chapter 6**, we explore how the majority of small and midsized businesses consider technology as their key to growth, and how convergence can accelerate their journey to sustained success. The takeaway for anyone in a small organization is that if you can identify a genuine need, the technology to meet it already exists today. The heavy lifting comes in creating an appropriate business model. And in order to do that, you have to see things differently.

Chapter 7 introduces the concept of "The Transformation Triangle." It's a construct for achieving sustained and persistent agility, innovation, and efficiency as a means to achieving greater success. A transformed company develops the necessary management capabilities to create a comprehensive picture of itself as it is today and where it wants to be in the near—and distant—future, and creates the structures, processes, and information necessary to achieve it. This chapter, which speaks of BTM's concepts of Business Agility, Sustained Innovation, and Operational Excellence, provides the foundation for the three chapters that follow.

Chapter 8 defines and explores Business Agility, the potential financial value that can be derived from it, and the steps that must be taken to create agile organizations from business/technology convergence. Business leaders often use the word "agility" to describe their business plans and strategic initiatives, but it's often little more than just a word. To be agile, firms must serve ever-smaller niche markets and individual customers without the high cost of customization. Being agile requires the ability to sense-and-respond, and those capabilities are shaped by designing and managing business processes and technology enablers together.

In **Chapter 9**, we examine Sustained Innovation, the process of continual reinvention to create new markets and capitalize on new opportunities. Innovation only becomes effective when it's part of a process: A leader recognizes a need, assembles an organization and designs processes to meet it, and then applies business technology to make it work. It's not the invention of a new technology that matters so much as it is its application—understanding its role when developing a strategy or designing an organization or its processes.

In **Chapter 10**, we discuss the critical factors for Operational Excellence and the potential financial value driven from it, as well as the steps that must be taken to create effective organizations from business technology convergence. Creating this ability begins with establishing effective processes to provide feedback into the creation and formal expression of an enterprise's business strategy. A key element of this feedback is the clear articulation of the expected role that enabling technologies will play in achieving each business objective. The chapter discusses practical ways to decide when to invest, how to channel investments toward appropriate problem solving, and how to ensure that this leads to value.

Finally, in **Chapter 11**, we pull it all together to show the need for individual action to drive convergence in the modern enterprise. Doing nothing is not an option. The changes sweeping over corporations and other organizations will not stop because they make us uncomfortable. The only way to win is to get out ahead of these changes, to manage them in your favor. You can't do that today unless your business and technology are united as one. This chapter looks at the BTM Framework from the perspective of "Someone has to make convergence happen. Will it be you?"

We believe convergence in business and technology management is the answer for more than just greater returns and productivity. We believe it is the way to ensure that enterprises and economies remain viable and vibrant. Through convergence, organizations shed their inefficiencies in favor of collaboration, shared goals, and focused outcomes. Convergence is the antithesis to internal rivalries, segmented initiatives, and fragmented strategies. We are convinced that the future economy will be dominated by fully converged enterprises that will capitalize on the mistakes and inefficiencies of their nonconverged competitors. Our ultimate question to you is: Which camp will you fall in?

''The mind is everything. What you think you become.''

—BUDDHA

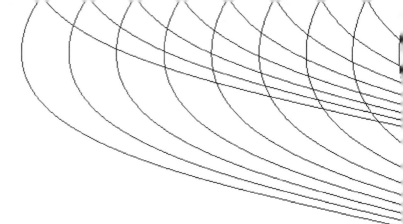

PART I

Business/Technology Convergence

CHAPTER 1

The Business/ Technology Disconnect

Do YOU REMEMBER the game *Battleship*? Two players face off on opposing game boards on which they have randomly arranged five model warships of varying sizes. The object of the game is to "seek and destroy" all of the opponent's warships. The players, unable to see the other's board, call out coordinates in an attempt to sink each of their opponent's pieces. Victory—or success—comes when all of the opponent's pieces are sunk.

Fun is one way to describe the game. Other possible descriptions are inefficient, random, and chaotic. Imagine for a moment a naval commander using the same technique in combat, randomly firing shells over the horizon in the hopes of hitting an enemy ship. Victory is possible, if not inevitable, if the battleship captain fires a sufficient number of rounds to blanket enough of the ocean surface that the enemy has no chance of survival (and assuming, of course, that the enemy isn't firing back). But at what price would victory come? A simple answer is that the cost and potential loss would be so enormous that no reasonable person would engage in such randomness.

Yet, business executives play *Battleship* all the time. They throw millions of dollars at new business models, technologies, infrastructure, and business development without clearly defining their targets, properly allocating resources, and managing execution. This is not a new phenomenon. For many years, many companies have simply thrown money at business technology investments with little apparent concern for whether it was put to good use or even met the objectives they were attempting to meet in the first place. Imagine that each of the coordinates you called in a game of *Battleship* cost a million dollars. Do you think you and your opponent would be more judicious in the shots you took?

Leaving business and technology investments to chance, assumptions, and randomness costs organizations billions of dollars annually. In worst cases, this chaotic approach to technology investment fatally wounds projects, products, and entire businesses. A look at failed business and technology initiatives provides evidence that companies have faced this problem since they launched their first technology project. As the scope and risk of these initiatives increased, so too did the effect of the disconnect. By the time the Internet burst onto the scene, the scale of technology projects had increased to the point that recognizing the correlation between business/technology convergence and the success of innovation (or lack thereof) became unavoidable.

This forces us to ask why we aren't getting real business value out of technology. Most organizations fail to capitalize on the technologies they already have, and many more are poised to meet this same fate with the next big technology fad. Whether it's wireless, Web services, or the latest and greatest in nanotechnology, companies will never get value— real or perceived—without first solving the business/technology disconnect. One thing is sure: organizations that continue to repeat the mistakes of the past will never reap the rewards of the future.

The Business/Technology Disconnect Phenomenon

A business/technology disconnect can manifest itself in any organization. By examining some celebrated business and technology failures in aviation, computer software, heavy manufacturing, and government, we'll see how these examples reveal an unequivocal truth: to understand, communicate, and plan how organizations should utilize technology, they first need to converge the management of business and technology.

Airbus Grounded by Disconnects

The blue yonder of commercial air travel—and its supporting ground network of airports—has been getting crowded for the better part of the last three decades. In the early 1990s, European aviation giant Airbus recognized the growing congestion and came up with what it thought was a logical solution—a new super jetliner.[1] Initially, Airbus's goal was simply to break American rival Boeing's dominance in large jets. As time passed, the project morphed to one in which Airbus would single-hand-edly transform the aviation industry by creating the A380, a double-decker, four-engine jumbo jet that had nearly twice the floor space and one-third more seating capacity than the famed Boeing 747. Its size (up to 850 passengers) and range (8,200 nautical miles) would enable air-lines to transport more people over longer distances than with any other aircraft in the world.

It was a tremendously attractive idea, but one that proved difficult to develop and execute, especially in light of the nature of this particular manufacturer. Airbus is a unique consortium backed by the govern-ments of France, Germany, The Netherlands, Spain, and the United Kingdom. For this reason, its manufacturing and operations are distrib-uted across Europe. The wings are made in Wales. The belly and tail are constructed in Spain. Some sections and mechanics are fabricated in China. All the components—from fuselages to tray tables—are shipped by land and water to the assembly facility in Toulouse, France.

The Airbus A380 has suffered numerous setbacks and problems over its two decades of development. Keeping these design and manufac-turing centers in sync was exceedingly challenging, and a lack of man-agement coordination on technology standards and investments nearly scuttled the project. But arguably the most significant foul-up was the errant use of computer-aided design (CAD) software. In October 2006 Airbus was forced to concede that the A380 production would slip off schedule because of a software snafu. There was nothing wrong with the advance aircraft's avionics package. The problem was in the design software used to create the engineering plans for the plane. Airbus stan-dardized on Dassault Systems' Catia computer-aided design software. CAD applications and their complementary software Product Lifecycle Management (PLM) vastly simplify the engineering and design process by automating and digitizing mechanical drawings. CAD makes designs easier to create and manipulate. PLM maintains the bill of materials. The two, when working in concert, ensure engineers and manufacturers have the right directions and list of materials for smooth production.

CAD and PLM software was an absolute necessity for the A380 pro-duction process. These software packages would allow local engineers to view and modify their respective piece of the giant puzzle and keep the overall design consistent. At least that's what they thought. However, assembly line workers in Toulouse, France, discovered to their horror how wrong their assumptions were when components didn't fit together. What happened was that the wiring bundles that delivered power for everything in the plane from lights to in-seat entertainment systems to galley appliances didn't fit as intended from the rear fuselage to the forward nose cone.

The design discrepancy resulted from two design centers using different versions of Dassault's Catia. Engineers at the French assembly facility used version 5 of the CAD software. Unfortunately, the German manufacturing facility that built the rear fuselage used the older version 4, and the two versions calculated measurements and scales differently. The result was the design discrepancy. At first, assembly line workers tried to run the 300 miles of wires by hand through the fuselage. But try as they might, they couldn't easily rectify the error. Airbus was forced to redesign the wiring system at a cost of billions of dollars, time on the production schedule, and penalties due to airlines for late delivery.

The engineering and mechanical problems were eventually resolved, and as of 2010, the first A380 were being delivered to airlines. But Airbus suffered a tremendous loss because its business management teams and technical design centers did not align their objectives and converge their tasking to not just guard against technical disruptions but ensure all departments were working in unison to meet the company's prescribed objectives.

Symantec's Failed Systems Upgrade

By the early 2000s, Symantec was the undisputed king of the security software world. It was twice as large as its next closest rival, McAfee, and its millions of users that nearly automatically renewed their annual subscriptions provided Symantec with the revenue and profits to invest in new lines of business. But business analysts were seeing the company approach a ceiling where revenue would no longer grow at an appreciable rate. In 2004, then–chief executive John Thompson embarked on what was seen as an extreme deviation from Symantec's success path— the acquisition of Veritas, a rising star in the storage software management market. The blockbuster $13.5 billion deal that brought the two companies together was (and remains, as of this writing) the largest IT merger ever.

Industry and technology analysts saw tremendous logic in the

Symantec-Veritas marriage. By integrating the two technology domains, Symantec would provide enterprises with the tools for managing and securing the vast amounts of data they produced and stored. The perceived benefits ranged from greater operational efficiency and improved regulatory compliance to a lower total cost of ownership related to the acquisition and ongoing operation of disparate systems used for managing data storage and security.

Symantec and Veritas couldn't have been any more different, however, the disparity in culture and operations firmly rooted in their legacies. Symantec was born as a consumer software company that grew into the small business and—eventually—enterprise market. In fact, much of Symantec's $2.5 billion in security software revenue at the time came from consumer and small business sales and subscription renewals. Veritas, on the other hand, was part of a new breed of software companies that was created to meet the data storage management needs of large enterprise. Consequently, the management systems—commonly known as enterprise resource planning (ERP)—were designed very differently, making for an impossible management of the combined companies' 250,000-plus products. The first step in bringing these two houses together was Project Oasis, an IT project undertaken in 2005 to upgrade and consolidate Symantec's ERP system.[2]

Symantec worked with Oracle in designing and implementing its new software system that was intended to make ordering simpler for both Symantec's legacy reseller partners and its newly acquired army of enterprise integrators that supported Veritas. Symantec didn't undertake the project blindly; under the direction of the chief information officer, the company consulted with hundreds of partners that would use the ERP system to determine their needs and desires. Ideas gathered quickly brought form to the system that would provide Symantec reseller partners with greater transparency into their orders and accounts, as well as provide Symantec with deeper visibility into its pipeline and partner ecosystem of 40,000 resellers and integrators. And, for the first time, the ERP system would reconcile and consolidate the numerous account entries; no longer would "ABC Corp.," "ABC," and "ABC Corp. of Wisconsin" have different lines within the system—a huge advantage for companies trying to streamline account activity management.

On paper, Project Oasis would produce the most sophisticated ERP system in the IT industry. The features and accessibility made it possible for new actors in the partner organization to use the system to gain insights into product availability, ordering activity, and account status.

This was a chief desire expressed by the partners, and precisely where the project began to unravel.

When the system went live in November 2006, Symantec encountered the usual hiccups inherent in any new software deployment. Despite numerous communications to partners about the system's launch and instructions on how to use the new ordering system, partners were ill-prepared for the changes. The hiccups quickly escalated to a full-blown crisis as users couldn't figure out how to navigate the new system and the system failed to correctly process orders. Making matters worse, the company's support network of help desk and technology call centers was overwhelmed by cries for assistance.

Symantec would eventually discover that a confluence of errors and poor management assumptions led to the Project Oasis crisis. The ERP was designed precisely to the desires and needs of the legacy users of both the Symantec and Veritas ordering systems, and included the ability to add more users. What Symantec failed to account for was the group of new users that had never used its or Veritas' old ERP system. They had a different set of information needs, operating requirements, and accessibility desires. Not only did Symantec not know what these users' needs were, they had no knowledge that they existed. Consequently, they didn't have any mechanisms for communicating, training, or collecting feedback from this group of stakeholders, who as it turns out were highly influential in their organizations and among their downstream customers.

ERP projects are rarely easy or go over as planned, but Symantec's Project Oasis has gone down as one of the worst-ever software implementations. The failure of Symantec's management to recognize the true need of aligning resources to meet the requirements of its sales teams and partners cost the company dearly. As a result, it took more than a year for Symantec to remediate the ERP problems, at a cost of tens of millions of dollars. Further, the initial problems threw off its revenues for at least two quarters. And the botched project delayed Symantec's full integration of Veritas into its systems framework by more than two years.

In retrospect, Project Oasis met all of its technical objectives, while failing to meet the business needs. A lack of transparency into the true stakeholders in the go-to-market logistics and value chain nearly derailed Symantec's grand future strategic design.

Covisint: An Idea in Search of a Mission

Nearly a decade before General Motors and Chrysler took tens of billions of dollars in government bailouts, they and other automakers sought ways to streamline their supply chains and lower product acquisition costs. Just as eBay and Priceline.com had revolutionized the concept of commerce by allowing consumers to bid on goods and services, the big automotive manufacturers sought to create an online marketplace where buyers and sellers of materials and parts used in vehicles would trade on variable commodity pricing. The vision was manifested in a new software company called Covisint.

Covisint—founded with tens of millions of dollars supplied by Ford, General Motors, DaimlerChrysler, Nissan, and Renault—was intended to create the world's largest online marketplace of parts and materials and supply chain management tools, as well as to stimulate collaboration between suppliers of raw materials and parts and their buyers—namely the vehicle manufacturers. The platform was based upon the notion of creating secure lines of communication between users that had a single account identification and password (or access credentials).

In theory, Covisint was precisely what the automotive industry needed. Even a decade before the great recession of 2008–09, the industry was reeling from a series of poor choices, bad products, and fierce competition. The American automakers—Ford, General Motors, and the Chrysler division of DaimlerChrysler—were losing billions of dollars annually as market share shifted to foreign manufacturers, who held the advantage of producing higher quality cars at a lower price. Foreign competitors were free of the burdens of legacy expenses such as funding retiree health benefits. The American carmakers were willing to try anything that promised to either contain or reduce their costs.

But Covisint, as it turns out, was just an idea that was way ahead of its time. Within four years of its founding, the company collapsed under its own weight. Its seed money was all but gone. Its systems were incomplete and difficult to use. And the amount of business—and cost savings—generated through its online platform were but a fraction of what was needed to make a difference in the multitrillion-dollar automotive industry and supply chain. Confidence in the company's ability to execute on its products and mission were compromised.

What went wrong with Covisint? Industry analysts and intended users say that Covisint never had a truly defined mission and that the only value seen in the venture was the commoditization of component pricing to the vehicle original equipment manufacturers (OEMs). When you think about it, the supporting OEMs—Ford, General Motors, and DaimlerChrysler—were all in crisis. Other manufacturers—Toyota, Honda, Volkswagen, Hyundai—which were in strong revenue and business positions, stayed clear of the joint venture. Suppliers who were supposed to flock to the online exchange saw it as nothing more than a mechanism for shaving value from their products and driving down their prices and—subsequently—their profitability. "Nobody liked the auctions. It's a crappy way of doing business," commented Peter Karmanos, chief executive of computer software company Compuware, which eventually bought Covisint and incorporated the useful bits of collaboration and security technology into its broader portfolio.[3]

Covisint's founders made the mistake of assuming that all suppliers and buyers wanted to use a single system. In fact, companies that participated in the Covisint network were put at a competitive disadvantage to those operating outside the system; the transparency in the auctions and exchanges gave competitors tremendous insights into their rivals' operations and allowed them to cut out-of-band deals with OEMs. This inconsistency left many supply companies confused about their future relationships with the OEM; they didn't know if the Covisint exchange would replace their legacy supply chain and product acquisition systems, so many were reluctant to fully adopt it. In fact, while Covisint was struggling to meet the supply chain needs of its patron founders, Ford was sinking hundreds of millions of dollars into a competing, internal supply chain management platform developed under the code name "Everest." Everest was canceled shortly after Covisint met its final demise, costing Ford $400 million.[4, 5] Fault for Covisint's failure doesn't rest purely on its management's shoulders. Bickering among the automakers made fulfillment of its mission nearly impossible. Each patron had its own idea of how the system was supposed to work and of the value it was to derive. The only consistency in Covisint's future, from the automakers' perspective, was building up to an IPO so they could not just reap the benefits of the collaborative platform but make money on the venture. In the end, Compuware bought Covisint in 2004 for an undisclosed amount—but assumed to be a massive loss compared to the investment made by the automakers. Some industry analysts estimate that in total, Ford, General Motors, and DaimlerChrysler sank more than $100 million into Covisint. Fast-forward and ask where Covisint is today and you'll find Compuware executing on its vision for the collaboration platform. When the acquisition happened, Compuware's CEO estimated that the Covisint technologies could generate up to $100 million annually if applied correctly and expanded into new markets. Compuware has leveraged the technology developed by Covisint to create secure collaboration platforms that are valued by the health care, financial services, and government sectors. It just goes to show how understanding market needs, focus on a business model, and tight development of technology lead to success.[6]

FBI Records Systems Becomes a Federal Disaster

Much to the chagrin of federal authorities and Congress, the Federal Bureau of Investigation announced in 2006 it was suspending deployments of Phase III and IV of Sentinel, a $305 million virtual case file management system intended to replace the agency's obsolete Automated Case Support (ACS) system. When completed, Sentinel will give agents in the field access to a repository of information, correlate data into actionable intelligence, and allow collaboration with peers. But problems with the software have forced a delay in the project that started in 2005; the system won't be fully operational until at least 2011—nearly a year past its original completion deadline.[7]

This isn't the first or the most celebrated failure by the FBI to modernize its information systems. Sentinel is actually a replacement project to the failed Virtual Case File (VCF) project that fell apart in 2004 after three years of work and more than $105 million in taxpayer expenditures. VCF is one of the best examples of how technology projects run awry when there's improper setting of goals and expectations, and a failure of project managers to govern development.

VCF was launched after the September 11, 2001, terrorist attacks that felled the World Trade Center in the worst terrorist or military attack on U.S. soil. Postmortem analyses found that plenty of clues existed that could have warned intelligence and law enforcement agencies to the pending threat. But the computer and information systems of the time were incapable of connecting the dots. VCF was intended to provide FBI agents with the ability to collect intelligence, correlate scraps of data, collaborate with other agents and law enforcement agencies, and ensure that there were no gaps in enforcement.

The task for building the system fell to Science Applications International Corp. (SAIC), one of the largest federal contractors. In 2004,

SAIC set about the task of designing the system and building the custom applications that would require more than 730,000 lines of computer code. What the FBI wanted was a system through which agents could take and act upon information in the field; would have the ability to search, mark, and annotate files for future reference; be able to sort data for easier correlation; and that would be network based to enable disparate users to access files and intelligence.

SAIC continued delivering product and project updates, and the FBI continued paying the bills. As far as anyone was concerned, the project was proceeding well and would be ready for deployment on schedule. That schedule was disrupted in 2003 when the FBI's chief technology officer, Zahmai Azmi, asked about error rates. Software problem reports, as they were called, were mounting in the hundreds of action items, and many of the basic systems had yet to be analyzed. Azmi raised red flags that the project was in trouble and within a year, FBI Director Robert Mueller III canceled the entire program.

VCF's failure set off a firestorm in the FBI and in Washington, D.C., power circles. Congress wanted answers as to why the FBI didn't have the computer system required to combat modern crimes and counter terrorist threats. Budget hawks wanted to know why tens of millions of taxpayer dollars were squandered without question in the pursuit of a botched IT project that never had any hopes of succeeding. And everyone wanted to know what needed to be done to prevent such a catastrophic failure from happening again. In this celebrated IT failure, both the FBI and SAIC shared the blame, auditors and investigators concluded.

The FBI's fault in this project boils down to three simple elements: it didn't know what it was asking for, it didn't have the in-house expertise to design the scope of the project, and it didn't have the means to properly oversee the project's development. In short, the FBI lacked the human expertise for a project of such complexity.

Over the last decade, the FBI and other federal agencies have suffered from a "brain drain," as veteran civil servants depart the government for lucrative private sector jobs. This exodus has made government agencies more dependent on contractors such as SAIC to develop and implement systems. While the FBI knew it needed a better information repository and collaboration system, it didn't have the depth of knowledge to truly understand what it needed and what was possible. And, most damning, investigators determined that the FBI lacked the rigor to oversee a project as complex at VCF. In fact, SAIC said that the FBI project manager's indecisiveness and inconsistencies in what they asked for was the largest culprit in the project's failure.[8]

Auditors would later discover that what the FBI asked SAIC for was simply impossible. There was little hope that SAIC—or anyone else for that matter—could deliver VCF in the manner specified by FBI project managers. However, that didn't stop SAIC from accepting the $170 million project. This is not to say that SAIC didn't think it could deliver a working system; it would deliver a product to the government. But SAIC's vision for what VCF should be and what it would take to produce it was vastly overstated, investigators found. SAIC assigned hundreds of computer programmers to the task, and released modules and delivered progress reports, but even it knew the project was off track and wouldn't perform. Insiders at SAIC said that the company made the decision to keep working on the project as long as the FBI kept paying the invoices.[9]

By 2005, after a year of trying to salvage the project, VCF was officially scrapped by the FBI at a cost of $105 million. Money wasn't the only loss, as Congressional investigators noted. The Bureau would remain reliant on a recordkeeping system that was largely paper-based and unchanged since J. Edgar Hoover established the FBI to combat bootleggers and gangsters in the 1920s. What concerned lawmakers on Capitol Hill was that VCF's failure could leave the door open for another terrorist attack on the scale of September 11.

In 2006, the FBI then turned to Lockheed Martin to pick up the pieces and start over with Sentinel. The difference between VCF and Sentinel is that Lockheed Martin would use off-the-shelf software to build the system and implement it in phases to ensure the Bureau recognized incremental benefits. While the FBI is using some aspects of the system that were rolled out in Phases I and II, the delay in Phases III and IV will keep the agency from realizing the system's full benefits and could add another $30 million to the price tag. Assuming Sentinel is successfully completed, the upgrade of the FBI's Automated Case Support system will prove to have cost U.S. taxpayers more than $450 million over ten years.

Why the Business/Technology Disconnect Continues

The business/technology failures in the previous examples all share a common problem: the complete and utter failure of management to properly align technology implementation to business objectives. Airbus's failure to ensure common adoption of computer-aided design software cost it billions of dollars in inconsistent design specifications that derailed production. Symantec's botched enterprise resource planning upgrade not only disrupted orders, but it threw its entire sales channel into chaos for two quarters. And the FBI's failure to govern its data systems upgrade leave it exposed to further intelligence and law enforcement failures that—as many in Congress fear—could ultimately cost lives.

Our ability to manage business technology has not kept pace with our creation of new technology. Let me stop for a moment to define "business technology" as we use it throughout this book: the application of technology to deliver a business capability or automate a business operation, in other words, the *right* technology to meet the business objective. In many organizations there are still two camps—technophiles and technophobes—and if they aren't at war, they are at the very least wary of each other. In too many organizations, the "business side" comes up with a plan and throws it over the wall to the "technology side" for implementation. Because technology is so embedded in the way things work today, these two sides should have been sitting and planning together from the very beginning.

To say technologists and business managers haven't been sitting at the same table discussing business plans and objectives is a bit of a misstatement. The disconnect that leads to gaps in business intent and technology execution often happens when these stakeholders leave the table. Technophiles will interpret the directives and desires of their business counterparts through their lens, and independently make modifications. Why? Most technophiles believe they know technology better than their line of business managers. Thinking like that leads to systems that are suited best for the designers and not the users.

These outcomes threaten to marginalize technology's role in value creation at the very time that it should be brought closer to the business than ever before. What appears at first blush to be the fault of the technologist ("Can't you make this stuff work?") is really an organization's failure to unify business and technology decision-making managers.

Imagine for a moment that you have finally decided to build your dream house. After some research, you have selected Janet, a prominent architect, and Robert, a respected contractor. To kick things off, you invite them over to your apartment to discuss the project. After brief introductions and some cursory small talk, the three of you sit down and get to work.

YOU: As the two of you know, I'm interested in building a house. Not just any house, but my dream house.

THEM: [Nodding]

YOU: For years now I've been picturing this house in my mind, so I know exactly what I want. First, it's got to feel like home. I'd like a breakfast nook, a Jacuzzi in the master bathroom . . .

THEM: [They jot notes]

YOU: . . . a deck off the family room. And a dramatic two-story entrance, of course. Also, I just love our neighbor's fireplace . . .

THEM: [Scribbling furiously]

YOU: So what do you think?

JANET: It sounds to me like you'd love the Colonial revival style. We could include a portico with ionic columns, and dentil band to add an air of sophistication.

YOU: A dentil what?

ROBERT: And I know an importer who gets beige Breccia marble direct from Karnezeika.

YOU: Karne-where?

JANET: . . . and a hipped roof . . .

ROBERT: . . . cantilever wall in the family room . . .

JANET: . . . with sidelights and transoms . . .

ROBERT: . . . tensile grade, ASTM A-615 . . .

At this point, you're probably lost. Or, at the very least you feel like you're no longer in charge. How does all this technical jargon relate to your vision of a dream house? What do "tensile grades" and "dentil bands" have to do with "feeling like home"?

The problem here is common: you've hired two skilled associates who instinctively view the project from their own specialized perspectives—which you definitely don't share. But despite all this, you're still the boss, and you need to figure out a way to make sure that everybody comes together to achieve your vision—no matter how limited your architectural and structural engineering vocabulary.

Not to worry, because architects and builders have faced this problem as long as they've been building for style as well as shelter. To help communicate issues, Janet and Robert will follow an established approach that helps them to collaborate and ultimately capture the design for your dream house in the form of an architectural blueprint. The three of you will then use this blueprint to bridge the gaps between their technical knowledge and your overall requirements: Janet could point out the portico and the simple yet elegant design of its ionic pillars, Robert could explain how advanced structural engineering allows them to include continuous open spaces through multiple rooms, and you could envision what it would be like to actually live in the home. Without this approach, designing your house would mean ceding control of the project to Janet and Robert; the end result would presumably look impressive and be structurally sound, but there would be no way to ensure that it matched your vision.

Now let's revisit this scenario, but with a twist. Instead of a prospective homeowner, you've become a senior business executive. And instead of building a house, you're managing an organization.

Your company is an aggressive market leader, quick to change to achieve competitive advantage. In recent years this has meant defining new business models, optimizing processes, and embracing technology to provide the infrastructure that lets you get ahead. To plan, deploy, and manage these investments you've hired Janet (now a high-powered consultant) and Robert (this time a respected process and technology manager). As before, the three of you are sitting and talking.

You: As the two of you know, we're beginning a project to get closer to our customer base. This project has been in the works for some time now, so I've got a pretty good idea of the things we need to accomplish.

Them: [Nodding]

You: First, we're interested in improving customer segmentation. This means we'll have to gather information across all our customer touch points . . .

Them: [Jotting down notes]

You: . . . and analyze this raw data. Also, we'd like to automate some field support activities and maybe do something with our call center . . .

Them: [Scribbling furiously]

You: So what do you think?

Robert: This sounds like a CRM installation to me . . .

Janet: . . . with analytics

ROBERT: . . . maybe WAP
YOU: Huh?
JANET: . . . and load balancing . . .
ROBERT: . . . distributed architecture . . . on the cloud . . .

Once again, things seem to have spiraled out of your control, from business subjects you understand and appreciate—"customer base" and "segmentation"—to the arcane technology details required to implement your vision—CRM, WAP, load balancing, and cloud computing.

In our dream house scenario, you (the homeowner) were able to rein in the project by collaborating with the architect and contractor to produce an architectural blueprint. Inexplicably, most organizations don't employ an analogous management approach to help you (the executive) visualize scenarios and incorporate multidisciplinary domain knowledge in order to overcome a similar dilemma.

What businesses need today to survive is information, which can be analyzed and turned into knowledge, which can then point them to growth and innovation. We get there by connecting, disaggregating, and reaching out in new ways.

Information, knowledge, and innovation might be considered the "what." Connectivity, disaggregation, and partnerships might be considered the "how."

Information ▶ Knowledge ▶ Innovation
Connectivity ▶ Disaggregation ▶ Partnerships

It is not the invention of a new technology that matters so much as it is its application—understanding its role when developing a strategy or designing an organization or its processes. As much as enterprises need a plan and strategic direction in developing and deploying technology, they also need a common language that's bound by common objectives.

From Alignment to Convergence

For many enterprises or operations, *alignment* of business technology with the business has been considered the Holy Grail. Alignment can be defined as a state where technology supports and enables but does not constrain the organization's current and evolving business strategies. It means that the technology function is in tune with the business thinking about competition, emerging threats, and opportunities, as well as the business technology implications of each. Technology priorities, investments, and capabilities are internally consistent with business priorities, investments, and capabilities.

When this is the case, then the organization has reached a level of business technology management maturity that relatively few have achieved to date. Alignment is a good thing, and is sometimes sufficient to serve a particular business situation.

But there are higher states to consider and for some enterprises, *synchronization*—technology and business initiatives progressing in parallel—of technology with the business is the right goal. At this level, business technology not only enables execution of current business strategy but also anticipates and helps shape future business models and strategy. Business technology leadership, thinking, and investments may actually step out ahead of the business (that is, beyond what is "aligned" with today's business). The purpose is to seed new opportunities and encourage farsighted executive vision about technology's leverage on future business opportunities. Yet the business and technology are synchronized in that the requisite capabilities will be in place when it is time to select the most appropriate strategic option.

Finally, there is the state of *convergence,* which assumes both alignment and synchronization, with technology and business leadership able to operate simultaneously in both spaces. Essentially, the business and technology spaces have merged in both strategic and tactical senses. A single leadership team operates across both spaces with individual leaders directly involved with orchestrating actions in either space. Some activities may remain pure business and some pure technology, but most activities intertwine business and technology in such a manner that the two become indistinguishable.

Is this actually possible? Absolutely! Examples are abundant for alignment, although less so for synchronization, and still fairly rare for convergence.

BTM Corporation's research since 1999 illustrates what leading organizations around the globe have learned about innovation through business technology convergence and not simply through innovating new technology. These include Global 2000 corporations, government agencies, small to medium businesses, and social enterprises. We looked into these organizations to better understand how they create innovative business models—models that can adapt to as opposed to suffer from unexpected shifts in the market.

FIGURE 1–1 ALIGNMENT, SYNCHRONIZATION, AND CONVERGENCE.

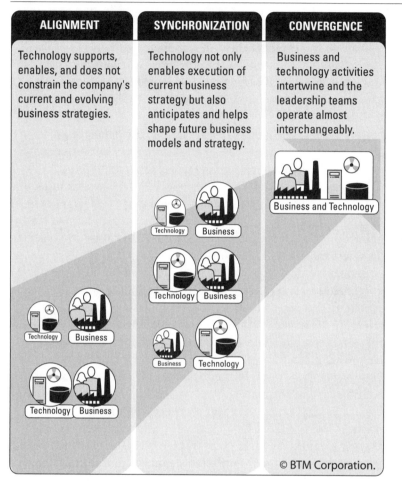

The three states of alignment, synchronization, and convergence demonstrate different relationships between business and technology.

As we discussed in the Introduction, BTM Corporation's research further suggests that leaders who place a focus on converging the business management and technology management disciplines of their companies attain far greater financial success than those who continue to treat them as silos. There is demonstrable economic value in advancing business technology management maturity, and the payoff is greatest for those enterprises that are approaching convergence.

The ability for technology (in its purest sense) to give an enterprise a competitive advantage is limited by the similar adoption and application of the technology across the competitive landscape. The Convergence Index introduced in Chapter 3 shows that when enterprises place the business strategy and model ahead of technology, and use technology as a supporting piece of the strategy, the enterprise will continue to grow faster and with healthier profit margins than competitors who are using the same technology without drawing upon how it relates to the business.

There is hardly any more debate that in the best-managed modern enterprises, technology and business management will converge completely. Managing business and technology together, or as we call the discipline, "Business Technology Management (BTM)," takes a multidisciplinary, structured approach that creates a "whole-brained" enterprise. Increasingly, this approach will be the source of all competitive successes, and will be the engine that allows professionals to innovate sustainable business models.

We need convergence now more than at any time in history to make next-generation enterprises thrive. Our increasing energy, transportation, manufacturing, and labor costs are redistributing wealth and power across the globe at a historically unprecedented rate. The means for not only surviving but also thriving in the globalized marketplace is convergence. This is what we will discuss in the coming chapters.

Convergence often begins at the top, with the CEO and the board, where the organization's overall strategy is set. Is it to be lean? To be agile? Or both? Is it to protect a position in existing markets or to explore new ones? Each of these broad goals requires a different technology deployment, and the technology must be part of the planning. It is in such planning, and in the information generated to inform it, that organizations can create the unique business model and processes most likely to deliver success.

Do you think organizations have mastered such a strategic use of technology?

The term *convergence insufficiency* (a term from the medical field) occurs when your eyes don't turn inward properly while you're focusing on a nearby object. When we read or look at a close object, our eyes should converge—turn inward together to focus—so that they provide binocular vision and we see a single image. But if we have convergence insufficiency, our eyes do not move inward to focus normally. Today, convergence insufficiency occurs as well in enterprises when business and technology do not come together!

The Takeaway: Turning Ideas into Action

As we have seen in this chapter, poor utilization of technology and bad investment-related decisions made in regard to technology can make or break a project, if not a company—all because of poorly defined objectives, management oversight, and lack of situational awareness. In later chapters, we'll explore in more detail how effective business technology management and convergence can drive significant operational and financial improvement. For now, consider the following first steps when reviewing the management practices of business and technology initiatives in your company.

Using business technology to accelerate operational performance requires informed decision making to determine which investments best support an organization's strategic mission and as a result, improve its overall financial performance.

The following five steps detail how to analyze and shift investments among technology portfolios to strike a balance between those that deliver stability and those that support agility.

Step 1: *Review* your company's strategic position, as well as your business strategy and technology strategy formulation activities. Are marketplace and competitive analyses part of these activities? Is the role of business technology prominent in these analyses? Is strategic experimentation used to enable a better understanding of the roles served by business technology investment in acquiring and sustaining favorable market positions?

Step 2: *Determine* how both business and technology investments are handled in your company's strategic planning and budgeting activities. To what extent do investment levels across operating units reflect the role that business technology actually serves in enabling strategic positions? To what extent do investment levels across staff or support units reflect the role business technology serves in enabling these units to accomplish their mission? Are the baselines for such analyses founded on historical trends, industry benchmarks, or carefully selected (that is, strategically and operationally comparable) peer groups?

Step 3: *Assess* the existence and maturity of business/technology management capabilities across the enterprise. Which technology capabilities—given the role that business technology serves in enabling your firm's strategic posture—must be maintained at world-class levels? Has sufficient investment in business/technology management capabilities occurred at an enterprise level and within each business unit?

Step 4: *Evaluate* your enterprise's organizational synchronization. Are your business strategy and strategic position well communicated and clearly understood across the organization? Are your enterprise's business strategies reflective of exploitative strategic actions, exploratory strategic actions, or both? What roles do your business/technology investments play in enabling these strategic actions?

Step 5: *Develop* an appropriate mix of the kinds of business technologies needed to advance your firm's strategic agenda. Technology—and investments in new technology—will become a significant tool for the enterprise's executive team.

CHAPTER 2

Convergence: Concept to Value

I N MAY 2010 APPLE did what many people thought was impossible just five years prior. It surpassed Microsoft for the title of the world's most valuable company in terms of market capitalization. Through a combination of business execution and external stock market volatility, Apple's total valuation hit $222 billion while Microsoft's value shrank to $219 billion. Making matters worse is how fortunes have changed for these two companies over the past decade. When Bill Gates turned over the Microsoft CEO office in 2000 to longtime successor-in-waiting Steve Ballmer, Microsoft's market value was nearly $560 billion. That same year, Apple was just beginning to execute on its future vision and its market value was a mere $15.6 billion. Through a combination of building new business models, executing on an evolving and adapting technology strategy, and acting with a singular focus on customers, Apple toppled longtime rival Microsoft for the title, "king of the technology world."

There are many lessons to be learned from the juxtaposition of these two technology giants. Chief among those lessons is the value of enterprise-wide convergence of business and technology management. Throughout the course of the book, we discuss how convergence can be achieved through certain organizational "constructs," or, as some would say, "management behaviors." These constructs and behaviors are the foundation on which enterprises build innovative business models. And, interestingly, enterprises that operate atop such constructs yield superior financial performance than their nonconverged counterparts.

The fabric of these constructs is Business Technology Management (BTM), a management approach applied to business technology that unifies and improves decision making. BTM provides a structured approach that lets enterprises align, synchronize, and even converge business technology and business management, thus ensuring better execution, risk control, and profitability. It addresses business and technology as a holistic, structured management system. It covers critical management capabilities and a management maturity model to identify areas most in need of improvement and to specify the correct path for change.

The key to institutionalizing these principles and capabilities is that they are driven by a set of robust, flexible, and repeatable processes, executed by defined organization structures, informed by useful information, and enabled by business technology. By "business technology" we mean the application of technology to deliver a business capability or automate a business operation. Business technology can be thought of as the result of configuring, implementing, applying, and using technology to produce a business result. Business technology investments and business technology capital are investments related to the creation, use, and maintenance of business technology. Business Technology Management investments are those related to the creation and realization of Business Technology Management Capabilities.

Simply defining processes for technology adoption and implementation is insufficient. Many organizations maintain a set of documented, standard operating procedures that are rarely followed as intended—if at all—because they run counter to organizational interests, the right information isn't available, or compliance is too difficult. To achieve the full "concept to value" of convergence, enterprises need a management playbook and a collaborative decision-making process that is supported by a maturity advancement plan, which defines the steps through which an enterprise will realize its convergence goals.

In this chapter, we will introduce the essential BTM capabilities critical for successful integration and conversion of technology investments into business value. Without a single, comprehensive management science by which enterprises can manage technology in lockstep with the business, value and competitive advantage will remain unattainable. Increasingly, converged management capabilities are the source of all dramatic competitive success in today's marketplace. This is the ultimate lesson from the surging success of Apple and the flagging fortunes of Microsoft, as well as myriad other examples of businesses rising through the proper application of technology (or falling through the misapplication). Isolated technology development and implementation will lead to stagnation. The holistic use of technology—where technology is an equal partner at the management table—based on external intelligence and acted upon internally with singular focus will produce tremendous success.

The Role of Business Technology Management

Grounded in research and practice, BTM is an emerging management science that unifies decision making from the boardroom to the C-suite to the project management team. BTM aims to create a seamless management approach that begins with business priorities and goals and connects all the way through technology investment and implementation.

Enterprises have employed a number of methodologies and techniques to improve business and technology alignment. These range from the Software Engineering Institute's Capability Maturity Model (CMM) to Project Management Institute's Project Management Body of Knowledge (PMBOK) and the Information Technology Infrastructure Library (ITIL) for services management. Each of these methods has their own set of strengths and benefits, but they represent piecemeal solutions. None of these approaches focuses on integrating and enabling the capabilities necessary to achieve strategic technology management and the subsequent sustainable value. The danger of relying solely on downstream technology management methodologies is that by the time misalignment becomes apparent, it may be irreversible.

BTM, as illustrated in Figure 2–1, provides a set of guiding principles around which the practices of an enterprise are organized and improved. It builds bridges between previously isolated management tools and standards. Essentially, BTM sits strategically above operational and infrastructure levels of technology management.

The BTM Framework

The BTM Framework, as shown in Figure 2–2, identifies seventeen essential capabilities grouped into four functional areas. They are:

- ○ Governance and Organization
- ○ Strategic Investment Management

FIGURE 2–1 STRATEGIC POSITIONING OF THE BTM FRAMEWORK.

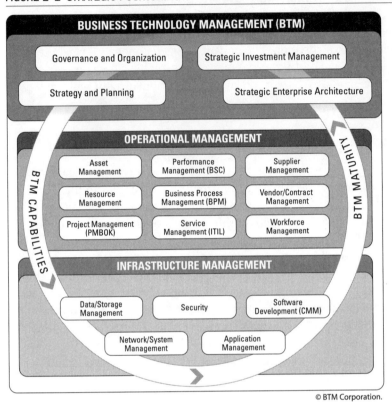

© BTM Corporation.

BTM strategically integrates with other methodologies and enables the capabilities necessary to achieve convergence of business and technology management.

- ⋂ Strategy and Planning
- ⋂ Strategic Enterprise Architecture

These capabilities are defined and created by four critical dimensions:

- ⋂ Processes
- ⋂ Organization
- ⋂ Information
- ⋂ Technology

FIGURE 2–2 THE BTM FRAMEWORK.

© BTM Corporation.

The BTM Framework is based on four functional areas comprised of seventeen capabilities, with each capability relying upon four critical dimensions.

BTM capabilities define a set of organizational competencies that enable an enterprise to manage business and technology together. Maturity in these capabilities is achieved through the implementation of well-defined processes, appropriate organizational structures, timely information, and appropriate technology automation.

These capabilities are interdependent and "networked." Successfully implementing any of them will move an organization closer to the goal of business and technology convergence. This progress accelerates as each additional capability is realized and continuously improved.

Standing alone, each of the seventeen capabilities represents a critical point of interaction in the enterprise between business and technology. More importantly, these capabilities—and the interactions between them—are the building blocks of solutions to the thorniest issues facing enterprises today, including achieving sustainable innovation, creating an agile enterprise, optimizing service delivery, building an extended enterprise, and maximizing growth.

The Functional Areas and Capabilities of the BTM Framework

Convergence occurs in the establishment of organizational structures, processes, information flows, and automation that unite enterprise business and technology process decision making. The BTM Framework is the management structure upon which business and technology are converged, and technology becomes a strategic resource. By establishing repeatable processes, it frees enterprises to make the best use of technology in pursuit of their business goals. Ideally, it becomes an enterprise's management standard.

An enterprise's path toward convergence begins by recognizing where it stands with regard to its true state of management maturity and making the commitment to real progress. Through this determination, management can focus on specific priorities, implement specific capabilities, and continuously improve upon and reorder those priorities. The journey starts with the four functional areas of the BTM Framework.

Governance and Organization

Governance and Organization, essential to the management of an effective enterprise, harmonizes and integrates the varied interests of all stakeholders within the enterprise. The capabilities within this functional area provide strategic direction in the overall enterprise as it matures and evolves its business and technology management. When communicated to the entire enterprise, these capabilities ensure that all actors understand and operate within the prescribed parameters. Governance and Organization is the catalyst for the enterprise's purposeful move to convergence. The following four capabilities comprise Governance and Organization:

- **Strategic and Tactical Governance** establishes what decisions must be made, the people responsible for making decisions, and the decision-making process. This capability touches on a broad range of decisions beginning with the most strategic, such as business direction and new product introductions, carrying through to the tactical direction of execution.

- **Organization Design and Change Management Capability** optimizes the organizational design necessary to support informed decision making across the enterprise and to provide for the changes necessary to put such an organizational model into place. It optimizes horizontal collaboration to accelerate the enterprise's move to convergence.

- The **Communication Strategy and Management Capability** crafts and delivers appropriate, effective messages on mission, strategies, initiatives, and programs to all members of the enterprise—including partners in an extended enterprise. It translates this information to the roles and responsibilities of the recipients; it measures to ensure the effectiveness of the message; and it provides for updating and refreshing the message on a regular basis.

○ The **Compliance and Risk Management Capability** ensures that government and regulatory requirements are understood and reflected in enterprise operations. This capability identifies the categories and sources of risk for the enterprise; addresses its internal, external, and inter-enterprise risk; provides for the enterprise's determining its own risk posture; and ensures that appropriate risk mitigation strategies are in place.

Strategy and Planning

Strategy and Planning is the intersection of business and technology management where the enterprise's strategic intent influences and is shaped by the technologies that are essential to moving it forward. These capabilities address the establishment and ongoing testing and validation of a BTM strategy, that strategy's grounding in sound financial practices, and the process of performance measurement. Strategy and Planning addresses the crucial decision as to which partners the enterprise will work with. It handles the challenging processes of consolidating acquired assets—businesses, intellectual property, people, and customers. It also standardizes the enterprise's use of these assets. Strategy and Planning is comprised of the following four capabilities:

○ The **Business Technology Strategy Capability** identifies and determines the appropriate strategic positioning, value discipline, and value type of the enterprise, infusing technology into business strategy. It tests and elevates strategy development and execution, establishing the interconnection of business and technology that is essential for enterprise success.

○ The **Strategic Planning and Budgeting Capability** makes an ongoing, adaptive strategic planning process fundamental to the operating stance of the enterprise, providing for the establishment of goals and milestones. It grounds the assessment of the effectiveness of the technology strategy in established financial measures.

○ The **Strategic Sourcing and Management Capability** supports the creation and management of relationships with partners best suited to the strategy of the enterprise. This includes identifying areas of strategic opportunity for outsourcing, co-sourcing, and vendor selection, resulting in the development and management of "value nets"—or as some would say, the ecosystem of the extended enterprise that includes internal and external stakeholders including suppliers, strategic contractors and consultants, and partners.

○ The **Consolidation and Standardization Capability** helps the enterprise identify the impact of acquiring businesses, products, customers, or other assets and provides the foundation for identifying opportunities for standardization and integration into its organizational and governance structure.

Strategic Investment Management

Strategic Investment Management applies the disciplines of asset portfolio management to business technology and other productive assets. It translates strategy into action by subjecting all initiatives to a consistent framework for approval and prioritization, requiring each to show why it's a superior investment in the mix of possibilities; it establishes the means for determining both the demand for the human, financial, and capital resources required for each investment, and its supply; and it establishes and empowers the investment management office, which is charged with maximizing the returns from each of the enterprise's investments. Lastly, it establishes and maintains a regimen for preparing, launching, and executing projects once approved, ensuring that all participants in the process are working within the same guidelines toward the planned result. The following four capabilities are the backbone of Strategic Investment Management:

○ The **Portfolio and Program Management Capability** provides visibility into the investment planning and results of the assets and programs portfolio of the enterprise—wherever technology and business intersect. It is focused on effective program monitoring and execution. It provides the management techniques for evaluating performance and identifying areas of strength and weakness. These techniques enable an enterprise to act decisively and preemptively to maximize returns on technology investments.

○ The **Approval and Prioritization Capability** establishes the criteria used for evaluating alternatives, specifying the decision-making process, and prioritizing technology investments. It provides a consistent framework for planning, proposing, and deciding upon proposed initiatives.

⟲ The **Project Analysis and Design Capability** applies technology to project execution throughout the entire implementation life cycle, ensuring that each major initiative maximizes existing assets and optimizes standards.

⟲ The **Resource and Demand Management Capability** provides for an appropriate and adequate mix of people and financial and physical assets to meet the demands of the enterprise. It supplies the foundation for analyzing the demand characteristics of the enterprise's technology initiatives.

Strategic Enterprise Architecture

Strategic Enterprise Architecture (SEA) defines the organization's business model and the technology environment necessary to support it. It outlines the technology standards the enterprise will—and won't—use in achieving its goals. And it provides the framework for categorizing, analyzing, managing, and rationalizing the applications the enterprise employs in enabling and executing its business model strategy. SEA consists of the following five capabilities:

⟲ The **Business Architecture Capability** defines the operating model for the enterprise, which includes strategies, competencies, customers, processes, and other elements related to the utilization of technology. It defines the operating characteristics and their interrelationships in a dynamic model used to identify opportunities to enhance business performance.

⟲ The **Technology Architecture Capability** systematically maps the technology required to optimize all elements of the business architecture. It dynamically represents information technology as well as all technologies leveraging the effectiveness, efficiency, and reach of enterprise business activities.

⟲ The **Business Technology Standards Capability** identifies and defines standards to maximize the reuse of technology assets. This includes a definition of guiding principles, usage and applicability, and definition of other governance requirements. Standards may include the reuse and retasking of software applications, processes, information architecture, and suppliers.

○ The **Application Portfolio Management Capability** establishes, categorizes, and manages portfolios of technology applications, consistent with business technology strategy, target architectures, and standards.

○ The **Asset Rationalization Capability** reduces complexity and cost by providing a repeatable process to manage and optimize technology assets consistent with the business and technology architectures and standards.

The Four Critical Dimensions of BTM

The famed three-ring binder is the embodiment of enterprise documentation. Few enterprises have a shortage of documentation—manuals, guidelines, standard operating procedures—that is captured and stored in three-ring binders or, nowadays, intranet portals. Yet in many enterprises all this documentation does little more than collect dust. Why? It's simply a matter of complexity and culture. Enterprise documentation is typically dense and impractical for day-to-day operations. Enabling enterprises to lapse out of proper procedures—or make exceptions to the rule—results from management's willingness to disregard procedures in the face of expediency. When management and staff are faced with the choice between procedural integrity and productivity, they'll typically default to productivity—and that failure to monitor goals results in a steady devolution of quality and cohesion that makes it more difficult to reach business objectives.

There are four dimensions defined in BTM that are critical components toward achieving and sustaining success. By adopting BTM, management is making a commitment to look beyond the holistic integration of business and technology disciplines to the *institutionalization* of practices that enable technology application toward business objectives and sustained, repeatable outcomes. The four critical dimensions that support BTM—across all functional areas and capabilities—include process, organization, information, and technology (automation).

BTM capabilities are defined as matured organizational competencies achieved by applying well-defined processes, appropriate organizational structures, actionable information for decision making, and supporting technologies in one or more functional areas. Successfully implementing any of these capabilities will move an organization closer to the goal of business and technology unification. This progress accelerates as each additional capability is realized and continuously improved. Although capabilities are interdependent, all of them should be implemented to maximize the business value of technology investments. But doing so requires a carefully orchestrated approach with top-down and bottom-up management support. It involves business and technology groups in equal measure. In this section, we'll review what each of these dimensions mean to an organization and how they're implemented to achieve superior business results.

Process

The first dimension for institutionalizing BTM principles is establishing sound, repeatable processes beyond simple definitions. Effectively implementing BTM requires the evaluation of processes to ensure general quality of business practice (doing the right things), efficiency (doing things quickly with little redundancy), and effectiveness (doing things well). Management processes are more likely to succeed when they are supported by appropriate organizational structures based on clear understanding of roles, responsibilities, and decision rights. Such organizational structures generally include:

- ○ Participative bodies, which involve senior-level business and technology participants on a part-time but routine basis.
- ○ Centralized bodies, which require specialized, dedicated technology staff.
- ○ Needs-based bodies, which involve rotational assignments created to deal with particular efforts.

Organization

Organization is more than just having a management structure—it requires a set of collective and collaborative working groups designated to establish and manage technology development and implementation. Call them steering committees, review boards, or management teams, organizational structures will vary from enterprise to enterprise, and are influenced by the enterprise's size, mission/purpose/value proposition, and its relative BTM maturity. The formalization of a technology management organization is the embodiment of BTM in an enterprise's strategic construct.

Persistence, collaboration, responsibility, and authority are many of the attributes that set BTM apart from what most perceive as conventional management hierarchies. BTM calls for the creation of working groups that operate in parallel with the management structure to ensure cross-discipline communication and collaboration. These are more than just temporary task forces. They are standing bodies that meet regularly to oversee both domain issues (macrotechnology management) as well as granular projects (specific tasks). Each working group should have a charter (or mission) for its responsibility and authority; a clear understanding of how it interacts with the executive team, line of business management, and other working groups; and intimate knowledge of the resources available for its activities.

They are typically comprised of representation from the executive team, lines of business, technology management or the CIO office, and line staff. Working groups are not temporary assignments. Participating management and staff should treat their designated working group as an extension of their jobs and scopes of responsibility. As such, supervisory management should make working group members' participation a part of their performance expectations and reviews.

Information

As the well-known phrase goes, "garbage in, garbage out." If you put bad information into a decision-making process, you'll get a bad decision. Information is more than just a collection of facts and figures; it is the fuel that drives business. In the BTM context, information is the refinement of data into intelligence for effective technology management decision making. After all, no good manager would make a critical business decision without having objective information to back her up. For the working groups within the BTM construct, information is the lifeblood that provides context for their deliberations and, ultimately, the material for their recommendations and directives.

The importance of clear and consistent information cannot be overemphasized. Making information actionable requires making it intelligible. In other words, information must not only be intelligent and complete enough to make sound business decisions, but also comprehendible to nonspecialists and laypeople in working groups. It's not enough to expect the specialists to interpret information for the group or the organization; that leaves too much margin for misunderstanding and the ability for specialists to sway decision making with their agendas.

Where does this information come from? Enterprises have no shortage of data; the metrics used to measure performance of productivity and processes churn out copious amounts of information. Metrics is essentially the process through which data (raw material) is refined into actionable intelligence (information). Data must be available, relevant, accurate, and reliable for metrics to produce a desired, useful product. And metrics must be designed to ensure they produce appropriate, valid intelligence for making decisions that drive the enterprise toward strategic and operational objectives.

It's often said that you can make numbers say anything you want them to say. This is why truth in business is often elusive; different groups will apply different measures to their activities in order to demonstrate their productivity and value regardless of relevancy to the total enterprise. Standardizing data and metrics across an enterprise's internal operations and extended network of partners and suppliers is critical to ensure all stakeholders and decision makers are dealing with the same intelligence. Equally important is designing metrics for use from one year to the next, one decade to the next; the product of metrics must be comparable over time to measure progress and performance. Management processes based on flawed information will fail when confronted with conditions that exploit the flaws.

Technology

Technology—such as management automation tools—can help connect all of these BTM dimensions. Technology helps make processes easier to execute, facilitates timely information sharing, and enables consistent coordination between elements and layers of the organization. It does this through the automation of manual tasks, reporting, the generation of analytics for decision making, and the integration of disparate management systems.

The simple addition of technology to automate existing processes leaves most of its potential value untapped. The largest gains result from the optimization of processes, organizational structures, and information flows. The complexity of managing the technology function and increasing demands of an ever-evolving business climate require more information transparency and operational synchronization than basic computing tasks provide. The appropriate use of technology should not only ease the development and reporting of information needed to fuel management processes across the organization, but also to achieve consistent horizontal and vertical management integration.

Advancing Capability Maturity

The measure for understanding where an enterprise resides in its convergence journey is what we call the BTM Maturity Model™, as shown in Figure 2–3. This model defines five levels of maturity, scored across the four critical dimensions of process, organization, information, and technology. Our research shows a distinct variance within organizations depending on their maturity level.

- ↻ At Level 1, an organization typically executes some strategic technology management processes in a disaggregated, tasklike manner.

- ↻ At Level 2, an organization exhibits limited technology management capabilities, attempts but does not fully assemble information for major decisions, and consults their technology group on decisions with obvious technology implications.

- ↻ At Level 3, an organization is "functional" with respect to technology management. This means that an enterprise has adopted many of the core principles of technology management, but hasn't implemented them consistently across the projects or the organization.

- ↻ At Level 4, an enterprise has technology management fully implemented across the organization.

- ↻ At Level 5, an enterprise has matured enough to know when to change the rules to maintain strategic advantages over advancing and nonconvergence competitors.

The BTM Maturity Model describes how well an organization performs a particular set of activities in comparison to a prescribed standard. This model makes it possible for an enterprise to identify anomalies in performance and benchmark itself against other companies or across industries. Establishing a baseline of management maturity is an essential starting point on the path to achieving business technology convergence. A baseline is generally defined as "a line or standard by which things are measured or compared." To be effective and meaningful, a maturity baseline must be inextricably linked to the entire environment being measured, and it must be built upon a set of critical observations or data used for comparison or a control.

What follows are sample self-assessment questions that can allow

FIGURE 2–3 THE BTM MATURITY MODEL.

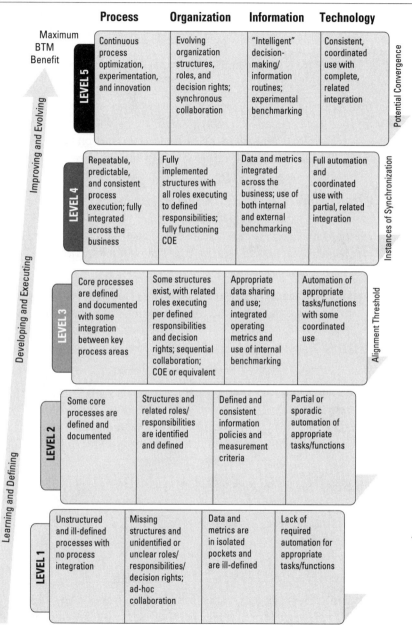

© BTM Corporation.

The BTM Maturity Model identifies areas most in need of improvement, fixes the starting point for the enterprise, and specifies the path for change.

an organization to create a baseline for its current management capability maturity level. These questions are based on the seventeen management capabilities identified and defined earlier in the chapter and arranged by dimension (process, organization, information, technology) in order to capture discrete data for each capability.

1. **Strategic and Tactical Governance**: To what extent does your enterprise have a formal decision body in place—with both business and technology management professionals participating—that can make decisions and enforce policy on the direction of its technology investments and standards?

2. **Organizational Design and Change Management**: To what extent has your technology organization been designed to support the demands of your business and technology strategies? How easily can changes be made to ensure that the technology organization adapts to changing needs?

3. **Communication Strategy and Management**: How effectively does your enterprise communicate the degree to which the technology organization supports business strategy and business technology strategy? To what degree are the technology initiatives being undertaken designed to meet business needs?

4. **Compliance and Risk Management**: To what extent does your enterprise ensure that government and regulatory requirements are understood and met, that appropriate risk mitigation strategies are in place, and that technology is an active partner in the governance of compliance and risk management?

5. **Business Technology Strategy**: To what extent does your enterprise work regularly to coordinate its business strategy with its technology strategy, reflecting both current and future business and technology trends? To what extent do senior business and technology leaders treat the technology strategy as a meaningful exercise?

6. **Strategic Planning and Budgeting**: To what extent does your enterprise conduct formal planning and budgeting activities using financial planning models? To what extent does your enterprise develop portfolio allocation targets to prioritize investments according to its technology strategy?

7. **Strategic Sourcing and Management**: To what extent does your enterprise identify and analyze areas of strategic opportunity for outsourcing, co-development, and knowledge partnerships? To what extent does it conduct the analysis of the capabilities of potential partners in a consistent and objective fashion? And has your enterprise entrusted this responsibility to a professional group within the enterprise?

8. **Consolidation and Standardization**: To what extent does your enterprise work effectively to make newly acquired assets fit within its strategic and operational framework and adjust its planning and decision cycles to rapidly develop and execute programs to comply with standards and to consolidate or eliminate redundant assets, resources business networks, and investments?

9. **Portfolio and Program Management**: To what extent does an enterprise utilize portfolio management to identify and examine current and future assets and resources, as well as risks to investments and operations? How does it map and track those elements to business drivers and other measurable criteria? Does it have a full-time professional group in place to ensure that the enterprise appropriately optimizes each portfolio?

10. **Approval and Prioritization**: To what extent do decision-making bodies in your enterprise employ objective criteria based on its business strategy, technology strategy, financial framework, and risk management stance to determine which technology initiatives should be approved and the order in which they should be implemented?

11. **Project Analysis and Design**: To what extent does your enterprise work to ensure that every proposed technology initiative fits within the guidelines of its business strategy, technology strategy, and architecture standards?

12. **Resource and Demand Management**: To what extent does your enterprise work actively to ensure that technology resource requests and allocations are consistent with its required business capabilities, priorities, budgets, and capacity?

13. **Business Architecture**: To what extent does your enterprise work to capture and organize information about its business strategy and business processes, creating models of the operating steps of

each business process and identifying technology services required to support them?

14. **Technology Architecture**: To what extent does your enterprise work to capture, organize, and categorize information about its business technology assets (including their relationship to each business process), creating detailed models of the technology environment and the relationships between technology domains including infrastructure, hardware, and applications?

15. **Business Technology Standards**: To what extent does your enterprise work to establish standard business technology applications and tools, to review their compliance with architectural guiding principles and standards, and to ensure that future trends and directions in technology are reflected in those standards?

16. **Application Portfolio Management**: To what extent does your enterprise work to collect information on its technology applications, and to analyze each of these applications to determine its alignment with business and technology strategy, target architectures, and enterprise standards? To what extent is this process used to determine the desired future state of the enterprise's technology portfolio?

17. **Asset Rationalization**: To what extent does your enterprise work actively to identify and manage the elimination of redundant, obsolete, nonstandard, or underutilized technology assets? To what extent does it work to plan and execute initiatives that migrate the enterprise's portfolio of assets toward an "optimized" state?

Based on the enterprise's maturity level selected for the preceding questions, a convergence score is calculated that provides a composite measure of the technology management maturity.

Assessment results capture the requisite data needed to compute an individual score for each capability. Individual scores are aggregated and a baseline maturity level is determined according to the predefined metrics outlined in the BTM Maturity Model. The results produced by this model are a clear statement of the areas of strength and those in need of improvement. The model fixes the starting point for improvement, while describing the anticipated outcomes in terms of expected business results. The results of the assessment provide the input necessary to the creation of a Maturity Advancement Plan (MAP), which functions as a roadmap for advancing the processes and procedures of technology management through the stages of coordination, alignment, and convergence.

Realizing Critical BTM Capabilities

In seeking the right level of coordination, an enterprise must weigh the extent to which its business strategy and strategic initiatives help set the priorities for technology, including investments in infrastructure and services, application portfolios, and sourcing relationships. At the same time, this design must account for the fact that business technology is increasingly shaping future business strategies, processes, and initiatives. Establishing the appropriate organizational structure will facilitate true coordination between all areas of an enterprise. It will assist firms in exploiting technology-enabled opportunities, often leading to an innovative business strategy that may even result in the differentiation of an organization's product or service offerings. To be effective, there are a few things an organization must do to get itself in order:

○ **Organize and manage based on value-creating processes**. Don't set up committees for the sake of creating the *perception* of coordination and collaboration. Take stock of the value-creating processes that these organizational structures will support. Remember that the level of complexity associated with an organizational unit will vary based on the sophistication of the governance network it supports. Apply a modular organizing logic in designing critical technology structures across the organization. Consider explicitly assigning individual executives to each one of these modular organizational units.

○ **Recognize that Organization Design and Change Management is a critical BTM capability.** Organization design changes must be managed with care. Strong relationships need to be built with stakeholders. How can you promote "straight talk" in an environment that values commitment and relationships? How can you lead your team to accept that difficulties along the way are not failures, but rather a normal part of the change process? How will you resolve these rough spots and build on them to fuel the organizational change effort? Develop "bottom-up" change agents—rarely does change result solely from a top-down edict.

Lower-level employees must buy in as much as C-suite executives. Cultivating change agents can guarantee their support in selling their peers.

⊙ **Develop your Communication Strategy and Management capability.** Communications has significant implications for evolving organization structures. The board, senior management team, technology executives, and external partners are some of the numerous stakeholders that determine its success. Communications Strategy and Management is the responsibility of the entire senior management team, and should be supported by expert communications professionals to ensure that the communications strategy is based on behavior-based goals and objectives; that a path is defined to move target audiences from mere awareness to understanding, commitment, and action; and that the plan includes appropriate communications research, channel identification, key messages, timelines, and measurements of success.

A business technology strategy defines the capabilities required for an organization's success. Aligning technology investments with business strategy is accomplished by remaining focused on the type of value the enterprise seeks to create through technology. Technology investments require structured thinking about what the business wants to achieve. Consider the following items when developing a technology investment plan:

⊙ **Determine what specific technology capabilities must be put in place for you to meet your short-term and long-term business goals and objectives.** A mature business technology strategy is the most effective way to ensure that the technology group understands the specific business needs and enables the business strategy.

⊙ **Prepare the processes that need to be put in place to improve communications and educate the organization about each component.** Creating an effective strategy requires careful and complete communication. It also requires the integration of the enterprise business strategy (outlining the strategic goals, imperatives, and initiatives of a company), enterprise technology strategy (outlining the strategic direction of business technology), and technology function strategy (outlining how technology develops, deploys, operates, and supports the systems needed to deliver business technology).

○ **Decide what internal and external capabilities you need to execute on defined business strategies.** Prioritizing and focusing investments starts with understanding the type of value that will be created. Enabling stability and/or agility will require different levels and types of investments. Consideration must be given to the nature of this investment mix as it relates to supporting other critical activities.

○ **Understand and specify the business value discipline to be pursued.** What is the primary value discipline—that is, operational excellence, product leadership, or customer intimacy? The answer must be embedded in the enterprise business strategy, and cascaded through all stakeholders and levels of the organization. Doing so will prescribe the specific business capabilities required in a way that guides effective technology strategy creation.

BTM Corporation's research suggests that enterprises should apply a networked governance model. The role of the board of directors and the executive team is to articulate a vision for business technology, shaping the overall metrics architecture and providing oversight for strategic risks and compliance. Business management is primarily responsible for championing innovative applications of business technology, including making the business case for projects. Technology management is responsible for managing technology services, skill availability, and the technology infrastructure. Finally, external vendors—a key element of the governance network—provide access to needed expertise as well as economical and/or world-class services and skills.

Boards usually carry out their governance duties through committees that oversee critical areas such as audit, compensation, and acquisitions. It might be time for firms, particularly those in information-intensive sectors, to consider establishing committees that are responsible for technology strategy.[1] The charter for such a committee would be twofold. First, it would be involved in decisions related to the envisioned role of business technology, the metrics architecture, and strategic risks and compliance. Second, it would have the role of monitoring significant technology management decisions, including portfolio and project and sourcing risks.

Complementary to this board-level committee is an executive committee that has become common in most firms: the technology executive committee. This committee often consists of the chief executive, chief financial officer, head of operations, senior sales executive, chief technologist, the leader of research and development, and the chief information officer. Executive-level committees such as these are responsible for executing the strategic role of business technology in decisions about investment, applications prioritization, and infrastructure build-ups; monitoring the risks of business technology and the effectiveness of the risk mitigation and control systems; communicating policies and standards about the use of technology assets, data management, and compliance management; and interacting with the board of directors on key technology issues.

Finally, the Office of the CIO has emerged as another important organizational mechanism that complements the effectiveness of the board and the executive management team. Key responsibilities of this group include monitoring the technology portfolio, value metrics, and technology capabilities (staff, infrastructure, services) of the enterprise. The CIO group is responsible for tracking emerging technologies and managing an appropriate research and development posture toward these technologies.

Relationships with key vendors and supplier partners are usually managed by the CIO group. Technology vendors rely on feedback from customers in developing the next generation of their products and services. Likewise, it's through strong relationships and lines of communications that enterprises and vendors are able to craft customized versions of technology that meet specific needs within the BTM strategy. In many cases, this customization serves a research and development function; vendors may provide cost breaks for customization if it shows promise for later monetization in the form of a marketable product.

Only a small percentage of organizations have adopted a technology governance structure, even though they may realize the issues they face could be resolved this way. However, those companies that have adopted formal approaches with a strategic perspective are mitigating risks, delivering on the value of their technology investments, and improving the alignment, synchronization, and even convergence between business and technology.

The Takeaway: Turning Ideas into Action

So, where does an enterprise begin? The job of implementing seventeen BTM Framework capabilities and measuring progress using the BTM

Maturity Model can seem overwhelming. After all, every enterprise starts from a different place, with existing investments in systems and business processes that make starting over virtually impossible.

So don't start over. Start anywhere.

The right way to approach capability implementation is iteratively. Fundamentally, an enterprise must determine where it is—its starting point—in order to get focused on specific priorities; it must design and implement specific capabilities with those priorities in mind, and it must execute the appropriate steps and continuously improve. Senior management must begin by recognizing where its enterprise stands with regard to BTM maturity. Only by respecting what is can you make real progress toward what *is to be*. Then you cycle again, using five steps to continuous management improvement:

Step 1: *Assess management maturity.* Establish a baseline (assess BTM maturity levels, confirm opportunity areas, identify high-priority functional areas and key stakeholders).

Step 2: *Create a management playbook.* Detail how management will lead the organization forward.

Step 3: *Model and analyze your future state.* Identify the optimal future state for the organization and describe it in a holistic manner, from strategy through service delivery.

Step 4: *Develop, execute, and track implementation programs.* Develop a set of implementation programs and necessary supporting investment proposals to reach the desired future state. Those investment proposals must be rationalized and filtered through a collaborative approval process, and their execution must be tracked and managed.

Step 5: *Manage performance and capture value.* Implement metrics for measuring the operational effectiveness delivered by investment and solution programs. Enterprises must ensure that poor performance is detected and remediated as early as possible. Conversely, superior performance should be identified and incorporated into the management playbook to advance organizational learning and BTM management capability maturity.

Smart enterprises today are rightfully pursuing alignment of technology with the business, and that in itself is no small achievement. But for some, the right level is really synchronization, where technology *shapes* (not just enables) strategic choices. And at the highest level of achievement, business and technology leadership actually converges, reflecting an executive and management team that has achieved an extraordinary level of cross-understanding and vision for the future. Assembling the components of the BTM Framework yields unprecedented capacity and opportunity for success in a marketplace where competitive advantage is increasingly defined through technology.

CHAPTER 3

The Financial Value of Business/Technology Convergence

THE FORD MOTOR COMPANY gave birth to the modern automobile industry. Its founder, Henry Ford, perfected the art of assembly line production and early forms of automation. Ford Motors was also among the first companies to pay workers a living wage so they could afford to consume the products they produced. It is that legacy that made the automaker an industrial powerhouse the world over.

Today, few are ignorant of Ford's troubles. Like many of the major American automobile manufacturers, Ford Motors fell on hard times—many of its own creation. After decades of missteps, poor products, and shoddy investments, it had finally reached its breaking point in 2005. After William Clay Ford Jr.'s restructuring plan, "The Way Forward," failed to reignite the company's business fortunes, it turned to former Boeing executive Alan Mulally for leadership. He wasn't Ford's first choice; car industry vendors such as DaimlerChrysler's Dieter Zetsche and Renault/Nissan Motors's Carlos Ghosn had turned down the chief executive's post. Bringing in an aerospace executive to run a car company seemed pretty desperate, but times were desperate given that Ford had lost $12.7 billion in 2005 alone.

An engineer by trade, Mulally is a process- and precision-oriented executive. He wanted efficiency and focus on execution. One of the first tales to emerge from Ford after Mulally took the reins in 2006 was his disbelief that the company used so many nonuniform parts. As the story goes, Mulally scattered dozens of hood hinges across a conference room table and challenged product management and design teams to explain why they couldn't design just a few that could work in multiple vehicles. Whether this particular incident actually happened or is just another piece of Detroit lore isn't important. What is important is that Mulally uncovered and disrupted the underlying problem holding Ford back from success: balkanization.

As it turned out, Ford had more than thirty unique platforms for building its products. No two vehicles in the Ford portfolio used the same basic pieces of equipment—headlamps, mirrors, springs, wheel rims, or, as noted, hood hinges. In fact, Ford had developed a culture in which engineers and product teams would spend more time rationalizing their poor decisions than implementing changes that would produce a better product for the customer and result in better revenue for the company. Mulally's goal was to reduce the number of engineering platforms to a half dozen or less—which was more in line with the rest of the industry. Doing so was an imperative, since the balkanization was adding billions of dollars to Ford's cost structure and putting it at a competitive disadvantage.[1]

Although Mulally did a number of things to revive the flagging automaker, standardization on the technology (products and components) Ford used to build cars was among the more significant changes. The results were most telling during the economic collapse of 2008 and 2009, when General Motors and Chrysler were forced to take more than $50 billion in government loans to stay afloat. Ford, on the other hand, took no government money and is now the United States' largest automaker by revenue and unit volume.[2] Technology—whether its personal computers or hood hinges—is a major expense for companies. Technology investment and expenses are embedded in every aspect of doing business. As shown in the Ford example, it is a critical enabler of strategic imperatives—agility, resiliency, and innovation—as well. Using technology as an advantage in today's hypercompetitive global economy requires converging business and technology.

In our Introduction, we introduced the concept of "convergence"—and discussed some classic failures that resulted from its lack. In this chapter we will focus on the role of technology/business convergence and its effect on financial performance. Moving toward convergence should be the lesson derived from what Mulally did at Ford by making technology decisions based on business objectives—namely operational efficiency (saving money) and quality output (making cars that people want to buy). We will show how converged companies are more resistant and resilient to vagaries of fluctuating markets—just as Ford weathered the 2009 recession that nearly swamped General Motors and Chrysler.

Convergence can be achieved through certain organizational "constructs," or management behaviors, which have been identified in research and confirmed in practice. These constructs establish a foundation on which corporations can build innovative business models. They ultimately yield superior financial performance for the enterprise as a whole. BTM Corporation's initial *Business Technology Convergence Index I* study, published in 2007, showed that Business Technology Management maturity at the alignment level—the level at which business and technology management teams are operating on parallel paths—correlated with superior economic performance.[3] The updated *Business Technology Convergence Index II* study (see Figure 3-1)—published in 2009 and incorporating data from one of the worst economic downturns in our history—shows that superior economic performance in such a period requires a disproportionately higher level of technology maturity.[4] In other words, maturity beyond alignment—and approaching convergence—is necessary to achieve superior economic performance.

Agility, Innovation, and Convergence

When Adam Smith wrote *The Wealth of Nations* in 1776, he described the characteristics and benefits of a free market, in which wealth was transferred between the producers of raw materials, manufacturers, and consumers of refined goods. Smith argued that a free market would ensure competition that resulted in higher quality goods at lower prices. The underlying presumption is that manufacturers would always have to create or respond to changes in the market to ensure their viability and success. In Smith's era, however, change came at a glacial pace; it would take years, sometimes decades, before change rippled across global markets.

The modern economy—global, domestic, and local—is fast and dynamic; the market is in a constant state of change. The greatest overarching challenge facing business leaders and their enterprises is to be able to quickly respond to market change; they must be the catalyst of

FIGURE 3–1 BUSINESS TECHNOLOGY CONVERGENCE INDEX II, 2003–2008.

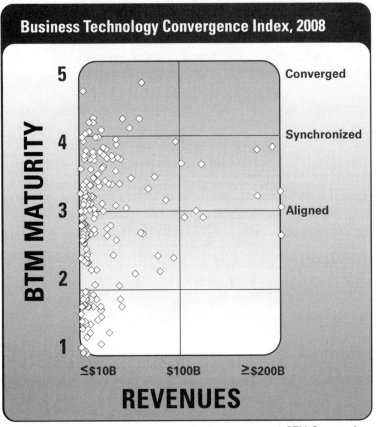

© BTM Corporation.

This figure represents the maturity levels of corporations assessed by the BTM Corporation in its second Business Technology Convergence Index. As you will note, alignment and convergence are not dictated by a company's revenue, but rather its management structure.

organizational change that will guide their businesses to market leadership. The pressure for change requires enterprises to be resilient, innovative, agile, and adaptive.

- ⌒ *Resilient:* able to bounce back from shock.
- ⌒ *Innovative:* able to push the envelope and develop new products, services, and methodologies that advance beyond the competition.
- ⌒ *Agile:* able to act nimbly to seize opportunities.

↻ *Adaptive:* able to sustain innovation through repeatable processes and organization that ensure advancements happen due to planning, not happenstance.

Actually, these seemingly distinct concepts are interrelated and interdependent. As an analogy, think of the Internet. In 1973, the U.S. Defense Advanced Research Projects Agency (DARPA) initiated a research program to investigate techniques and technologies for interlinking packet networks of various kinds. The objective was to develop communication protocols that would allow networked computers to communicate transparently across multiple, linked packet networks.[5] Its creation made communications resilient, and allowed for the increased ability to bounce back from shock. Yet it does so much more: the Internet allows organizations to be agile, to be able to act nimbly to seize opportunities. It has been the enabler of endless innovation in business models, processes, and global collaboration.

In the same way, a firm that is adaptable—agile and resilient—will be equipped to experience "sustained" innovation, meaning the innovation is not solely the result of happenstance but rather continuous and evolutionary. Sustainable innovation involves solutions to problems that reflect a commitment to economically, environmentally, and socially sound business practices. The connection among these concepts should not be surprising. Innovation, after all, is doing something new that creates value in the marketplace. Agility and resilience imply the ability to react to something new.

Organizational design and behaviors directly affect how the enterprise can react to and recover from forces beyond its control. Our research illustrates what leading organizations around the globe—including Global 2000 corporations, government agencies, and social enterprises—have learned about innovation. We looked into these organizations to better understand how they create innovative business models that can adapt and overcome unexpected market shifts. Successful organizations all moved toward the convergence of business and technology, applying similar and interrelated organizational designs and behaviors. Technology is now basic to all business activities, but if not managed as fundamental to an enterprise—if the management of business and technology are not "converged"—efforts to be adaptive and innovative are easily undermined.

In the best-managed enterprises, technology and business management converge completely. This occurs when business and technology

activities are intertwined and the leadership teams operate almost inter-
changeably. Our research further suggests that leaders who place a focus
on the convergence of business and technology disciplines within their
companies attain far more success than those who continue to treat
them as isolated functions. There is demonstrable economic value in
advancing maturity of technology management, and the payoff is greatest for those enterprises that are approaching convergence.

BTM's *Business Technology Convergence Index I* study (2002–
2006) showed that enterprises operating in the same economic environment with a more converged technology management structure
exhibited superior revenue growth and net profit margins as compared
to their nonconverged peers. The numbers spoke for themselves:

- 4 percent average higher return on equity (ROE).

- 8 percent average higher return on assets (ROA).

- 13 percent higher return on investments (ROI).

- 7 percent higher earnings before interest, taxes, and depreciation
  (EBITD) than those delivered by their industry groups.

- 36 percent average annual earnings per share (EPS) growth in
  contrast to 8 percent for their industry groups.

- 12 percent average annual revenue growth as compared to 1 percent for their industry groups.

The *Business Technology Convergence Index II* study further confirmed the durability, persistence, and value of converged outperformance. Of particular interest was the performance of convergence leaders
in the second five-year period (2004–2008), which coincided with the
economic downturn. This updated study employed the same methodology as the initial study and covered the succeeding two five-year periods,
2003–2007 and 2004–2008 (see summary chart of the latter period in
Figure 3–2).

The following performance highlights demonstrate the continued
resilience and performance advantages of convergence leaders:

- In 2004–2008, leader organizations delivered a dramatic 58 percent outperformance in annual ROE; the 2003–2007 advantage
  was 9.2 percent.

FIGURE 3-2 LEADERS' FINANCIAL OUTPERFORMANCE, 2004-2008.

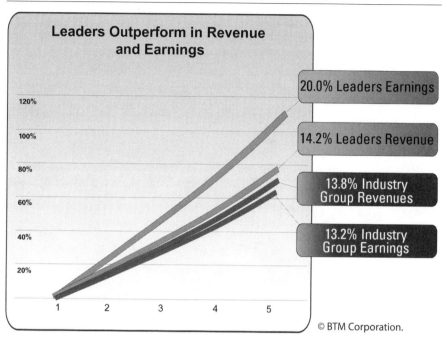

© BTM Corporation.

The *Business Technology Convergence Index II* study showed the monetary benefits of convergence. In the period 2004–2008, leaders in the convergence index had substantially better earnings and revenues than their laggard rivals.

○ The 2004–2008 ROA outperformance held by leader organizations was an equally dramatic 47 percent; the 2003–2007 outperformance advantage was 2.7 percent.

○ The 2004–2008 ROI outperformance for the leader organizations was 44.7 percent; the 2003–2007 advantage was 20.4 percent.

○ In the 2003–2007 and 2004–2008 periods, leader organizations delivered a 3.6 percent and 1.0 percent respective advantage per year in EBITD margins from operations, versus the 6.9 percent previously seen.

○ For 2003–2007, average EPS growth for leader organizations held steady at 37 percent per year, versus the 36.2 percent seen in the prior study, each representing a more than 3.5X outperformance over their industry peers. In the 2004–2008 period, the leaders' growth advantage decreased to 52 percent outperformance—reflecting the impact of the economic downturn.

⟳ Average revenue growth for leader organizations held steady at 11.5 percent per year in 2003–2007 and increased to 14.2 percent in the 2004–2008 period, tracking the 11.7 percent seen in the prior study. Outperformance versus the leaders' direct competitors varied significantly, moving from 11 percent in 2002–2006, through 2.4 percent in 2003–07, to 0.5 percent in the 2004–2008 period.[6]

By developing converged technology management capabilities, an organization creates an environment for strategic exploration and business agility. This occurs in the context of a clear understanding of technology's potential to accelerate development of both effective strategic positioning and innovative business models.

Constructing the Business Technology Convergence Index

To understand what these successful companies were doing differently, we evaluated them against a set of essential management capabilities for effective technology convergence.

These capabilities are grouped in four functional areas—Governance and Organization, Strategy and Planning, Strategic Investment Management, and Strategic Enterprise Architecture—which were discussed in some detail in Chapter 2. Each capability, as evaluated in four critical dimensions—Process, Organization, Information, and Technology—is marked by repeatable processes, executed through appropriate organizational structures, and enabled by the right information and technology. By developing these management capabilities, an organization creates an environment for strategic exploration and business agility. It has a clear understanding of technology's potential to accelerate the development of both strategic positioning and innovative business models.

Business and technology convergence happens when an organization is integrated into a "whole-brained" enterprise that creates connections between innovation, resilience, and agility. This organizational maturity supports innovative thinking through carefully designed processes, calculated risk taking, and information architectures that serve as a knowledge base for building and testing opportunities. Convergence provides an enterprise with the platform to thrive on marketplace change rather than just reacting to keep pace.

The Business Technology Convergence Index—an unweighted database of the enterprise-wide management maturity levels of approximately 100 commercial enterprises and public sector entities—was created to measure the prevalence and effects of convergence. Enterprises in the Index were included because their maturity levels had been validated, not because of any desired set of operating characteristics. Their organization and management activities were evaluated using the Business Technology Management (BTM) Framework, which describes and standardizes the capabilities cited above.

Not all of the enterprises in the Index were explicitly practicing the tenets of the BTM Framework; however, the Framework was the tool used to understand and define the activities we observed. The assessment validated the extent to which each enterprise had:

- ◑ Developed and implemented process maturity.
- ◑ Established and empowered decision-making bodies.
- ◑ Gathered, standardized, and put to use its information.
- ◑ Used automation to facilitate decision making and management.

The examination of these companies focused primarily on the foundation capabilities, whose maturity underlies overall technology maturity: Strategic and Tactical Governance, Organizational Design and Change Management, and Portfolio and Program Management. However, analysis was also conducted in the higher-level capabilities, those that are often developed later in the maturation process, such as Communications Strategy and Management, Compliance and Risk Management, and Resource and Demand Management.

The information gathered about these organizations was analyzed using the BTM Institute's BTM Maturity Model, which defines five levels of maturity—Initial, Repeatable, Defined, Managed, and Optimizing— scored across the four critical dimensions—Process, Organization, Information, and Technology.

Our research shows (see Table 3–1) that Level 1 enterprises typically execute some strategic Capabilities in a disaggregated, task-like manner. A Level 2 enterprise exhibits limited Capabilities, attempts to assemble information for major decisions, and consults the technology

TABLE 3-1 MATURITY LEVELS AND CAPABILITY DIMENSIONS.

Process Dimension Maturity	Characteristics
Level 1 Initial	Unstructured processes.
Level 2 Repeatable	Some core processes identified and documented.
Level 3 Defined	Some integration between key process areas.
Level 4 Managed	Consistent processes with integration across the organization.
Level 5 Optimizing	Continuous process optimization.

Organization Dimension Maturity	Characteristics
Level 1 Initial	Missing organizational structures.
Level 2 Repeatable	Structures, roles, and responsibilities are identified and documented.
Level 3 Defined	Structures exist, with roles and responsibilities being executed.
Level 4 Managed	Fully developed structures with roles being executed.
Level 5 Optimizing	Organization structures are optimized.

Information Dimension Maturity	Characteristics
Level 1 Initial	Isolated, relatively poor documentation of data and metrics.
Level 2 Repeatable	Documented and consistent information policies and measurement criteria.
Level 3 Defined	Effective data sharing; internal benchmarking.
Level 4 Managed	Organization-wide metrics; internal and external benchmarking.
Level 5 Optimizing	Fully data-driven decision making.

Technology Dimension Maturity	Characteristics
Level 1 Initial	Lack of required automation.
Level 2 Repeatable	Partial or sporadic automation.
Level 3 Defined	Growing amount of automation with some coordinated use.
Level 4 Managed	Full use of automation with some integration.
Level 5 Optimizing	Consistent, coordinated, integrated use of automation.

function on decisions with obvious technology implications. Level 3 enterprises are "functional" with respect to the Capabilities, and those at Level 4 have the Capabilities fully implemented. Level 5 enterprises are responsive enough to rapidly adjust the rules to maintain strategic advantages over competitors.

Enterprises at lower levels of maturity will score lower for technology productivity, responsiveness, and project success than those enterprises at higher levels. As the enterprise's maturity increases, the resulting synchronization of business strategy and technology delivery makes the enterprise more agile and adaptable. As a result, they are able to sense and respond to emerging opportunities more quickly.

The Business Technology Convergence Index is comprised of approximately 250 organizations, an increase from the 100 covered in the first study. The data shows that maturity is not dependent upon an enterprise's industry or size. We assessed corporations across dozens of market sets and sizes by top-line revenue. The performance of these companies ranges from Level 1, with incomplete or missing elements across the process, organization, information, and technology dimensions, to Level 4, operating in a state of synchronization. Only a few enterprises were fully converged or approaching a Level 5 rating.

The Financial Effects of Convergence

The *Business Technology Convergence Index II* study revealed a striking linkage between success in progress toward technology convergence and an enterprise's financial and operational performance. The financial performance benefit of technology convergence is evident. Here are a few of the highlights.

- ◑ Synchronization-level maturity (BTM maturity of greater than 3.9) is required for superior economic performance over industry peers during the five-year period that included the downturn. In the previous study periods, economic outperformance was achieved at lower maturity levels—3.6 and 3.7, respectively.

- ◑ Alignment-level maturity proved to be an economic liability during 2004–2008. At the 3.6 maturity level in the 2006 study, economic performance declined in each of the six measured financial categories, the amount of the decline ranging from 7.8 percent to more than 52 percent.

- ◑ In 2004–2008, convergence leaders demonstrated remarkably superior performance in ROE, ROA, EPS, and ROI—the outperformance advantage ranged from 200 percent to over 600 percent.

Leaders enjoy a marked advantage in the average annual rate of increase of amounts returned to their bottom lines, and to their shareholders; it more than quadrupled that of their competitors in the first two study periods, and, in the midst of the economic downturn, convergence leaders were able to sustain a 50 percent advantage over their competitors.

Between 2002 and 2006, leaders generated 12 percent average annual revenue in growth versus 0.7 percent for their own industry groups. Between 2003 and 2007, the leaders' growth figure held steady at 11.5 percent versus the industry group figure of 9.1 percent. In 2004–2008, although the leaders' growth figure increased to 14.2 percent, the advantage decreased to 0.5 percent. These figures are not limited to any one area within the enterprise. They are not technology-specific and do not measure returns on any single project. Rather, they measure enterprise-wide returns, and they reflect the growth rates and the entire enterprise EBITD. These figures tell the story that these leaders have discovered and implemented a business model superior to their competitors—one in which business and technology work cohesively for the benefit of the enterprise.

The financial effects of technology convergence are enterprise-wide because the capabilities that drive them are enterprise-wide. Key management capabilities are interconnected and require the active shared ownership of decision making and execution by both business and technology professionals.

Other essential business improvement steps are equally grounded in the key capabilities. Whether building an environment that fosters sustained innovation, designing an enterprise to achieve consistent execution and measurement, extending the enterprise's boundaries to establish and exploit business partner networks and indirect sales channels, or optimizing service delivery, convergence is clearly key to ensuring superior operational performance and financial outcomes.

The Common Characteristics of Convergence Leader Enterprises

The enterprises in the Index have a level of technology maturity that marks them as leaders at or above 3.9, at the high range of synchronization and approaching convergence.

As a group, leader enterprises have achieved synchronization, but only a small number are approaching convergence. They cover a wide range of sizes, with revenues that range from approximately $2 billion to about $100 billion, and are spread across eighteen industry sectors. This diversity of size and industry demonstrates that BTM maturity does not constrain itself to a particular size or industry—all organizations can achieve the benefits of technology convergence.

Alignment, synchronization, and convergence do not happen by accident; it's a very deliberate, step-by-step progression through the phases as the enterprise moves toward convergence. And, as with all cases of business, each enterprise is unique in how it actually operationalizes convergence. Market conditions, competitive landscape, internal organization structures, and the skill sets of management all contribute to this advancement. But each of the leader enterprises in the Convergence Index II shares some common characteristics.

Consistency

Enterprise management processes—lines of communications, project oversight and authorizations, project reviews, and financial accountability—are consistent across the entire organization. This consistency also means that management—strategic, operations, and technology—is consistent in how they deal with issues. The "enterprise view" is fully developed, and the enterprise has the means of addressing a broad array of issues. Consistency is the one characteristic that permeates through each of the other characteristics.

Governance

Leading enterprises have consistent processes for ensuring that business management is fully engaged in decisions regarding technology. They have a clear and articulated understanding of the execution of organizational change management. They demonstrate clear communication of technology initiatives. And there is both a risk posture for the organization and a clear appreciation of what must be done to ensure regulatory compliance.

Strategic Investment

The management within these leading enterprises has established and maintains consistent processes for sponsoring, selecting, and managing business initiatives. They have standardized how projects are structured and managed. They have standard management of resources—human, financial, fixed—for the approved initiatives. And they have a management entity that actively monitors and manages the performance of all initiatives according to a commonly accepted framework; this management layer is also an "early warning" system for elevating issues to upper management.

Strategy and Planning

These enterprises have established close collaboration between business and technology professionals in the development of technology execution strategies. The enterprise's business strategy both reflects and is driven by its technology strategy. Financial matters are considered from inception, and there are active, mature budgeting and benchmarking regimes in place. The enterprises have an understanding of which of the organization's technology activities can best be delivered by its own employees or partners. They have a mature framework for ensuring transparency in service delivery. And, they have an established, mature set of processes for weaving disparate assets—including those acquired through mergers and acquisitions—into the enterprise fabric.

Strategic Enterprise Architecture

Leading enterprises have documented, integrated business and technology architectures that fully describe the organization and the technology necessary for reaching its goals. They have reasonable exceptions for technology practices and execution, as well as intelligently enforced standards. And, lastly, they have regimes for ensuring that the organization inventories its technology assets, schedules future acquisitions, and plans for an orderly transition to the future state.

Of course, these characteristics and processes are meaningless unless the enterprise has clearly defined organizational structure with roles defined and assigned to managers and employees. Depending on size, enterprises may have divisions or business units charged with decision making and oversight of technology strategy and execution. Leader enterprises consistently have governance bodies that place the responsibility of technology decision making in the hands of business and technology professionals. They have bodies focused on the approval and prioritization—and on the financials—of technology initiatives, and that similarly have cross-functional representation. They elevate to a direct reporting relationship to the CEO all those professionals ultimately responsible for the operational and productive technology, rather than limiting that information conduit to the chief information officer. In such organizations, these bodies are woven into the decision-making and execution fabric of the enterprise. They are not a "management superstructure," nor are they "overhead."

For these enterprises, data is more than information; it is refined and actionable intelligence. Such enterprises manage information effectively across the whole of the organization and can make reasonable, sound decisions based on information communicated through many layers and across divisional boundaries. And, in large measure, this information is available through and managed in an integrated, enterprise-wide automated system that facilitates decision making. These organizations understand both the specific strengths and the limitations of point solutions, and they have created management dashboards and other tools to make decision making and management consistent. While not every professional may have access to it, the system exists and is a management tool in effective use.

The topmost enterprises among the leaders have achieved convergence, the state in which the distinction between technology and business professionals has almost altogether vanished, and in which the enterprise is optimizing its management of the two. These enterprises have enhanced the process, organization, information, and automation described above, so that they now operate as a whole. For example:

○ They engage in continuous process optimization. They learn, adapt, implement, and improve, in an ongoing cycle.

○ Their organization structures are optimized, so that they have the right structures in place at the right level, and they make decisions appropriate to their status.

○ They conduct fully data-driven decision making enabled by consistent, coordinated, integrated use of automation. Every professional has an appropriate level of access to enterprise-wide information, analysis, and management tools, and the enterprise makes this uniform, data-driven model fundamental to its way of doing business.

Technology convergence occurs in leader enterprises as a fundamental element of best management practices. That these leaders do well financially should not be surprising. Their maturity in managing business and technology together mirrors their maturity in managing other areas—human talent, materials, supply chains, and finances. This is true to a different degree for each individual enterprise. Some are in industries in which firms spend more on technology in general, and on information technology in particular, than firms in other industries. Each must identify its place on the spectrum of enterprises that ranges from those for which technology is strategically critical to those for whom it will have less significance on performance and survival.

While every firm will benefit from better technology management, the primary area of focus for the boards and upper managements of certain enterprises may well have to be on industry-specific concerns such as government regulations. Large publicly traded companies are governed by the Sarbanes-Oxley Act of 2003, which mandates financial accountability in the wake of the Enron collapse that robbed thousands of investors of their equity through fraud. The entire health care industry is subject to the security and record keeping requirements in the Health Insurance Portability and Accountability Act of 1996. The financial services industry is governed by the Graham-Leach-Bliley Act, which mandates data security and accountholder privacy requirements. In such enterprises, technology decision making appropriately takes a secondary role.

Given the strategic role of technology and its potential to affect financial performance, however, boards of directors and top management in many companies are assuming larger roles in its oversight.

Their first "decision" must be to understand the strategic importance of technology to their particular firm. They must link technology investments to their firms' business models and product market strategies.

The Strategic Roles of Technology

To understand why the convergence of business and technology can have such an effect on financial performance, consider first the subtle yet significant shift in the role of technology itself. It's now basic to all business activities. Many companies routinely spend as much on information technology alone as on all other capital investments combined. In some large enterprises, the budget for information technology can exceed $1 billion.

Organizations that are mature in their technology management spend huge amounts of money on technology, not because they see it as an efficient and cost-saving tool (which of course it is), but because they recognize its strategic role. For such enterprises, technology investments are planned and evolving. Systems are not simply deployed and decommissioned as point solutions; they are layered, built upon, and developed into systems that stand the test of time and user expectations. A primary difference between a converged and nonconverged enterprise is how each views technology at the end of its life—a converged enterprise will have future-proofed its investments against cost shocks and obsolescence; a nonconverged enterprise must engage in costly "rip and replace" exercises.

But just how does technology enable a business? How do technology investments and implementations move a business toward its strategic goals? Technology—developed and deployed in a technology framework—fulfills four critical, strategic roles—automation, empowerment, control, and transformation—as discussed below.

Automation

Technology plays a critical role in transaction and work process automation, enabling the business goals of higher productivity, lower cost, and improved efficiency. Automation enables the goal of being easy to do business with by allowing employees, customers, and business partners to access services with speed, convenience, and personalization. Examples include deployment of customer self-service (self-checkouts at retail stores, Internet check-in for airlines), employee self-service (desktop-based self-procurement, self-management of benefits), and online sales.

An automation directive signals that the firm's technology focus will be on seamless enterprise and inter-enterprise services, global process connectivity, and the quest for more digitization. Key business value metrics will focus on productivity and costs.

Empowerment

Technology is critical to the facilitation of fast, effective, and accurate decision making across the enterprise and its partnership network. It is performed through investments in decision-support tools and technologies (for example, data warehousing, data mining, and online analytical processing), intranets for dissemination of best practices, and extranets for rapid sharing of information with business partners. Empowerment supports this process by providing front-end workers with intelligence and decision support in their interactions with customers, business partners, and external stakeholders. Many of these interactions (especially those that take place in a customer call center) require problem or dispute resolution. Examples of empowerment include decision support scripts for call centers and customer service agents and visibility tools in supply chain and logistics processes. An empowerment directive signals that the firm's technology focus will be on decision support and knowledge management. Key business value metrics will focus on partner satisfaction, problem resolution productivity (number of problems resolved, cycle time to resolution), and resolution costs (cost per customer call).

Control

Technology augments a firm's control by facilitating efficient and real-time monitoring of business operations and business partners through practices such as daily close, operational alerts, and dashboards with drill-down capabilities. It is performed through investments in monitoring tools and technologies (data warehouses, portals) and through enterprise risk management processes. Control enables the business goals of enhancing transparency of business operations, rapid detection and resolution of management control issues, and accurate reporting of the key metrics of business performance. The emphasis of the control vision is on strong financial performance management systems. Key business value metrics will include the completeness, accuracy, validity, and integrity of the firm's transactions and decision-making processes; the accuracy, speed, and economy of financial reporting; and the effectiveness of financial audits and fraud detection.

Transformation

Technology, in its role as agent of transformation, facilitates the innovation of new business models (for example, direct to the customer, multiple-channel integration, whole of the enterprise or "one face" integration, value net integration), new products and services (digital products and services, digitized customer service through online chats), and new modes of organizing work (globally distributed work practices). The focus is not on investment in specific business technologies as much as on the development of digital options, digitization of products and services, and experimentation with new technology-enabled business ideas. Transformation enables the business goals of continuous innovation, agility, and competitive disruption. Key business value metrics include the rate of product, process, or business model innovation and the comprehensiveness and richness of a firm's innovation portfolio.

The Takeaway: Turning Ideas into Action

Our research suggests that the convergence of business and technology is a logical first step for enterprise leaders facing a rapidly changing world, needing new management structure and response approaches, trying to predict and realize the unknown, and seeking profitability in a hyper-competitive environment. Whatever the nature of the firm, the management practices that create convergence can enable the firm to attain its strategic mission.

Using the right metrics to assess the business value derived from technology is critical in demonstrating the effectiveness of business technology investments and achieving convergence. Senior executives increasingly demand an understanding of how business/technology convergence can improve operations, enhance managers' decision making, and place the organization in a strong position to compete.

The following eight steps can help create a foundation to provide evidence of a positive relationship between business technology investments and overall financial performance:

Step 1: *Establish* the business purpose of each investment in technology: Is it to enable growth, maintain the infrastructure, or manage risk?

Step 2: *Determine* whether the metrics you use have changed along with changes in business processes and technology.

Step 3: *Agree* on new metrics that show how your organization creates agility, sense-and-respond capabilities, and digital options. This agreement will ultimately lead to metrics that accurately measure business value.

Step 4: *Understand* the business environment and how the company adjusts its strategy to changes in the environment. This often requires real-time adjustments in operations, placing a greater onus on business technology executives to develop a well-oiled system for gathering information and presenting business alternatives.

Step 5: *Leverage* management capabilities, such as BTM's Approval and Prioritization capabilities and its Consolidation and Standardization capabilities. These can be used to manage and define the information requirements to support a high information-orientation culture.

Step 6: *Translate* the business strategy into tactical plans for which information and communication technologies can be deployed. It is increasingly the role of the technology executives to make this connection. Executives must take the lead in communicating the areas in which business technology can add value. Employees must be made aware of how these opportunities relate to their jobs.

Step 7: *Identify* the complementary investments necessary to get full value out of technology investments.

Step 8: *Instill* in employees the behaviors and values that will lead to the best use of information to support and enhance customer, supplier, and partner relationships.

PART II

Convergence in Practice

CHAPTER 4

The Nimble Giants: How Converged Business Models Drive Successful Large Enterprises

BLOCKBUSTER DIDN'T CREATE the video rental market. By the time Blockbuster emerged in 1985, tens of thousands of video rental clubs and stores dotted strip malls across the country. But the early video rental business was immature and its model expensive. Video stores would charge "membership dues" and exorbitant late return fees to cover their high expense for buying tapes through movie distributors. Blockbuster was different because it made video rentals easy and affordable. It didn't charge membership fees, which lowered the barrier to consumers. But what really made Blockbuster different was the change it brought to the video rental model. Rather than paying a large upfront charge for movies, it brokered a revenue sharing arrangement with studios and distributors. The revenue split lowered costs and increased returns to all parties in the supply chain. Blockbuster's bulk stocking of new releases made it a better choice for moviegoers, and revenues soared. At one point, Blockbuster grew so large that it attempted a merger of equals with entertainment giant Viacom.

All good things must come to an end, and Blockbuster reached its tipping point in 2009, when it lost nearly $560 million as year-over-year revenues plummeted 21 percent.[1] The fall was unprecedented considering that rentals usually climbed during a recession—and 2009 was one of the deepest economic recessions on record—as people seek low-cost entertainment alternatives. Confusing the equation was the increase in DVD sales during the same period. While home entertainment was becoming increasingly popular with budget-conscious consumers, Blockbuster was shutting stores and cutting staff. What changed was technology, specifically the Internet and high-speed home broadband connections. And it's that platform that the chain's rival, Netflix, has rode to overcome its own growth challenges and disrupt the Blockbuster model.

Netflix was disruptive from its start in 1997. Through its subscription-based service, members would order the movies over the Internet and Netflix would deliver the selection to them via the postal service, with a paid envelope for easy returns. Making Netflix appealing were its no-late-fee policies, allowing members to keep movies as long as they wanted, and a recommendation feature that made suggestions to members based on their previous ordering history and what people with similar profiles watched. Netflix still isn't challenging Blockbuster or competitors in terms of revenue; it generated $1.3 billion revenue in 2009 to Blockbuster's $4 billion take. But the model was enough to scare Blockbuster and retail giant Walmart into attempting their hand at similar services. Both failed, and Blockbuster's decline is paralleled by Netflix ascension.[2]

Success hasn't come easy to Netflix either. The subscription rental model was never a guarantee of success, and the company faced numerous logistical challenges throughout its operating history. It invested millions of dollars to keep its technology and model ahead of the competition. Most notable of its quest to stay fresh is "The Netflix Prize," a contest open to any software developer that can produce a 10 percent performance improvement in its movie recommendation engine. In September 2009, Netflix awarded its $1 million to "BellKor's Pragmatic Chaos"—a team of AT&T Labs researchers—for producing an algorithm that produced substantial performance gains.[3] Programs like this prize help keep Netflix competitive. Netflix isn't sitting idly by as new challenges emerge. The Internet is disrupting the model it pioneered by allowing cable companies and other Internet-based providers to enable rentals to be downloaded and played on PCs and Web-connected televisions. Netflix is adapting its model, and was one of the early pioneers of

Web streaming of videos and limited-time online movie rentals. It has even created an app for the Apple iPad, giving its users the ability to download movies for these ultra-portable devices. And its concept for streaming rented video over the Internet has inspired copycat offerings by Amazon, Apple, Microsoft, and Sony.

While Netflix hasn't always gotten its model right and has suffered numerous setbacks over the years, it has demonstrated a lack of complacency that would leave it vulnerable to shifting market dynamics and competitive pressures. Unlike Blockbuster and other competitors that were laggards in developing next-generation business models and responding to changing market conditions, Netflix constantly pushes for ways to enhance and expand its business model to stay ahead. It didn't just implement technology; it transformed itself by harnessing the power of technology and business modeling to create a new dynamic. As Netflix founder Reed Hastings so aptly described the guiding philosophy, "We tried not to get drunk on the future, but actually to predict it accurately."[4]

The Innovation Imperative: Adapt or Die

"How did you lose your money?" starts an old joke in business. "First, very slowly. Then all at once." In other words, complacency bred by success is what often leads companies to their doom. Engrossed in the approaches that made them successful, they fail to evolve their business model to meet changing market needs or take advantage of new technologies. As we saw in the Blockbuster/Netflix example, a business's failure to adapt often opens the opportunity window for would-be competitors.

Big, innovative companies share several common characteristics. The most important in our view is that they have brought the management of their business and their technology together. Let's look at UPS as an example. It's the world's largest package delivery company. It invests $1 billion a year in technology and owns the world's ninth largest airplane fleet. It moves nearly 15 million packages—or two percent of the world's gross domestic product—through its global network daily. UPS's business and technology convergence begins with a mindset buried deep in the culture. Technology is an equal player at the strategy table. Technology and the business are partners in a collaboration-driven strategy that results in greater efficiencies, cost controls, and revenue opportunities.

UPS's business/technology convergence takes physical form in the organizational structure. The chief information officer sits on the Management Committee, the top executive group that oversees operations. The CIO also chairs the Program Project Oversight Committee, a cross-functional group through which all projects, technology and otherwise, come for prioritization. And he chairs the Business Technology Governance Committee, a group of business and technology people that considers all major technology initiatives. Presenting to that committee are portfolio managers, each of whom has a business partner. Other groups within the company undergo a continuous study of emerging technologies. One is the Information Technology Steering Committee, which looks for innovative uses of new technologies. Only a handful of its thirty members are technologists. This cross-functional collaborative approach means that business executives have to become comfortable with evaluating and advocating for technology. In other words, technology ideas can come from any quarter, so all are given a fair hearing regardless of their source. Conversely, by the way, technologists have to learn to talk in business terminology.

When establishing governance, corporations have to define the specific structures, their memberships, and their roles to achieve and maintain consistency in oversight and output. There is no one absolute way to do it. However a company chooses to frame its structure, successful innovators like UPS systematically bring all parts of their organizations together to consider and implement new ideas. The converged management of business and technology is no guarantee that a company will become innovative. Nevertheless, convergence is a prerequisite to holistically seeing a company's interrelated parts. Once those parts are identified and integrated, a company can better position itself to seize new opportunities.

With the management of business and technology converged, the organization becomes a seedbed in which new ideas can take root and grow. The organization becomes nimble in exploiting new ideas. Everything can—and typically does—move faster.

Architecting Business Models: A Blueprint for Convergence

Technology is more than tools and automation. As economist Carl Schramm wrote in his book *The Entrepreneurial Imperative*, technology is both an equalizer and enabler. It provides enterprises with the ability to simplify tasks, maximize efficiencies, lower costs, and expedite delivery systems. Technology in this sense is a positive business enabler that offers an enterprise a competitive advantage. At the same time, widely adopted technologies provide the same objective benefits to all, and therefore little competitive advantage. As Schramm wrote, "Technology isn't the answer, since everyone now either has the same technology or can easily obtain it. By definition, when everyone has access to the same asset, the asset itself can't supply an edge. Only innovative, entrepreneurial ways of employing that technology can provide a comparative advantage."[5]

Technology properly aligned with an organization's business needs, goals, and objectives makes the difference between an enterprise on the path to extinction and one that's able to stay aloft during turbulent economic times and remain consistently, progressively successful. Take, for example, the innovation that keeps UPS the leader in the parcel and package delivery industry. When a big brown UPS truck pulls into your driveway, what you see is, well, a big brown truck. What you don't see is the driver's wireless connection to the global network of one of the world's most innovative companies. It has chosen brown trucks as a symbol, but it has found its competitive edge in technology. The blueprint of that competitive edge is the business model.

"Business model" is one of those terms that takes on the meaning of its user. You can't always be sure that one person's "business model" isn't another's "value proposition," "business case," "revenue model," or "strategy." Before explaining what the term ought to mean, let's point out a couple of ways companies incorrectly use "business model," ways that have little bearing on converging the management of business and technology.

Companies sometimes treat the term "business model" as little more than a cocktail napkin one-liner. Choose your metaphor for how it's conveyed—cocktail napkin, back of an envelope, elevator pitch, etc. It's a thumbnail, not a business model. Although the gross simplification encapsulated in this thumbnail is too shallow to form an effective basis for business/technology convergence, it does echo one of the crucial attributes of a proper business model: a big picture of the business, its operations, and expected outcomes.

Ironically, the second way that people misapply the term is almost exactly the opposite of the cocktail napkin mistake. Rather than oversimplify, they dive in at a level of complexity that precludes a big-picture view. This happens when a business model is equated with a financial model. Before you can build even the most basic financial model, you have to first make some important assumptions (industry and vertical specialization, target customer, geographic service area) that preclude the unbiased, big picture that is integral to our purposes.

For the purposes of this discussion, a business model is something different from both the cocktail napkin one-liner and the financial model in disguise. It's a big picture that captures a snapshot of the enterprise and communicates direction and goals to all stakeholders. BTM manifests this business model in what we call "Strategic Enterprise Architecture" (SEA).

SEA: Architectures to Action

Businesses have plans and organization charts, but those instruments don't necessarily translate into execution. For that, we turn to the Strategic Enterprise Architecture, which defines the organization's business model with details of the technology resources and operating procedures. An SEA frames the business intent (model, purpose, mission) with specifics of the technology and governance process for successful execution of a business model. Executives should not confuse SEA with an organization chart, since it transcends typical business hierarchies by providing the conduits between executives and operational groups to ensure cooperation and converged oversight of technology adoption, implementation, and management.

Just as the term "business model" carries multiple definitions and meanings to different people, so too does the term "architecture." Let's narrow the scope of what BTM means when it says "architecture." Enterprise architecture isn't just about technology or technology assets. The best way to visualize SEA is how it adds value to the business through four broad filters: identity, strategy, asset assignment, and competitive positioning.

Identity

Businesses have names and brands, but identity is the all-encompassing value derived from the business's net assets and operations. Identity consists of intangible perceptions as much as tangible assets. It includes such elements as mission statements, division and product brands, market reputation, competitive market position, and what differentiates the business from competing offerings. Toyota, for instance, enjoyed years of unblemished corporate identity buoyed by high-quality cars that performed well and retained their value. Its products, work ethic, competitive positioning, and market performance fueled the company's identity. Even when Toyota's reputation and identity were tarnished in 2010 following the massive recalls of its best-selling hybrid Prius cars, it was able to leverage its strong identity to rebound quickly. A combination of its speedy response and its track record for engineering excellence enabled it to repair its troubled cars and restore sales volumes after a momentary decline.

Identity might also include elements that describe the company's unique culture, such as values, office rules, and employee behavioral expectations. Companies such as Google and Microsoft tout their position on *Fortune*'s annual 100 Best Companies to Work For list for a reason—it helps them recruit top talent and it gives customers a sense that they care about their workers.

Strategy

This simply is a company's mission and values translated into concrete action. An important component is the coordination between multiple business units, each of which plays a unique role to help meet common goals. Strategy includes elements such as goals, a time frame for achieving goals, required resources, and performance indicators.

Strategy is basic to growth: It requires a clear organizational vision, a clearly defined and effectively communicated roadmap to the future, and the measurement of outcomes against predefined criteria. Through proper execution, it allows for an increased ability to define a differentiating competitive advantage, and to ensure that its technology initiatives originate from its overall business strategy.

Asset Assignment

Assets are all the resources a company needs to pursue its strategy. These might be products and services; organizational assets, including the reporting structure, geographic distribution, roles/responsibilities, and individual resources; financial resources; intellectual property; distribution channels; and physical assets like real estate, and operational and information technology. These assets, in whatever form, collectively support the direction a company chooses to follow. It is important to note that the decisions made on which area call for the most investment often vary based on the priorities deemed most critical according to the overall strategy at any given time.

Competitive Positioning

This is more than just who a company competes against, but also how it's differentiated, how it ranks among its competitive set, and the composition (and value) of its extended ecosystem (suppliers, partners, and resellers/dealers). In addition, it could include market demographics such as potential entrants, emerging technologies, availability of resources and supplies, and general trends that influence the company's position in its market.

Each of these four elements, as shown in Figure 4–1, has subjective and objective—textual and numeric—attributes (metrics, priority, and feasibility) that help give the SEA the depth of description and interaction that distinguish it from a simple diagram. These attributes could include additional characteristics such as a contextual description of who is considered a high-value customer and numerical values that describe the estimated number of customers that fall into this category and the revenue a customer needs to account for to qualify as high value.

FIGURE 4–1 SEA-BASED BUSINESS MODEL.

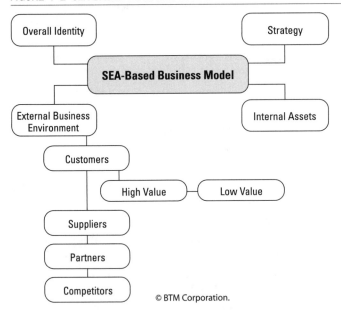

© BTM Corporation.

Strategic Enterprise Architecture goes beyond a basic business model by incorporating a depth of detail that provides assessments on where a corporation stands in the market, what it's trying to achieve, and who and why different actors are assigned tasks.

This information provides an important basis for developing business scenario models. Scenarios could vary according to the revenue required to qualify as a high-value customer.

Keep in mind that explaining a business model poses somewhat of a problem. There is a common misconception that an SEA is a singular, one-size-fits-all architecture. Nothing could be further from the truth. The specifics of a given business model differentiate one company's SEA from another's. Companies aren't limited to one empirically correct set of elements. The categories and elements expressed in Figure 4–1 shouldn't be considered a cookie-cutter mold for patterning every SEA. Each company's culture and business model will inevitably produce a unique approach, none of which is necessarily better or worse than any other.

SEA's direct benefits come from two sources: the composite elements and the process of researching and defining the SEA. The deliberate act of creating the SEA compels management to think through the complete business landscape and ultimately uncover hidden opportunities for improvement. This is obviously not a matter for a two-day meeting or even a week-long off-site retreat. Nor is it the province of some ad hoc committee. It is a matter for everyone, and it's an ongoing activity. Assessing, evaluating, and understanding oneself is the essence of an SEA.

The benefits of SEA are seen in many innovative, disruptive, and evolving companies that have leveraged technology to their competitive advantage. Consider these famous examples:

- ○ Walmart had humble beginnings in Arkansas, where it was little more than a small chain of mom-and-pop stores in the 1960s. Where other retailers focused on product lines and sales models, Walmart evolved around logistics. It bought product in bulk and mastered the art of distribution, ensuring that low-cost goods reached the stores where they are in the highest demand. The model has left many retailers on the wayside while Walmart has become one of the biggest companies in the world.

- ○ Microsoft in the early 1980s was just one of many software companies publishing operating systems for personal computers. MS-DOS, the operating system that ultimately made Microsoft a powerhouse, wasn't particularly remarkable in its design or performance. Microsoft rocketed to success with its creation of software licensing (a business innovation that leveraged technology), which produced royalties from every computer running its code. By the end of the 1980s, Microsoft was the world's dominant operating system company and founder Bill Gates was on his way to becoming one of the richest men in the world.

○ Michael Dell, while a college student in the early 1980s, started assembling personal computers in his University of Austin dorm room. He hit upon the idea of a direct sales model where consumers could choose different PC configurations. The result is a model that both delivered high customer satisfaction at lower costs, and that completely disrupted the staid PC marketplace then dominated by IBM, Hewlett-Packard, and Compaq.

○ Pierre Omidyar, a France-born Iranian computer programmer, sat down one weekend in 1995 to begin writing the code to make it easier for people to trade goods over the Internet. In essence, he was creating a virtual garage sale. What he produced was eBay, today one of the most recognizable brands, and one that revolutionized the dealing of new and used goods, created new sales channels for small retailers, and, in the process, completely disrupted the newspaper classifieds market.

○ Larry Page and Sergey Brin were just two Stanford University students that had an idea for organizing information on the rapidly growing Internet. In 1996, they came up with an idea for a search engine. At first, they didn't think of it as a company, but as a tool that another company could leverage. They presented their concept to Yahoo!, then the dominant portal on the Web, which passed on buying the technology. Undeterred, Page and Brin struck out on their own and founded Google, which is now the world's dominant Web company.

Every industry has stories of how an unsuspecting innovator with a new business model came along and completely transformed the market. In hindsight, it's easy to see the wisdom of a Bill Gates or a Pierre Omidyar, but it's harder to discern the value of a concept when it's new and unproven. It's especially difficult to accept a new idea when the current conventional model and product is performing well. It is often the case that innovation and disruption don't happen when a product or business model is in decline, but rather when it's peaking. SEA not only provides the enabling framework for optimizing the use of technology to reach business objectives, but the recurring impetus to question, re-assess, and adjust the use of technology in meeting new goals.

Organizations have used a variety of resources to document bits and pieces of the way they operate over time, yet much of this information is disjointed, incomplete, and of little value. This is often the result of not using commonly agreed-upon standards and terminology, or of architectures that are not complete. This makes it difficult to formulate a cohesive picture of the business and technology architectures.

A valid business architecture allows an organization to express its key business strategies and their impact on business functions and processes. Typically the business architecture is comprised of both current and future state models that define how the organization maintains its competitive advantage. Business architectures are linked to technology architectures that include applications, data, and infrastructure elements. The joining of these architectures comprises the SEA. It includes the capabilities necessary to design the enterprise from business, process, application, data, and infrastructure perspectives. These are the Business Architecture (business strategies, operating models, and processes) and Technology Architecture (applications, data, and infrastructure) capabilities. These capabilities bring order to the islands of information that exist typically in large organizations, as shown in Figure 4–2.

Leadership Starts at the Top

In December 2001 the world eagerly awaited the end of what had been one of the worst years in memory. The United States' sense of security was shattered by the September 11 terrorist attacks that included two planes hitting the World Trade Center in New York, one crashing into the Pentagon in Washington, D.C., and a final plane that went down in a field in rural Pennsylvania. The global economy was already trending toward recession, and the terrorist attacks were enough to push the global economy over the edge. And in the technology world, the computer systems of commercial enterprises around the world were being ravaged by viruses such as Nimda and Code Red that attacked and destroyed the data on the Windows operating system.

Computer viruses and worms—also known as malware—had been around since the late 1980s, when researchers produced proof of concept viruses to demonstrate how computer systems could be invaded by and manipulated by malicious software. Malware threats had been fairly con-

FIGURE 4–2 STRATEGIC ENTERPRISE ARCHITECTURE.

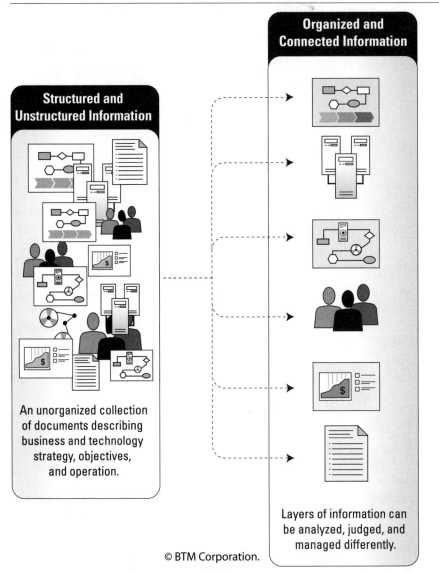

© BTM Corporation.

SEA transforms structured and unstructured information by organizing and aligning it.

tained by the limited mediums for moving between computer networks. But the commercialization of the Internet, the broadening use of e-mail, and the rise of persistent Internet connections opened new conduits for malware creators to disburse their wares. In 2000 and 2001 malware hit the Internet like a tidal wave, causing billions of dollars in lost data and productivity. The target of opportunity was Microsoft's Windows because it was filled with security vulnerabilities and was the most widely used computer platform in the world. Enterprises were tiring of the malware problem and placed the blame squarely on Microsoft for selling them software that was so easily corrupted. Fortune 500 executives and government officials petitioned Microsoft to fix the problem or else they would find another operating system.

It was December 2001 when Microsoft founder and spiritual guru Bill Gates issued an edict that Microsoft's top priority was fixing the security problem and making its products the most secure in the computer industry. The edict—literally an e-mail that read like a manifesto—called for the creation of Trustworthy Computing, an initiative to diagnose software security problems, retrain software developers in secure coding techniques, and create new products that had embedded security features. Microsoft took the extraordinary step of halting development of new products and retrofitting products already in the field. The estimated first year cost of Trustworthy Computing ranged from $100 million to $200 million. A decade later, Microsoft still has security flaws in its software, but it's no longer the primary source of all security woes. Further, Microsoft has contributed more to advancing the state of computer security than any other company.

Part of the problem that created all the security issues in Microsoft's software was misalignment. Microsoft programmers were rewarded not for meeting business objectives, but for how many applications they were able to get into a new product release. Quality control, interoperability, and the impact on security were secondary to functionality. The result was a hodgepodge of functions and applications that created security vulnerabilities that hackers and malware creators used to make Swiss cheese of Windows. Getting the whole of Microsoft on the same page required Gates to issue the edict from on high and make alignment a priority for everyone—executive, manager, and developer.

Business and technology alignment starts at the top. Unfortunately, not every CEO or executive team understands that concept. Executives have different notions about what makes a good—and likely successful—technology strategy. In many organizations, though, technology investment and decision making is either decentralized and/or fragmented by a bottom-up approach. As a result, technology discipline falls apart, and technology no longer works for the benefit of the enterprise. Worse, the cost of maintaining technology becomes a distraction from focusing on the true business objectives, as was the case at Microsoft. Business strategy must start at the top, with the board of directors, executive committee, and office of the CIO being the key stakeholders. Without this level of involvement, management teams are far more likely to experience technology-related failures. When that happens, they tend to focus more on the symptoms than the root cause. When a person says, "Technology just doesn't understand the needs of the business," "They don't deliver," or "They're giving us stuff we don't need," what they're pointing to are the symptoms of an organization without a business technology strategy.

A proper Business Technology Strategy—in the BTM context—begins with the executives articulating necessary steps to execute the business strategy and achieve goals, followed by the technology needed to enable those execution points. Intimate knowledge of the business architecture, operating models, capabilities, and processes constitute actionable inputs for an astute, converged management team. In its purest form, a Business Technology Strategy incorporates three critical strategic elements: an Enterprise Business Strategy, an Enterprise Technology Strategy, and a Technology Function Strategy.

The Enterprise Business Strategy outlines the strategic goals, imperatives, and initiatives that the company is pursuing, including specific business capabilities that make it all happen. There may be an overarching corporate strategy that applies to all business units (for example, shared services across multiple business units); however, each business unit is likely to be pursuing unique strategies based on their mission and objectives.

The Enterprise Technology Strategy outlines the strategic direction for technology. It specifies a plan for deploying the technology to meet business capability needs and to support the business strategy. It can actually help shape the Enterprise Business Strategy when enabling technologies are available to create sustainable competitive advantage.

The Technology Functions Strategy outlines how the technology function develops, deploys, operates, and supports the systems needed to deliver business goals. Consequently, it is driven by both the Enterprise Business Strategy and the Enterprise Technology Strategy. In turn, these higher-level strategies may be limited or enabled by the capacity and abilities of the technology function. The function level includes technology assets that support processes and infrastructure across organizations and locations, including centralized technology groups, satellite technology groups, and people performing technology roles in the business users' areas.

These strategies create a strong and cohesive framework for the adoption and implementation of an Enterprise Technology Strategy that is aligned with both corporate needs and business objectives. The important thing to remember is that even the best strategy is near useless unless it has the endorsement and support of senior leadership. Fragmented technology strategies will produce fragmented results.

Advanced Thinking for Better Business Technology Investments

Business managers get tricked often by the features and functions of technologies rather than the potential output and benefit of technology adoption. Technology investment decisions require more than just identifying possible technologies for acquisition. Decision makers must understand—and be able to explain—why those technologies are needed—in a business context. This requires critical examination of business needs compared to business objectives. Executives should think about technology investments as a four-step process: defining business goals, determining business and technology capability needs, prioritizing capability acquisition and deployment, and deciding on technology investments.

On the surface, these steps seem relatively straightforward and practical. That perception masks the complexity and importance of each of these steps in the technology investment decision-making process. In the BTM context, these steps are designed to ensure that cross-functional management teams are collecting the right information, conducting group deliberations, and making decisions that are aligned with the business's mission and objects. More importantly, the process ensures that decisions are made in the best interest of the organization and not just one discrete department.

In execution, this four-step process is a complex undertaking that requires a thorough analysis of the business strategy, operations, processes, stakeholders, and objectives. While some managers may find the process and its discrete components tedious, collecting the information and gaining the participation of the stakeholders is essential for producing an optimal technology investment plan. Let's take a look at what each step looks like in detail.

Step 1: Defining Business Goals

As we've discussed, the defining of business goals is an essential component to all of the BTM capabilities. How can a business determine technology investments when it doesn't know why it's making those investments? How can a business acquire technology capabilities if it doesn't know why it needs those technologies? Decision making without knowing the desired outcome is like searching for a needle in a haystack in the dark (yes, it's a mixed metaphor, but it reflects both the absurdity and complexity of not having business goals).

What a management team needs to know at this stage of the process is what its short- and long-term objectives are, and what will enable—in general terms—its business to drive toward those objectives. Defining business goals is more than just stating a growth rate, a new market to penetrate, or an EBITDA target. It requires an organization to select its "value disciplines" and "value types." Value discipline is the primary advantage the company seeks to achieve in the marketplace. The value discipline selected is directly correlated to the competitive environment, whether the company is operating in a stable period in which it focuses on improving internal processes and strengthening relationships with existing partners and customers or an agile period in which it must improve processes (internal) and products (external) to capitalize on new market trends or respond to competitive threats.

Business objectives are relatively simple to discern and should be relatively self-evident at the beginning of this process. However, it's always a good idea to restate even the obvious; make sure everyone on the team understands the starting point and the target. Determining what will enable the business is a little more difficult to define, but likewise should be relatively simple to pull together since it's usually about general items—people, processes, resources, etc. Determining the enterprise's operational state is tricky, but is particularly important since it will determine the level and extent of investments. We say "tricky," because crystal balls aren't provided as you ascend the corporate ladder, and most investment decisions are made in advance, whether according to budgetary requirements or fiscal year. In order to plan accordingly, part of that process requires determining which of the two your company falls under—and as a result, what funds go where. If a business is operating in a steady state—meaning that it's relatively free of competitive threats—its goals, priorities, and investment needs will differ greatly than in a volatile market where agility is a necessity.

Step 2: Determining Business and Technology Capability Needs

Moving beyond identifying general business needs, this step requires the management team to specify the precise capabilities required to meet their goals and objectives. Where in the first step a team may state that it needs more automation manufacturing to decrease costs, in this step they'll start to identify the automation technologies and their specific applications to roles and processes. Building off the defined operating environment (stable or agile), the team will be able to draw upon examples of automation used by competitors or—in some cases—they will be a first-mover or early adopter.

Determining business capability needs is a crucial step in the decision-making process because the outcome of this team is directly related to how competitive and innovative a company will become. It's during this step that the management team will identify technologies that will improve processes and procedures, and that will enhance existing assets and previous investments. The team may also discover through this process marketplace opportunities that can be capitalized upon through the adoption of new technology. At the very least, the team uses this stage to identify technologies that will improve the product development process, interaction with partners and suppliers, and relationships with customers.

Step 3: Prioritizing Capability Acquisition and Deployment

Military commander Frederick the Great said that when you guard everything, you guard nothing. The same is true in business, albeit in a different context. No enterprise—no matter how wealthy—can invest in every project or technology it desires. It must have choices for investing in capabilities that will produce the best outcomes, which are typically measured in market share expansion, operational efficiencies, and profitability. Through this step, the management team will prioritize the technology capabilities it needs to reach business objectives. This prioritization is based on the evaluation of goals and technology requirements according to enhancements and shortcomings in the existing portfolio. This step makes the decision-making process more transparent and easier for the management team.

Step 4: Deciding on Technology Investments

Once the business goals are restated, capabilities identified, and technology priorities identified, the management team can make its investment decisions. It will use all the available information in a portfolio approach to decide which projects will receive funding and support. Beyond just making the investment decision, the team will prioritize investments, giving emphasis to more critical technologies while giving development—or secondary support—to technologies that are needed but not critical.

No business can make technology investments without first going through these logical discovery, examination, and deliberative steps. This orderly process is about optimizing technology investment. It's equally about ensuring that businesses maintain focus on what's truly important—the execution of a business plan, not the shiny objects of technology that often distract us. The output of this process ensures that the organization invests in the tools that will enable the business strategy and, ultimately, power the achievement of business objectives.

The Takeaway: Turning Ideas into Action

Changing strategic direction and ensuring optimal enterprise performance is like turning a supertanker at sea—it doesn't turn quickly, and sudden movement can result in catastrophic results. Masters of change have demonstrable track records for leveraging technology to capitalize on new market opportunities. One of the best examples of such a company is Cisco Systems, which is driven by the leadership of CEO and Chairman John Chambers.

Cisco Systems was founded in 1984 to provide equipment for computer networking. As technology evolved, it morphed into the chief provider of routers and switches that leveraged Internet Protocol that carries Web traffic. Cisco wasn't the first and still isn't the only company that markets this technology. However, under Chambers's leadership Cisco has morphed into what it calls "a platform company," or the foundation for all things computing. In the past decade, Cisco has acquired more than sixty companies, and is now a major provider of products in computer security, virtualization, software as a service, video conferencing, telephony, and unified communications. It has an entire division—what some describe as an in-house venture capital lab—devoted to building the next billion-dollar business. Chambers's pursuit is to ensure Cisco continues to grow and stay ahead of the competition. Many have criticized Chambers's vision and questioned his ability to fulfill it, but Chambers and Cisco have repeatedly demonstrated tenacity for innovation and evolution that few others can match, and that's what makes Cisco so scary to both longtime and would-be competitors.

As Cisco demonstrates, a business seeking to use technology to accelerate operational performance requires informed decision making to determine which technologies best support the organization's strategic position. Decisions on business technology investments require structured thinking about what the business wants to achieve. This clear understanding of business requirements dictates the technology plans and the appropriate business technology investments needed to execute the firm's business strategy.

Determining such investments must begin with a solid understanding of an organization's strategy, goals, and objectives. Ultimately, a well-articulated business-driven technology strategy will not only recognize the uniqueness of varying organizational capabilities, it will balance with its desired strategic positioning by adhering to the following basic tenets:

Step 1: *Ask* what specific business technology capabilities must be put in place for you to meet your short-term and long-term business goals and objectives. A mature business-driven technology strategy is the most effective way to ensure that the technology group understands the specific business needs and enables the business strategy.

Step 2: *Prepare* the processes that need to be put in place to improve communications and educate the organization about each component. Creating an effective strategy requires careful and complete communication, and the integration of the Enterprise Business Strategy (which outlines the strategic goals, imperatives, and initiatives of a company), Enterprise Technology Strategy (which outlines the strategic direction of business technology), and Technology Function Strategy (which outlines how technology develops, deploys, operates, and supports the systems needed to deliver business technology).

Step 3: *Decide* what internal and external capabilities you need to execute on defined business strategies. What is the relative priority of stability and agility with regard to the business capabilities you need to have in place? Prioritizing and focusing investments starts with understanding the type of value that will be created. Enabling stability and/or agility will require different levels and types of investments. Further, consideration must be given to the nature of this investment mix as it relates to supporting other critical activities.

Step 4: *Understand* and specify the business value discipline to be pursued. What is the primary value discipline—that is, operational excellence, product leadership, customer intimacy? The answer must be embedded in the enterprise business strategy, and then cascaded through all stakeholders and to all levels of the organization. Doing so will prescribe the specific business capabilities required in a way that guides effective technology strategy creation.

CHAPTER 5

The New Face of the Public Sector: How Governance Leads to Greater Government Efficiency

THE UNITED STATES GOVERNMENT is arguably the world's largest consumer and patron of technology. In 2010, federal agencies—including the military—spent nearly $82 billion on information technology assets, services, and administration. Since the dot-com era of the early 2000s, the Clinton, Bush, and Obama administrations have made technology modernization a priority in their domestic agendas. Politicians and bureaucrats alike see technology as a giant panacea for inefficient government functions ranging from health care and social services to homeland security and national defense. In 2005, the Government Accountability Office (GAO)—Congress's fiscal watchdog—did a comparison of the responsibilities, operations, and authorities of federal chief information officers and their private sector counterparts. The conclusion of that report was government CIOs had greater levels of involvement in and authority over technology programs than their private sector counterparts. If only that were true.

In the five years between 2005 and 2010, government information technology spending increased by $27 billion. Yet, despite the steady growth in technology expenditures, federal agencies cannot readily exchange information, consolidate systems, cut costs, or ensure data security to the standards prescribed by Congress. Correcting the technology ills of years of mismanagement and misdirected efforts doesn't happen overnight. The U.S. government is now engaged in a comprehensive program to coordinate and converge its technology management structure into cross-domain project teams to ensure that strategic objectives are met across the twenty-seven major departments. As part of the new paradigm, all departments must complete reviews of technology projects prior to submitting their budgets, and all high-risk projects must undergo detailed reevaluation before proceeding. Agencies are also required to submit plans for consolidating data centers and analyses for the adoption of alternative, cost-saving technologies such as cloud computing. And, with all plans, agencies must document security plans for ensuring the integrity of computing systems and confidentiality of government records. The government's effort to improve its use of technology is evolutionary, not revolutionary.

Forget for a moment the stories of the government spending $600 for a toilet seat, $90 for a hammer, and other wasteful spending. The U.S. government is more than just a consumer of technology; it's a patron of technology innovation and development that will benefit both the public and private sectors. In the past, government-sponsored research and development programs have led to innovations such as personal computers, the Internet, cellular phones, and microwave ovens. As stated in a report from the National Research Council:

> Effective federal research has concentrated on work that industry has limited incentive to pursue: long-term, fundamental research; large system-building efforts that require the talents of diverse communities of scientists and engineers; and work that might displace existing, entrenched technologies. Furthermore, successful federal programs have tended to be organized in ways that accommodate the uncertainties in scientific and technological research.[1]

In this chapter, we will review the many ways government can use technology to better defend its borders and for disaster responsiveness and public service delivery. We will also show how the convergence of business and technology management can improve the government's application of technology, and will look at the consequences of technology failures resulting from poor management structures.

Inefficiency: The Government's Claim to Fame

Everyone's heard the expression "Not bad for government work" or the more dismissive "I'm from the government and I'm here to help you." These idioms reflect the poor public perception of the quality and efficiency of government projects and services. The popular belief is that the government is populated with people who couldn't hack the private sector, so they live in the shelter of civil service where they're not held accountable to performance standards. Even when the government engages private sector companies, the public belief is that the outcome will be of poor quality or that there will be high cost overruns—because contracts go, often by law, to the lowest bidder. The truth is the government isn't made up of incompetent administrators and its private sector contractors are not merely trying to rip off the public treasury. A few bad apples tarnish the reputation of the whole system. But there are numerous inefficiencies in the government caused by nonconverged oversight, insufficient (or nonexistent) management and accountability structures, and spending programs that are misaligned from intended outcomes. These inefficiencies aren't a reflection of the government, but rather the complexity of managing numerous complex projects within large organizations.

An understanding of how government isn't like a private sector corporation is important. In the private sector, shareholders measure the success and value of corporations by the revenue and profits they generate. Management is measured by the efficiency by which they execute product and project programs that result in revenues and profits. Private sector workers are rated by proficiency of their skills and the quality of the goods they produce. Government, on the other hand, is a bifurcated dysfunctional system of politicians and bureaucracies that is built on expenditures rather than income.

Whenever the public asks the government to do something, it's asking the government to spend money. When running for reelection, U.S. senators and representatives often woo voters with records of the bills they supported, laws enacted, and, above all, the funding they secured for their states and districts. Department of Defense, Health and

Human Services, Agriculture, Interior, Transportation, Commerce, and other bureaucracies are the instruments by which politicians funnel money back to their districts. As a result, Congress regularly authorizes programs that don't produce a true public benefit other than to maintain the flow of money out of Washington, D.C., to the hinterlands. The result is often gross inefficiency in the execution of programs that, because of government commitments, require further spending.

According to GAO, the federal government spent about $70 billion on information technology projects during fiscal year 2008. Of the 778 major information technology projects, which account for the bulk of the technology spending, GAO estimates that about half have been "rebaselined." That's the government's way of saying that these projects underwent changes in cost, schedule, and performance goals. Rarely does rebaselining result in lower expenditures.

"Managing technology is big and complicated, and it seems to reflect all the complexities that the organization encounters in any of its other dimensions," said Lester Diamond, then assistant director of the GAO. "When I see technology management fail in a broad way, I usually look to the organization. Technology doesn't often fail by itself. I believe technology more often fails as a result of other organizational problems."[2]

Perhaps no place in the country understands the consequences of poorly implemented government technology programs than the Gulf Coast states of Louisiana, Mississippi, and Alabama, which in the last five years have been ravaged by more than one massive natural disaster—Hurricanes Ivan (2004) and Katrina (2005).

Meteorologists called Hurricane Katrina "a 100-year storm," meaning that its strength and destructive power was so rare that such an event happens only once a century. Katrina unleashed a fury so great on the Gulf Coast that there was serious talk about abandoning the devastated city of New Orleans. Wrecked homes and roads were the most obvious signs of Katrina's destructive power, but the hurricane also took out government and civilian lines of communications. Landline and cellular phone networks were disabled or unreliable. The government spent billions of dollars in the aftermath of the 9/11 terrorist attacks to ensure military and local first-responder units could communicate. However, on the Gulf Coast, the Federal Emergency Management Agency (FEMA), Department of Homeland Security, National Guard, and local police and fire departments quickly learned that they hadn't overcome these communications gaps. And, worse, government computer systems couldn't talk to each other, which slowed the distribution of supplies and relief teams to the affected regions.

If FEMA didn't shine in its response to Hurricane Katrina, one private individual did, demonstrating how innovative thinking can rise above chaos. In the parking lot of a Wal-Mart in hurricane-ravaged Chalmette, Louisiana, just outside of New Orleans, Dr. Enoch Choi examined a newly homeless woman who could remember only that she took "blue pills." He pulled a microcomputer from his belt and wirelessly connected to a network created in just days by 150 corporations and nonprofits. From it, Dr. Choi retrieved her prescription records and safely restored her medication. In this hot parking lot, hundreds of Katrina refugees began to see some order replacing the shattered circumstances of their lives.[3]

It was not so much the technology Dr. Choi used, although that was critical, but how he managed it that mattered. He was sponsored by a Presbyterian church in California, worked under a tent erected by the National Guard, hooked into a prescription database through a cell wireless connection set up by Verizon, used five microcomputers he borrowed from OQO Inc., a new California company pioneering microcomputers, and treated up to fifty patients a day. Passionate about his quest to solve a real human need, he reached out to organizations to get what he needed, and he just made it up as he went along. As he looked around, however, he saw no other such innovation. "FEMA," he said, "was using paper and pens."

The U.S. federal government has a long list of technology-based projects that are either languishing in development, stalled by bureaucratic malaise, or simply underperforming or nowhere near meeting their stated goals. Such projects include:

- ○ Upgrading the Federal Aviation Administration's air traffic control system to improve commercial flight management and ease congested travel corridors.

- ○ Implementing port security to scan the millions of cargo containers entering the country each year for explosives, and for chemical, biological, and radiological threats. (Currently, less than 10 percent of containers are inspected.)

- ○ Deploying systems for digitizing medical records and facilitating electronic collaboration among health care providers. Some experts estimate electronic medical records would save the country more than $81 billion annually in health care costs.

○ Extending broadband Internet access across the country—a modern version of the Rural Electrification Administration of the Roosevelt New Deal era. The Obama administration has earmarked more than $7 billion for this program, but disagreements between the Federal Communications Commission and telecom carriers has stopped the project dead in its tracks.

○ Protecting the nation's government computing networks and critical infrastructure from cyber attacks by hackers, terrorists, and hostile nation-states. For years, Congress through the Office of Management and Budget has required government departments to report their information technology security posture. Since the program began in 2002, federal agencies have consistently earned subpar ratings. While many officials recognize the computer security threat, not one program has resulted in a significant improvement in security status, readiness, or response posture.

These projects aren't "nice to have" or pork barrel projects. They are integral to the delivery of public services, maintaining a high level of commerce, and ensuring the security of the country. According to the GAO, the problem is plain and simple. Their analysis showed that agencies do not have comprehensive rebaselining policies.[4] To put it another way: It's the management—not the technology—that makes a true difference.

Propelling Innovation: The DARPA Way

Perhaps the answer to the government's challenges in designing and implementing technologies can be found within its own house. We have previously looked at how private sector organizations create structures that encourage innovation. They actually share many common characteristics with the Defense Advanced Research Projects Agency—better known as DARPA. It is instructive to see how this nearly fifty-year-old, enormously successful organization operates.

DARPA is small compared with most corporate R&D labs. It has only 240 employees on the inside who enlist project team members on the outside. The organization is flat—only one layer of management between top and bottom. For a government agency, it enjoys remarkable freedom from bureaucratic control. The technical staff is made up of world-class scientists and engineers from industry, universities, and government labs—and they stay only three to five years, so that the agency is regularly recycled with fresh thinking. As such, everything at the agency is project-based. Projects typically last three to five years and are focused on end goals.

DARPA officials meet regularly with military and civilian leaders in the Department of Defense to ask, "What keeps you up at night?" To these critical, near-term needs, DARPA then seeks to match solutions from its forward-thinking research. The agency thus not only has its eyes on technologies of the future—what the next generation of commanders will need—but also its ears to the ground for solutions to current problems.

Unrestrained consideration is encouraged, failure is not punished, and thinking big is the norm—but at the same time there is an emphasis on producing a result. Program managers are selected for their technical excellence, their entrepreneurial spirit, and because they are freewheeling zealots in pursuit of their goals. Because they are only around for four to six years, they feel free to change direction from their predecessors. Two other salient facts: There is little overhead (no physical facilities such as labs) and there is little institutional impediment to focusing purely on innovation. How often in corporations and other organizations do existing fiefdoms stifle any attempt to do something differently?

DARPA is a prime example of the convergence of business and technology management and goals, and what can result when convergence is achieved. What lessons can enterprises learn from DARPA? Consider the following:

- *Listen.* Members of an organization's internal and external community often have tremendous insights and ideas that lead to new innovations.

- *Stay open.* Ideas don't always come from experts. Sometimes the greatest innovations come from novices and backroom tinkers. Open-minded organizations often convert off-the-wall ideas into marketable products.

- *Collaborate.* No organization holds all the cards in developing new technologies. Collaboration with outside groups—complementary corporations, universities, government agencies, and think tanks—often brings new perspectives and ideas to the innovation process.

- *Go flat.* A flat management structure doesn't have the long approval processes and disjointed lines of communications that impede innovation. Organizations that can't go flat in management can achieve the same results by empowering workers to act independently.

○ *Embrace failure.* Many of the greatest innovations and technology leapfrogs were unintended results and, oftentimes, created by accident. Breakthroughs such as the discovery of penicillin or the power of microwaves were the result of accidents.

These organizational characteristics show up often enough in genuinely innovative organizations that we can safely recognize them as first principles of innovation.

One of the people to receive DARPA funding was Dr. Eric Brewer, a professor of computer science at the University of California–Berkeley. Brewer created the search engine Inktomi based on his government-funded work, and in 1966 created Inktomi Corp. to develop the search engine commercially. The search engine became one of the biggest in the market before succumbing to the dot-com bust of 2000–2001. In 1999, the federal government set about to build "FirstGov," a Web portal to more than 40 million government Web pages on more than 20,000 federal, state, and local websites. Brewer donated his search engine to the effort, free for three years. President Bill Clinton decreed that First-Gov would be up and running in just three months—an almost impossible deadline in the government—but it was accomplished, in large part, because of Brewer's donation. FirstGov has received numerous awards for innovation.

While the Inktomi search engine was innovative, and a massive Web portal would have been considered innovative in 1999, the real innovation of FirstGov was not the technology—it was the process through which FirstGov came into being.

Dr. Patricia Diamond Fletcher, associate professor in policy sciences at the University of Maryland–Baltimore County, teaches and conducts research on government information policy and system management. She and colleagues conducted a case study of FirstGov and came to some interesting conclusions about the success of the portal.[5]

First off, the project was high on the agenda of President Clinton and had not only his full support but also his sense of urgency. The program stayed high on the presidential agenda when President George W. Bush took office. Responsibility for the portal was given to the General Services Administration (GSA). It set up a working group outside of the existing organization; the group had access to GSA resources but didn't have to follow standard operating procedures. "Thus," Fletcher writes in *Library Trends*, "team expertise and enthusiasm were not hampered by the red tape of bureaucracy."[6]

The team's small size gave it flexibility and agility. The team enlisted the Federal CIO Council to be part of the project. These CIOs brought their professional expertise and knowledge of their agencies. Some twenty-two agencies actually contributed funding. Perhaps most important, however, the project now had their buy-in. "The agency CIOs were also co-opted to be change agents to convince agency personnel of the necessity of being a part of FirstGov," Fletcher writes.

Everyone involved in building FirstGov, Fletcher says, considered it a necessary and important public service—the first step toward true e-government. They just knew "it was right." Fletcher sums it up this way:

> This was not a typical government project, mired in procurement and acquisition regulations and constrained by the federal budget. . . . The FirstGov project was much more like that of a start-up "dot-com" fueled by the energy and engagement of its members and their belief in the project's goals and objectives. Unlike most information technology projects in government, where procurement and acquisition law often contribute to lengthy, drawn-out, and costly information technology developments, FirstGov was not subject to many of these instances of red tape. The requirement of a ninety-day project development meant that, to be successful, the team had to creatively, while legally, procure the necessary technology to launch the portal on time. This created a sense of urgency that spurred the team to exceed their performance expectations.[7]

If we translated this story to the corporate world, we would have a CEO committed and driven to create some new thing to meet a real need; vice presidents all signed on, even providing financial support; a small, tight-knit team operating outside bureaucratic procedures and passionately determined to succeed; and an atmosphere of urgency, creativity, and enthusiasm. Does this sound like a dream? Well, it happened, right in the bowels of our greatest bureaucracy.

A Process Approach: A Roadmap to Success

Clearly defining the mission and vision of a public sector department/agency, effectively creating and communicating a roadmap to achieve the desired outcomes, and then validating the actual results is a simple enough concept. Yet many government agencies display only limited success in creating an environment in which the development of strategic goals is reinforced by processes that organize and align their activities in support of achieving goals. It's even more rare that the government agency effectively manages its business and technology together and with predefined metrics to achieve mission goals.

Just as we have discussed in previous chapters regarding the management of technology in enterprises, establishing governance in government organizations begins with establishing effective feedback and review processes of the agency's strategy. A key element of this feedback is the clear articulation of the role that technologies will play in achieving each organizational objective. An equally important component is the definition of the criteria that will be used to judge the success of each initiative undertaken to achieve a strategic goal.

Documenting planning assumptions and success metrics is a prerequisite for establishing an effective strategy. Done well, this becomes a truly "mission-driven" technology strategy, which is the result of a predictable planning process used to define and document the specific business technology capabilities that must be put in place to achieve mission goals and objectives. Once an agency has decided on its course, it must communicate the expected outcomes to its internal and external stakeholders. The agency needs to be clear about the initiatives and their expected business results to give each person a sense of ownership. It must also establish the linkage between making technology investments and achieving superior business results. These linkages must be "executive sponsored and senior management ready." That means that in addition to documenting and planning for the execution of strategic initiatives, an agency must monitor the outcomes of each decision using business-focused metrics that measure success in terms suitable both for agency executives and oversight groups.

A process approach provides a roadmap for technology impact and value creation, and statistical methods provide the tools to capture, isolate, and measure such impacts. Senior agency executives need to understand how technology can lead to improvement in operations and enhanced decision making. They need practical ways to decide when to invest, how to channel investments, and how to ensure that investments lead to value.

Governance: Defining Who's in Charge

No government official or business executive can assume technology will cure their organization's woes or automatically lead some nirvana-like success. A screwdriver is little more than an object that is essentially useless until it's properly applied in a task for which it was designed. All forms of technology are the same in that regard—they require intent and direction to produce a proper, valuable outcome. The direction is governance.

Who precisely should govern technology direction and implementation? We believe the ultimate responsibility for all organizational initiatives and productivity resides squarely in the executive corner. Without executive buy-in and support, major strategic initiatives and even many operational programs will stall or fail. In the U.S. government, executive endorsement comes directly from the White House, and one of the greatest instruments of project prioritization is the president's annual State of the Union address. For generations, presidents have used the State of the Union to set their domestic and international agendas, set government priorities, and lead the nation in new initiatives. Franklin Delano Roosevelt's New Deal, Lyndon Johnson's Great Society, Ronald Reagan's anti-communist agenda, George W. Bush's War on Terrorism, and President Barack Obama's health care reform received their anointment in the State of the Union. It's for this reason that department heads, cabinet members, White House staffers, special interest groups, and corporations spend months lobbying to get their projects and initiatives mentioned in the State of the Union address. They know that a mention—even if it's just one line—means the difference between getting support for their projects and having their initiatives land on the "nice to do" list.

Executive endorsement isn't enough to make projects work. Putting technology plans into action requires the vigilance of management to ensure projects are carried out according to the organization's needs and goals. This means active involvement in articulating the business vision and the role of technology, establishing metrics for technology deployment and operations, and providing oversight of risks and compliance management. Management must adopt and develop the key BTM capabilities of Strategic and Tactical Governance and Compliance and Risk Management, which we discussed in Chapter 2. These capabilities ensure that required decisions are identified, assigned, and effectively executed. A coherent and disciplined approach to technology management is important for several reasons.

First, technology is a force multiplier and efficiency enhancer. In the private sector, it's a means for gaining a competitive advantage in the marketplace and creating wealth. In the public sector, technology is a tool for creating efficiencies in government organizations, which lead to better services for the citizenry. In both applications—private and public sector—technology has the potential for containing costs. But technology is only effective in attaining this benefit if management has the temerity to implement initiatives to exploit strategic opportunities in which technology can enable innovation and ensure government programs are executed with the highest outcome at the lowest cost.

Second, technology provides significant opportunities for productivity enhancement. However, the value in these productivity improvements is not just from the investments in technology as much as the complementary innovations in business practices. To enhance productivity through technology, organizations must target the right opportunities and appropriately sequence investments in business process, organization restructuring, and incentive system redesign. In the government context, this means that no single investment in technology, no single innovation in process or practice is likely to produce sustained productivity gains as much as a continuing program of synergistic improvement initiatives. An agency-wide perspective is required to ensure that specific technology and change initiatives are being managed as part of an overall program of productivity enhancement.

Third, maximizing return on capital employed requires oversight of how well these assets are deployed to generate stakeholder value. In the government context, this refers to the design and execution of technology implementations that produce a cost savings or improved service delivery. The Internal Revenue Service (IRS) implementing computer services that enables the electronic filing of personal tax returns is an example of a system that both increased service delivery and reduced operational expenses. What governance does is to prevent precious and limited budget resources from being expended on programs that lead nowhere. When that happens, it reduces confidence in an organization's ability to execute and, subsequently, lowers probability for future support for strategic initiatives.

Fourth, governance is a function of risk management. Technology, as with all things in life, has no guarantees of success. In some cases, it actually increases an organization's risk exposure, whether the organization is an enterprise or a government agency. The strategic importance of information and the nature of current technologies have raised the stakes regarding privacy, security, and confidentiality. It's vital that organizational leadership appreciate the material risks inherent in the creation and use of technology. Governance through management policies and procedures ensures that risk is accepted, assigned, or deferred.

Fifth, governance is about regulatory compliance. Heightened concerns about risk management, auditing and fraud detection, and public sector governance—similar to the reporting requirements seen in the private sector—have sensitized supervisory boards, government officials, and top management teams to adopt an even more active role in the oversight of business strategy and technology activities. Significant regulations including Sarbanes-Oxley, the Health Insurance Portability and Accountability Act (HIPAA), and the USA PATRIOT Act have raised the stakes. In the government, these regulatory requirements come from laws such as the Federal Information Security Management Act (FISMA), Federal Information Processing Standards (FIPS), and Common Criteria requirements. Failures to meet the required attestations, unintended violations of privacy and confidentiality, or heightened vulnerabilities to identity thefts are likely to invite adverse reactions from regulators and stakeholders. As technology becomes embedded in core organizational processes, control systems, and decision support systems, it is vital that supervisory boards appreciate the material risks due to technology and understand the risk mitigation strategy.

With new technology initiatives requiring larger amounts of capital, investment processes must permit a consistent way of evaluating the business value of these projects and investments across the government. These investment processes must be linked with metrics so that administrators can find it easier to champion critical business and technology investments. These metrics must relate to key processes and operations, such as customer relationship management (customer satisfaction, propensity to engage on a recurring basis), procurement (cost containment, operational efficiency), financial management (cash flow, cash reserve, lines of credit), and human capital management (skill development, retention).

A company that does technology governance very well and is worth emulation by public and private organizations is Intel. The computer chip manufacturer has implemented an approach that categorizes the business value of business technology into seventeen categories called "value dials" that deal with either bottom line savings or top line growth. Most of the value dials are based on metrics already used by Intel's business groups to measure business performance. As part of the dials approach, Intel executives first identify a baseline value for the metric that is likely to be impacted by the proposed business technology investment. As a next step, executives specify the likely value of this metric as a result of the successful implementation of the initiative. Finally, the improvement of this metric is monetized on the basis of prior experience with business value management. As an example, if a proposed CRM initiative aims to improve customer satisfaction by two points over the current value, this improvement can be monetized on the basis of an understanding of the relationship between customer satisfaction and future customer revenue. In other cases, the business metrics are more directly monetized (for instance, procurement, customer acquisition, or recruiting costs).

These value dials provide Intel's executives with a consistent, enterprise-wide means of evaluating the business value of technology investments. These principles are equally applicable to government agencies, since they enable senior agency administrators to prioritize their technology needs and champion investments. Whether in the private or public sector, management teams must direct an enterprise-wide perspective on the organizational value of business technology investments. Such a perspective must identify value metrics that are appropriate for the function of the government agency or department and should provide a process for judging the potential impacts of business technology projects and investments on those metrics. Without a coordinated investment philosophy that has the backing of the board, the metrics and the valuation process will lack the needed credibility to guide investments.

An organization-wide perspective is needed to guide the use of technology in implementing effective and economical enterprise risk management systems that facilitate both management control and performance. With greater complexity in the processes and structures for managing technology (such as cloud computing), there is a need for more sophisticated models of risk assessment that factor in not just the internal risks, but also the risks inherent in sourcing and external partnering. Administrative teams must provide active oversight over how business technology risks impact the business, and ensure the effectiveness of the governance systems in mitigating these risks.

Oversight without measure—or metrics—is essentially fruitless. A metrics hierarchy should consist of three elements that direct attention toward different types of technology investments, identify appropriate business variables, and relate to the management of strategic risk and regulatory compliance.

Metrics: A Measure of Success

How does an organization derive appropriate metrics? First, the business mission and profitability model must be well understood. Metrics established with such an understanding will most likely provide a clear link from technology investment to business value.

Metrics fall into three broad categories (see Figure 5–1)—productivity, profitability, and consumer value. Technology's ability to reduce operational costs and improve internal coordination can lead to higher productivity. A likely outcome of improved productivity is passing on the gains to consumers through better service, enhanced products and/or programs, and improved interaction. Therefore, for each of these categories of metrics executives must take a holistic approach, understanding all of the contributors to business value.

However, not all technology investments are the same, and the business value created by each varies as well. Different technologies are adopted for different reasons and will produce unique outcomes. In their research, Jeanne Ross, Director and Principal Research Scientist at the MIT Sloan School's Center for Information Systems Research, and Cynthia Beath, Professor Emerita of Information Systems at the McCombs School of Business, University of Texas, discovered four major types:[8]

1. Process improvement, where the goal is to enhance business solutions (such as greater customer personalization and self-checkout in stores).

2. Renewal, where the goal is to improve the delivery of business technology services (for instance, web services and intrusion detection).

3. Transformation, where the goal is to build a platform for future business capabilities (for example, data mining).

FIGURE 5–1 SELECTING APPROPRIATE METRICS.

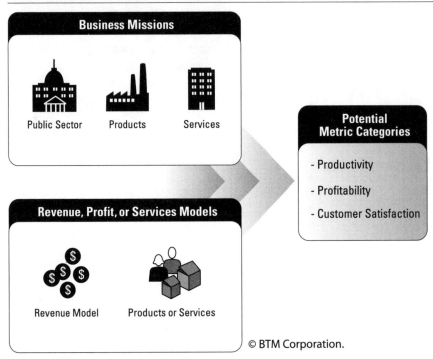

© BTM Corporation.

An organization must adhere to its mission and operating models to effectively determine relevant business metrics.

4. Experiments, where the goal is to engage in R&D and learning about the option value of an emerging technology (such as RFID).

After categorizing the type of investment, an organization must then identify appropriate operational and organizational variables that will be impacted by each of the above types of investments. Collectively, variables across the four types of investments should comprise the technology value dials. While the board usually must approve transformational types of investments, the other three types of investments are funded either out of business budgets (process improvements and experiments) or technology budgets (renewal investments).

Metrics are essential in the quantification of strategic risk and regulatory compliance. Strategic risk refers to the risks facing the firm due to poorly envisioned or executed business strategies. In particular, within BTM, the focus is on risks at the intersection of technology and business strategy. Regulatory compliance refers to corporate adherence to different regulatory expectations related to financial reporting and data management. Poor regulatory compliance invites liabilities of civil or criminal punishment, administrative actions against managers, and, in the case of government agencies, human resource actions such as termination. There are other forms of risks as well, including those involving systems and sourcing. While those forms of risk are likely to be managed by business and technology executives, the management of strategic risk and regulatory compliance must reside at the board level.

The things that plague our society, economy, and government the most—terrorism, the economy, health care, even just a better commute—have technological solutions. People expect the government to come up with solutions. Politicians and bureaucracies will succeed or fail largely on how well they manage the technology. The government is taking steps to open lines of communications and converge technology management. But by the admissions of many in government, much more work is needed and the road to convergence is long. Metrics are the means for measuring performance and making adjustments in the execution of strategic plans.

The Takeaway: Turning Ideas into Action

How does an enterprise become more sophisticated in its use of governance and organizational design? The seven practical "how to" steps of addressing this area are to:

Step 1: *Establish* a decision-making body (a Business Technology Council) that brings together business and technology professionals to review, approve, and prioritize technology requests, and then put into place an upper management body (a Business Technology Investment Board) that sets policy and serves as an escalation point to settle disputes. Involve management actively both as sponsor and partner with technology.

Step 2: *Create* a Program Management Office that will have authority over the process of bringing investment proposals forward.

Step 3: *Tie* the decision to approve or deny a proposed investment directly to items of strategic importance to the enterprise's business— measure proposals on the basis of business drivers and expected impact.

Step 4: *Remember* the importance of architecture! An Architecture Review Board needs to review the architectural compliance of proposals, and to advise the Business Technology Council on their fit. An Office of Architecture and Standards needs to establish standards, draft architectural roadmaps, and ensure that the gulf between architecture and business is closed.

Step 5: *Realize* that an enterprise that uses technology to meet its business goals will need professionals who *understand both business and technology.* Designing such an organization, finding these people, and letting them prosper requires an active partnership with human capital professionals.

Step 6: *Communicate* frequently, openly, and in business terms. For technology to work as an enabler it must be on the radar, not "under" it.

Step 7: *Focus* on compliance and manage risk. These areas should be understood and managed for the organization's benefit by a formal compliance and risk management function. Managers and administrators need to participate in governance bodies and advise decision makers with consistency.

None of these things will happen overnight, and pitfalls and challenges are attached to each. An organization—private enterprise or government agency—setting out to improve the way it manages business technology must realize that changing its governance and the organization will require time and attention. Changes here are immediately visible, and the results can be quickly realized.

Perhaps more than any other area, governance requires business and technology managers to work together, because it provides the forum for business and technology leadership to make decisions together that drive an organization's direction. What is required is to set goals and work with determination toward reaching them; anticipate and address potential pitfalls in each activity; establish a plan to increase maturity and work according to this playbook for improvement; and, put into place durable operating models, policies, processes, and procedures that will ensure that the changes made in the enterprise during its process of maturation become a way of life.

CHAPTER 6

Size Doesn't Matter: How Small Enterprises Benefit from Strategic Investment Management

I N JULY 2010 THE TASTEE SUB SHOP, a small, nondescript eatery in Edison, New Jersey, was host to a summit on unemployment and jobs creation. Rather than pulling together the titans of industry from the Fortune 500 who dominate Capitol Hill with lobbyists, President Barack Obama broke bread with a group of average small business people and entrepreneurs. On the agenda: talk of tax incentives, federal financial assistance, and training programs that would aid small businesses like the Tastee Sub Shop in creating permanent jobs.

The first two years of the Obama administration included double-digit unemployment rates across America not seen since the economic malaise of the 1970s. More than 8.4 million Americans lost their jobs to the economic downturn. It's easy to point to the large enterprises and multinational corporations that eliminated jobs as the primary source of this individual recessionary pain. After all, many well-known and established companies including Circuit City, Lehman Brothers, Linens 'n Things, Washington Mutual, and Aloha Airlines virtually disappeared overnight and took tens of thousands of jobs with them. But small businesses—in the aggregate—were the greater source of layoffs and decreased economic activity. In the United States alone more than 660,000 small businesses shut down because they couldn't sustain themselves.[1] The inability to secure credit, decreased business-to-business spending and consumer spending, and general uncertainty of economic prospects conspired to destroy many businesses ranging from sole proprietors to mid-market companies.

President Obama traveled to this suburban blue-collar restaurant because he knew that the overall U.S. economy—two-thirds driven by consumer spending—would not return to its prerecession robustness unless small businesses started expanding and hiring workers. If consumers don't have jobs, or if they feel as though their livelihoods are in constant jeopardy, they won't spend on new cars, homes, electronics, clothing, and durable goods. Reigniting the jobs engine is the first step in reigniting the economy.

Why target small businesses? President Obama and economists have long acknowledged that the small business community drives a large part of U.S. economic activity. The truth is that since 1985 small businesses have created virtually all of the net-new jobs.[2] The United States is home to more than 27 million businesses, of which more than 99 percent are considered small.[3] While large Fortune 500 companies employ tens of thousands of workers, the number of net-new jobs they create is a fraction of the jobs produced by small businesses, entrepreneurs, and startup companies. Although many small businesses employ fewer than twenty people, just imagine what would happen if one-quarter of all small businesses were to hire just one person this year. The unemployment rate would be cut by half.

Accelerated creation of jobs that pay well comes from the small businesses that break out and become large enterprises. Take computer storage company NetApp, for instance. When David Hitz, James Lau, and Michael Malcolm founded NetApp in 1992, it was just the three of them with a couple of engineers and a small support staff building a company from scratch to compete against an entrenched competitor, Sun Microsystems, with a product that redefined the data storage marketplace. In those early years, the founders weren't drawing paychecks as they pumped everything they had into the business. Their efforts paid off. In the company's first eight years, it grew from nothing to a $1 billion enterprise. Today, NetApp is a global corporation with more than $3.4 billion in gross revenue and employs more than 8,300 people.[4]

When President Obama ordered his sub in New Jersey, he wasn't looking to spur the creation of the next NetApp, Google, or Walmart, but rather to get small businesses thinking about growing. And in the middle of 2010, growth wasn't on the minds of many businesses. Signs of improving economic conditions did little to speed the pace of recovery and restore business confidence. Small businesses especially were reluctant to invest in expansion for fear of being caught without the revenue to pay for the people, inventory, and credit they would assume for growth. As a result, American businesses sat on more than $1.2 trillion in cash reserves rather than invest in expansion, innovation, and, ultimately, new jobs.

Despite the economic challenges, the United States will produce anywhere from 500,000 to 1 million new small businesses annually.[5] By far, the United States is the most industrious and entrepreneurial nation on Earth. The open economy, relative ease of doing business, and access to technology and financing makes business creation more possible than in most countries. Unfortunately, this high rate of entrepreneurship comes with an equally high business failure rate. According to the U.S. Small Business Administration, roughly one-third of new businesses fail within their first year, and only 44 percent survive longer than four years.

Why do small businesses fail in their first year or even when they're still midsized and relatively mature companies? Myriad reasons exist, but it often comes down to a lack of access to relevant information, internal transparency, and defined processes that enable them to make sound business decisions and advance to a higher level of growth and performance. Business Technology Management is designed to provide businesses of all sizes with the frameworks and processes to keep them from stalling and to grow. In this chapter, we'll focus on the BTM capability of Portfolio and Program Management (PPM). This part of the BTM Framework is of particular importance to small and medium enterprises, since they are at the greatest risk exposure to failure because they often lack the resources to make the sound strategic decisions that will make their businesses successful and, ultimately, put them among the ranks of the Global 2000.

Redefining Enterprises

What exactly is a small enterprise? It's not easily defined. Business analysts often measure the size of an enterprise by the number of its employees. Walmart, for instance, is the world's largest private sector employer with more than 2.1 million people on its payroll. By comparison, Facebook, one of the world's most recognizable brands, only has 1,200 employees. Another common measure of the size of a business is revenue. ExxonMobil, which had $284 billion in gross revenue in 2009, is clearly an enormous multinational enterprise. What about Nutrisystems, the dieting and weight-loss company? It's well known through its national television advertising and celebrity endorsements, so it must be an enterprise. But by many definitions, Nurtisystems is a mid-market company; it generated $528 million in annual revenue in 2009 and employs just 612 people. Defining it as a small enterprise—much less an enterprise at all—is anything but trivial.

For the purposes of this discussion, we're going to call any business entity with more than $25 million in revenue but less than $2.5 billion a small enterprise. That's a huge gap of 1,000 percent difference, but it's a logical range. Small businesses usually take on certain structures and divisions of labor when they reach the $25 million mark. They begin to have division of labor and responsibilities. The owner/operator is no longer a journeyman who covers multiple activities. And the organization has a certain level of internal governance over its processes and operations. By the time a company passes the $1 billion mark, those constructs are substantially defined. When a business passes the $2.5 billion mark, it's most likely operating as a collection of businesses, with divisional leaders holding the same charge as a chief executive over their domains.

This definition of small enterprise isn't so rigid and must include even businesses below $25 million in revenue. The reasons are clear: every large enterprise was once a small business. Microsoft started as a small software publisher. Hyundai was founded as a small construction company. Archer Daniels Midland has humble roots as a linseed crushing concern. And only time will tell what businesses and size Facebook, Google, and the next generation of businesses will become. Entrepreneurs, people who have a zeal for growth and arm themselves with goals and plans, founded all these businesses. They are distinctly different from "lifestyle" businesses, which are small operations designed and operated as self-sustaining entities whose purpose is to maintain the desired lifestyle of the owner/operator. Entrepreneurs look to the future and plan for the growth they want to achieve, which is far different from the lifestyle business that often only accidentally finds true success.

Technology is the factor that enables entrepreneurs and small enterprises to compete and succeed against entrenched enterprises. Never before in the history of business or economics has technology played such a critical role in leveling the playing fields. In the twenty-first-century global economy, a small business has the ability to reach across oceans to source product and sell goods with nearly the same efficiency as a large multinational enterprise. As Thomas Friedman wrote in *The World is Flat*, "The world has been flattened. As a result of the triple convergence, global collaboration and competition—between individuals and individuals, companies and individuals, companies and companies, and companies and customers—have been made cheaper, easier, more friction-free, and more productive for more people from more corners of the earth than at any time in the history of the world."[6]

The truth is that if a small enterprise can identify a genuine need, technology exists to fulfill that need locally and globally. The heavy lifting comes in creating an appropriate business model.

Strategic Investment Management

As we discussed earlier in this chapter, most startup companies fail in large degree because they are unable to correctly assess their market opportunities, develop a strategic plan, and exercise discipline in execution. The same is true for technology implementation; many technology projects either fail in execution or fall short of their full potential because they were never holistically managed as a piece of the business. These instances lack a logical approach of identifying and evaluating the critical elements required within a project.

As previously outlined in Chapter 2, Strategic Investment Management is comprised of four capabilities that include Approval and Prioritization, Portfolio and Program Management, Project Analysis and Design Standards, and Resource and Demand Management. For the purpose of this discussion, we will focus on Portfolio and Program Management (PPM), which provides enterprise-wide focus on defining, gathering, categorizing, analyzing, and monitoring information on corporate assets and activity as they relate to technology implementation and management.

PPM offers top managers a centralized and balanced view of various business technology projects that lays out the benefits and risks of each. Effective PPM is only realized by focusing on organizational structures, processes, information, and automation and in the process, bringing order to chaos. If a business has any hope of transforming its technology management, it must first structure and organize all of the disparate pieces of information held by the organization. It's really no different than anyone trying to organize hundreds of photos on a hard drive or clean out a basement. Management must discover what it has, sort it into logical piles, and assess the value of the individual items against some larger goal.

Business technology portfolio management is critical. Managers of financial assets, for example, would not presume to act without a full understanding of all their holdings. Portfolio management is widely applied in other management functions as well, including strategic planning and new product development. Most business technology executives know of it, and many practice some form of it, but it has not often been granted the strategic role it deserves.

Many companies don't reap the full rewards because they see it only in financial terms, think of it as a software tool, or view it as a tactical approach for managing projects. At its best, however, portfolio management as advanced by BTM's Portfolio and Program Management capability takes all of a firm's assets and activities into account. It is truly a more effective means of giving an entire company better information to develop strategies, manage risk, and execute plans.

PPM unites an organization's efforts at every level. It is a completely different way of seeing, assessing, and planning the business— somewhat analogous to financial portfolio management. For example, in finance, an investor identifies and categorizes all assets to form a portfolio, which provides aggregated views of individual investments. The investor might see that the portfolio is weighted too heavily in one industry, has redundant exposure to one type of security, carries a certain level of risk, and promises a certain level of return. The investor can set a strategy and construct a portfolio likely to achieve an appropriate balance of risk of return. In much the same way, business technology assets portfolios reveal what technology a company owns and what its various arms are trying to accomplish. Management can use a portfolio approach to decide which activities are more likely to support the enterprise business strategy.

The strategic role of PPM is nothing short of providing an enterprise (regardless of size) with a tool for better aligning its technology spending with current and future business needs. PPM creates information and insight to help management make such decisions as:

○ Defining business improvement options and scenarios.

○ Analyzing implications and impacts of potential initiatives.

⟲ Setting target allocations for investment categories.

⟲ Evaluating and making decisions on project requests.

⟲ Evaluating the health of business and technology assets.

⟲ Determining appropriate sequencing of major programs.

⟲ Managing risk mitigation across the enterprise.

⟲ Identifying and resolving critical project-related issues.

Through its centralized view of all technology projects, a good business technology portfolio will make it easy to ensure that investments are well balanced in terms of size, risk, and projected (anticipated) payoff. Used wisely, it will actually increase business technology's value by exposing projects that are redundant or risky, while revealing how to shift funds from low-value investments to high-value, strategic ones.

PPM improves the allocation of resources and reduces project failures by creating a "single view of the truth" about an enterprise's operations. It generates a common vocabulary and metrics. It permits a comprehensive set of decisions to be made before action is taken, identifying and resolving conflicts. It allows strategic direction flowing down to meet suggested courses of action flowing up in a formal management process. PPM is, in fact, continuous: strategic planning informs portfolio managers, who reassess programs and projects. Information on the status of corporate assets, risks, and financial performance likewise influences subsequent strategic planning.

PPM provides information that links business needs with business technology activities—enabling a converged viewpoint that is simply focused on business outcomes, rather than advancing the interests of one group versus another. PPM allows an organization to get beyond the incomplete approach of computing the ROI of individual projects. With a portfolio viewpoint, the payback of a project can be evaluated within the context of many projects contributing to a business goal. The merits of individual projects are not seen in isolation but in consideration of their contribution to business capabilities that enable a strategy. In forward-thinking companies, business and technology portfolios become inseparable from other portfolios—R&D, product management, mergers and acquisitions—and become just another component of a business initiative. Through a PPM implementation, no one group or project's interest will advance at the expense of another.

The Anatomy of a Portfolio

Portfolios are more than just the correlation of information; they are the organization of disparate but interrelated sets of information. PPM creates a single truth by sorting information into logical groupings. It's really no different than when a person organizes their photo collection—they group by vacation locations, baby pictures, social gatherings, sightseeing, and work. The grouping of photos creates a master collection of photos. The same is true with PPM. Enterprises do not create just one portfolio, but a collection of portfolios—as depicted in Figure 6–1—that have different, logical views that reflect the assets and activities at different levels within the enterprise.

Enterprises should start their PPM process by developing portfolios of assets and activities. These portfolios provide an enterprise-wide perspective for executives and managers to ensure that the organization is

FIGURE 6–1 PORTFOLIO TYPES.

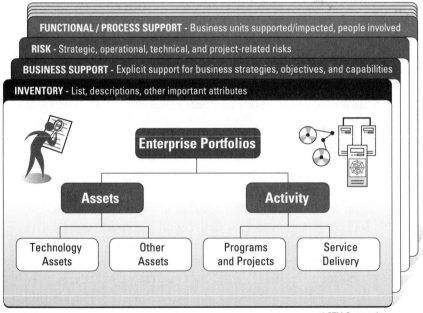

© BTM Corporation.

Different portfolios should be defined for various business and technology management purposes, ranging from accurately inventorying business and technology assets to managing strategic risk.

deploying resources in such a way that it will meet its business objectives.

Asset-related portfolios include technology assets and other (nonfinancial) assets such as technology asset portfolios. This would include business applications and tools, data, and infrastructure (hardware, operating systems, systems software, etc.). This could also include such nonfinancial assets as people and intellectual property.

Activity-related portfolios consist of discrete projects and programs related to continuous service delivery. These are a bit more complex in nature and execution, since different projects span different levels of an enterprise's operations. They include project-level, enterprise-wide, program-level, and service delivery portfolios.

Project-level portfolios include planned undertakings of related activities, which have a beginning and an end, to reach an objective. This type of portfolio enables better monitoring and exception-based management by creating a conduit where issues easily flow to decision makers. For example, a dashboard providing project-level status indicators across dimensions such as schedule, cost, scope, risk, and governance allows executives to focus on the exceptions rather than spending their time gathering and reviewing reams of data on all projects.

Enterprise project portfolios help with a variety of other activities such as identifying synergies and redundancies in projects; assessing the reuse of knowledge assets and intellectual property on different projects; and monitoring demand for resources, material, and support on projects.

Program-level portfolios include groups of related projects that all need to be completed to reach a certain level of benefit, and that are managed in a coordinated way to obtain a level of benefits and control not available from managing them individually. For instance, a program to improve customer retention via the Internet might contain individual projects such as website redesign, implementation of a new customer relationship management (CRM) process and system, and execution of an e-mail marketing campaign. Program managers would ensure that the interdependencies among these projects are well understood. This optimizes risk management that cannot be addressed by individual project teams. And it deals with other issues such as resource balancing across projects. Having a program view, with linkage to the underlying projects available to executives and managers, enables effective and timely oversight.

Service delivery portfolios include the operational, nonproject-related efforts required to support business operations. This is a critical piece of the overall pie when analyzing how well the organization is performing, and whether the company is working on the right projects based on business objectives. This information is critical when examining the enterprise resource portfolio and planning for changes to meet demand.

PPM is a critical enabler of many business activities and BTM capabilities. As illustrated in Figure 6–2, intelligence and perspectives PPM generates become an integral part of strategy creation, application management, resource and demand management, project approval and prioritization, and compliance and risk management—all critical components of BTM and each a BTM capability.

Compliance and Risk Management PPM supports Compliance and Risk Management by defining enterprise risk types and related portfolio structures, analyzing organizational vulnerabilities and business objec-

FIGURE 6–2 SUPPORT FOR OTHER CAPABILITIES.

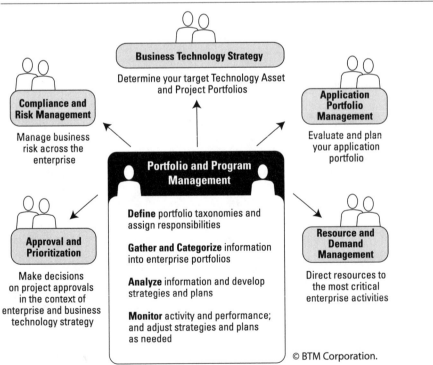

Portfolio and Program Management's impact extends well beyond its core focus.

tives, developing generic risk mitigation approaches, and identifying and categorizing enterprise risks. These portfolios might categorize risks as strategic, operational, technical, or project-related. PPM supports Compliance and Risk Management by allowing executives to review an overall enterprise risk map, which provides the ability to analyze and prioritize the risks to be mitigated.

Business Technology Strategy PPM aids in gathering information on the enterprise business strategy, its objectives, and desired capabilities. It does so by creating portfolios of current enterprise applications, data, infrastructure assets, and architecture, along with portfolios on current and planned enterprise initiatives. PPM allows the evaluation of technology assets and technology initiatives (existing and planned) against business objectives. It identifies technology enablers to help shape business strategy and guides the development of target architecture vision for applications, data, and infrastructure.

Resource and Demand Management PPM creates supply portfolios that identify resources and skills, and show their availability and allocation. A project demand portfolio should likewise be established for prioritized potential initiatives, planned initiatives, and currently active initiatives. An ongoing operational demand portfolio should be established for problem resolution, minor enhancements (nonproject), service requests, and other maintenance and general support. Using these supply-and-demand portfolios provides an effective assessment of the balance of risk and reward, while performing resource allocation and balancing at the same time. This includes assessing utilization and performance, determining a desired target resource portfolio, and planning resource portfolio adjustments.

Approval and Prioritization PPM creates an enterprise perspective on the expected business value of different projects, as well as the potential project risks. In supporting this task, program, project, and risk-assessment portfolios can address evaluation criteria such as project complexity; project uncertainty; the stability and quality of the information system development group; and, ultimately, the expected business capabilities that will be enabled.

PPM: Ideas into Action

Many companies are not prepared to adopt a portfolio-level perspective or manage the interdependencies among a large number of initiatives.

Often, enterprise executives think of portfolio management as strictly a project-based exercise, a province of the IT department with little connection to the rest of the business. An effective PPM capability, however, can only be realized through a balanced and thorough focus on organization structures, processes, information, and automation. The following four activities are how enterprises turn PPM concepts into actions that improve the output of projects and strategies.

Create Structures, Define Taxonomies, and Assign Responsibilities

A successful PPM capability requires that the right people perform the right processes. Ideally, an Enterprise Program Management Office (EPMO) will assume responsibility for managing portfolios, programs, and projects. Typically, an EPMO is a function found in large enterprises or organizations, and while there are certain core functions that most EPMOs perform, the role, the staffing, and the services or functions delivered vary to a surprising degree from one enterprise to another. Its responsibilities include educating the company and collaborating with key constituents on PPM processes. This group ensures that the organization has the appropriate tools and information available to perform portfolio analysis, and it's the source of an accurate inventory of initiatives and assets. The EPMO exercises control in defining and overseeing project justification and prioritization; it is the operational owner of project resources and is responsible for the allocation of scarce resources. This includes defining project management approaches and ultimately offering project-level oversight.

Owners, stakeholders, and customers of the EPMO include the Office of the CIO, Office of Architecture and Standards, and a line of business executives. Collectively, the owners and stakeholders must execute PPM in a way that ensures that project risks are being managed, process designs meet objectives, applications and requirements support processes, and standards and target architectures are followed. The leadership team and board of directors are customers of information provided by the EPMO, although much of their work is done in other bodies. A Business Technology Council (a cross-functional group of senior executives), for example, might be where these executives review the organization's portfolios for strategic fit. This group owns the overall strategy, ensuring that the portfolio of technology investments is in sync with the company's strategy and objectives and that major initiatives are receiving the right level of business sponsorship and attention.

Gather and Categorize Information into Enterprise Portfolios

For PPM to work properly, a discovery needs to take place involving an inventory of company assets and activity. A CIO, for instance, might be responsible for monitoring high-risk projects, collaborating with and providing status reports to business leaders, managing the overall budget, and collaborating with the organization's business and technology investment board to allocate investment dollars. To perform these tasks, the CIO would need a portfolio categorized by risk level, one categorized by country, one containing all initiatives, and one categorized by investment type.

Analyze Information and Develop Strategies and Plans

The actual analysis using portfolio information will vary depending on the area of activity. For example, if the Business Technology Council[7] is evaluating previously undefined project requests, the aggregate investment portfolio might be analyzed to determine alignment with the company's portfolio investment strategy. If the company planned to allocate spending at 50 percent to infrastructure, 20 percent to transaction processing, 20 percent to decision support, and 10 percent to strategic projects, their approval and prioritization decisions should support this distribution.

Another example might be where the company is developing its business technology strategy and is attempting to plan the resources to support the strategy over the next three years. In this case, the resource supply and demand portfolios would be analyzed to develop an appropriate balance of risk and reward given the desired business and technology targets.

Monitor Operations and Performance

PPM analytics should support the automatic roll-up of detailed data, which helps to shift the focus of managers from the administrative task of gathering and summarizing data to analysis and exception-based monitoring and decision making. As in the previous activity, the actual monitoring that should be performed will depend on the specific area of activity. Defining the appropriate metrics to measure performance is critical. Once portfolios are created, taxonomies defined, and information categorized, performance metrics should be used to measure portfolio effectiveness. These metrics typically are organized into categories such as financial (economic cost and benefit), business impact (contribution to business performance), likelihood of success or failure, and architectural fit (compatibility with guidelines).

PPM and its related activities may seem like the province of large enterprises, but the methodology is directly applicable to smaller businesses whether they are a manufacturing company, a media publisher, or a social network. In fact, in smaller organizations, PPM actually becomes easier to implement since many of the key actors in the process perform multiple roles. Consequently, those actors in small enterprises gain an equal—if not greater—benefit from PPM since it better organizes information for action in constructs with fewer resources. Without PPM, an enterprise regardless of size is simply guessing about the status of its projects, its available resources, and its prioritization decisions. PPM brings greater certainty to what enterprises can expect from their decision making.

Pharmaceutical Startup Prescribes PPM

When is a good time to implement PPM? As we stated earlier in this chapter, PPM and other BTM capabilities are applicable to businesses of all sizes. Small and midsized businesses, however, can use PPM when they need to avoid hitting a maturation ceiling. They can use PPM as a catalyst for taking their businesses through a logical and thought-out evolution that leads them to higher levels of planned growth and profitability.

Is PPM costly and time-consuming? Yes, no doubt about it. It requires commitment and discipline to enact and follow. But it's an expense well worth the investment when trying to grow a small business into a thriving mid-market company and, ultimately, into an enterprise. In fact, smart small businesses often discover that their investment in projecting and planning for their expected future states pays off when they achieve their growth goals. That was precisely what happened with Endo Pharmaceuticals Holdings, which made a conscious decision not to act like a small business when it started out in 1997.

From the beginning, Endo Pharmaceuticals wasn't a typical small business venture. For starters, the company's founders planned to focus on two widely used, non–patent-protected pain drugs, Percocet and Percodan. Observers thought the concept was pure suicide, since the entire pharmaceutical industry was built on the concept of profiting from patented drugs before they became available in the public domain as low-cost competitors. An equally challenging hurdle was the fact that even the smallest pharmaceutical company had billions of dollars in revenue. Endo would compete against the likes of Pfizer, DuPont, Merck, Abbott Labs, and GlaxoSmithKline. The company's three founders knew that if they made one mistake the gargantuan competitors would simply roll over them without notice.

Despite the perceivably insurmountable challenges, Endo founders Carol A. Ammon, Mariann T. MacDonald, and Louis J. Vollmer believed that if they focused on pain management medication, they could buck the conventional pharmaceutical market and build a billion-dollar business. The initial plan called for the company to take over management of thirty-five drugs from DuPont Merck Pharmaceutical, the joint-venture where they worked. Endo would focus on marketing commodity drugs rather than the expensive—yet lucrative—research and development model of developing new medications.

Endo's startup plan called for the fledging company to use DuPont Merck's computing infrastructure. Nesting inside the corporate patron's system would save Endo precious capital that would otherwise go toward building expensive data centers and acquiring software. It was a prudent, strategic move for a poor startup. But the company's technology leader, Eric Bloom, focused on Endo's desired future state of becoming a billion-dollar company, not where it was as a startup. He made the courageous decision to invest in expensive, complex applications that are typically reserved for large enterprises such as their competitors.[8]

Bloom's logic behind building for the future state was based in what BTM now calls Portfolio and Program Management. In 1997, Endo was little more than an idea with little money and big plans. Bloom assumed that it would grow as projected and would eventually need its own computing infrastructure. The more he thought about that migration out of DuPont Merck's infrastructure into their own systems, the more he realized that it might be better to just start out with its own applications and data center. He further rationalized that starting out on enterprise-class systems would better prepare Endo for the growth it desired. Essentially, they would grow up on the very technology that made their competitors great, thus leveling the playing field.

Endo did meet its own expectations and shattered notions that startups couldn't break into the highly competitive pharmaceutical market. At each phase of development, Endo's management team reviewed their technology assets, and reviewed and adjusted their technology needs against the growth and strategic plan. This process not only guided Endo through its build-out, but also smoothed its first acquisition and helped the company rebound from its missteps. It only took Endo four years to reach $100 million in sales. Today, Endo is a $1.4 billion pharmaceutical company that holds a legitimate place among the giants of its industry.

Endo is a prime example of how business vision, strategic planning, and proper Portfolio and Program Management can propel even the smallest companies in the toughest competitive and economic circumstances to sustained success.

The Takeaway: Turning Ideas into Action

Effective investment management does not simply happen. It comes about because of strategic intent, close collaboration between business and technology professionals, a deep appreciation of the need to invest optimally, and the creation and empowerment of decision-making and operational bodies focused on achieving excellence.

When faced with deciding how to select among the many "great technology ideas" presented, it's necessary to ask what the optimal mix of investments is for an organization's future. It must also be asked whether that future is based on the current strategy as set forth at that time.

The most effective means of answering those questions requires incorporating a business-based governance and investment management framework. Here's how it's done.

Step 1: *Educate senior executives and start small.* Begin to educate senior business and technology executives about the benefits of a portfolio approach. Consider developing a PPM capability for a small slice of the business to demonstrate the benefits and build consensus for embarking on an enterprise-wide effort.

Step 2: *Establish management commitment and vision.* Most of PPM implementation is not technical but managerial, and the commitment and strategic vision of top executives should be established and sustained. PPM involves many different people needing to do things differently within the organization and must be supported by senior management to achieve success.

Step 3: *Address new organizational structures early on.* Plan the creation of an Enterprise Program Management Office (EPMO), which in most cases owns PPM. The EPMO's responsibilities need to include educating the company on PPM processes and collaborating with key constituents to establish portfolio management approaches. This group will also provide the tools and information to analyze portfolios and gain access to the inventory of programs, initiatives, and assets. Plan the design of a Business Technology Council, the upper-level strategic decision-making body.

Step 4: *Explicitly design information management processes.* PPM will be an outright failure if information gathering is not performed adequately from the outset and if information is not kept up to date. Specific processes and responsibilities related to the creation, approval, and updating of information are critical.

Step 5: *Keep automation in perspective.* Don't focus your entire efforts on a PPM tool. The organizational processes and responsibilities to support PPM are far more important. Executives at many of these companies are not even aware of the PPM tools they own. It is critical to treat PPM as just one dimension of what needs to be addressed during a PPM implementation.

Step 6: *Sustain a high degree of focus on PPM end users.* More than any other implementation, PPM requires an intense executive focus, since PPM is at its core an enabler of other activity. Executives must have access to customized portfolios to support the activities they need to perform daily.

PART III

The Impact of Transformation

CHAPTER 7

The Transformation Triangle

T HROUGHOUT THE 2000s, Swedish carmaker Saab used the catchy tagline "Saab: Born from Jetfighters" in television commercials for their aerodynamic sports cars and luxury sedans: The sleek design of its flagship 9–5 shared an extremely low drag ratio lineage with several generations of Saabs. From early in its history, the company recognized that wind resistance—or the air buffer generated by a car's momentum—would affect engine and fuel efficiency. Its first car, Project 92—a prototype built in 1947—had a drag coefficient of 0.32, an impressive accomplishment even by contemporary standards.

But recognizing drag and wind resistance effect on cars isn't where "Born from Jetfighters" came from. Founded in 1938, Saab was commissioned by the Swedish Royal Air Force to produce military aircraft. War clouds were gathering in Europe, and Sweden didn't have the aircraft manufacturing capacity of other European powers. It started by building copies of American and German planes, but quickly developed its own designs. In 1941, the Saab 17 fighter and Saab 18 bomber took flight. They weren't perfect, but they were sufficiently functional. Sweden remained armed but outside of the conflict, but Saab continued to redesign its aircraft in case the country's sovereignty was violated.

By 1944, it was clear that World War II would end within a year or two with the eventual defeat of Germany. When that happened, Saab would find itself without a purpose. The military would no longer need vast fleets of aircraft, and its propeller planes would soon be rendered obsolete by jet aircraft. Management needed to diversify. Among the products it considered were trucks and commercial trucks, motorcycles, and household appliances. Volvo already made cars. Scania-Vabis led the Swedish market with trucks and commercial vehicles. And there were several motorcycle companies. Stoves and refrigerators were an option, but would take too much to reinvent the company. No, Saab decided to take what it knew about aerodynamics and apply it to a low-cost, highly efficient vehicle for the masses. Over the last six decades, Saab has built and fostered a reputation for efficient, reliable, and high-performing vehicles.[1]

Setting aside the challenges and setbacks suffered under General Motors' ownership over the last decade,[2] Saab remains one of the finest examples of rapid transformation in business. Were Saab's cars born from the same stuff as jetfighters? No, the company's first jets actually came after its cars were introduced. But its speed for diversifying and implementing change that kept the company from sliding into oblivion at the end of the war came at jet speed! Saab is but one example of how companies either transform or diversify from their original market intent. Here are some others:

- ↻ Raytheon started as a consumer appliance company that made radio tubes. Today, it's one of the largest defense contractors in the world, and makes microwave communications systems and cruise missiles.

- ↻ Symantec, a publisher of data security and storage software, was originally a maker of PC management tools and word processors.

- ↻ AT&T started out as a telephone network operator, but through evolving markets and regulatory mandates transformed itself into a global provider of Internet carrier services.

- ↻ Sony began as a recording equipment company; today it's the world's fifth largest media company.

- ↻ General Electric was founded as an electricity generator and producer of lighting components to create the power industry. But over its 132-year history, it has continually challenged itself to innovate and has produced everything from light bulbs to (shades of Saab) jet engines.

As economic conditions change and products reach market saturation, transformation is the only option for maintaining growth and financial viability. The difference between successful and extinct companies is the recognition and successful execution of this transformative process. Embarking on a transformation is more than just deciding to do something different or expanding into adjacent markets. It requires examination, planning, and execution. Companies that have mastered this trifecta are prepared for whatever the marketplace brings. At BTM, we call this process the "Transformation Triangle," and it codifies a methodology that enables enterprises to recognize the changes they need to undergo and to then manage their own makeovers. The triangle consists of three basic principles.

1. *Business Agility*—the ability to sense changes in economic conditions and competitive landscape, and proactively implement a response.

2. *Sustained Innovation*—the ability to develop new products, services, and methodologies that advance beyond the competition through repeatable processes.

3. *Operational Excellence*—the ability to consistently deliver cost-effective services at defined performance levels to internal and external customers.

Enterprises can apply these principles independently or in concert, depending on the response most appropriate for a company's market position, core competencies, and strategic imperatives. Each response relies on a select set of management behaviors and constructs. Business Agility, Sustained Innovation, and Operational Excellence each have a particular convergence pattern. Most organizations are not set up to meet the challenges—or for that matter, opportunities—these behaviors often present. These habits, which have made companies successful in the past, can sabotage them in the face of disruptive innovation. What is called for is a new business model, one that incorporates agility, innovation, and efficiency. Convergence is what enables transformation to happen.

In this chapter, we'll lay the foundation for implementing the transformative triangle to create innovative and dynamic enterprises. Before going into great detail about Business Agility, Sustained Innovation, and Operational Excellence in the chapters that follow, we'll first explore the need for continual transformation and evolution of business practices, products, and market penetration. It's only through growth that businesses achieve and maintain true viability, and viability translates into greater performance, profitability, and return on shareholder investment.

Why Transform at All?

It seems like a nonsensical question, doesn't it? Some would say that there are two kinds of people (or businesses) in the world: the quick and the dead. If your business isn't evolving—innovating, growing, or reinventing itself—it's in danger of failing. The business landscape is littered with the remains of companies that rose to great heights only to have their fortunes plummet because they were unable to transform themselves as times changed. Digital Equipment Corporation and Wang Computers, once the titans of the nascent information age, failed to innovate and were sold off to other companies. Woolworth's, once a fixture on Main Streets across the country, did not adapt its business model to the advent of mega shopping malls and big-box retailers and closed its doors in December 2008. Pan Am and TWA, once the standard bearers of the U.S. airline industry, could not overcome economic pressures and were forced to declare bankruptcy. Transformation was the imperative they all had missed out on.

Transformation is the management challenge of the twenty-first century. We are living in a transformative age, and no industry is immune to waves of change. The automotive and energy industries are racing to find the next stage of their evolution in a world that is challenged by the question of accessibility to oil in the face of global market demands. The media is grappling with the democratization of information resulting from the Internet, which has completely eroded the business models of film studios, music producers, and print publishers. The financial services industry tries to recover from the chaos resulting from bad risk taking and regulatory oversight failures, failures so bad that deep intervention by the U.S. government was needed, forever transforming banking, stock trading, and investment regulations.

Even Google, heralded as one of the great companies in the information age, is coming under pressure to transform and evolve. In August 2010, *Fortune* magazine published a cover story dramatically titled, "Is Google Over?" As of the article's publication, Google was generating nearly $24 billion in revenue and throwing off more than $6.5 billion in profits. It commanded more than 60 percent of the search advertising market. And it continued to grow at rates approaching 30 percent year after year. Yet *Fortune* noted several disturbing problems with Google's revenue and profit sources. Google earned roughly 90 percent of its revenue and 99 percent of its profit from search engine marketing. Despite its best efforts to create new businesses in cloud computing applications, Web browsers, and its Android mobile operating system, Google was essentially a one-trick pony that would mature into a healthy, but predictable company. *Fortune*'s conclusion was the organization would no longer innovate, but stagnate.

The fear permeating boardrooms and executive suites is that of disintermediation. Businesses can operate well and see healthy revenue and profit streams even during the challenging times. Today, however, lurking in the background is a new threat—a new entrepreneur, a new delivery model, or a new idea that can and will rip the legs out from underneath an otherwise stable and profitable industry. The newspaper and television industries were completely disrupted by the Internet. Software as a service and cloud computing is challenging software giants such as Microsoft, IBM, and Oracle. And social networks such as LinkedIn, Facebook, and Twitter are revolutionizing business-to-business and person-to-person communications.

Henry Ford once said, "Failure is the opportunity to begin again, more intelligently." Perhaps that was true in the early twentieth century, but today's economy is far less forgiving. Enterprises are beginning to understand that change is becoming a permanent way of life, that the status quo will never again be good enough, and that the biggest risk is not taking a risk at all. Companies must continually innovate to anticipate and adapt to new market demands and adjust their business models to capitalize on new and more efficient delivery systems.

This enterprise transformation means positioning an organization to manage its current business with increasing efficiency, discarding activities that no longer make sense, and constantly investing in new products, services, processes, and business models. It is not tweaking at the edges. It is creating a new organization, one that thinks and acts differently. It is a continuous process.

Disruption and transformation is nothing new. At the beginning of each new business era, the existing paradigm resists with vigor. When the automobile was first coming of age, the existing industry of horse carriages and the supporting infrastructure could not imagine a world without horse-powered transportation. In many cases, disrupted industries see surges in business as they begin their descent. Visionaries see through this fog and drive transformation. Agile enterprises are able to improve existing practices and develop new innovative processes on a regular basis. The notion that companies must continually renew themselves has appeared in management literature, with increasing frequency, since economist Joseph Schumpeter introduced the term "creative destruction" in his book *Capitalism, Socialism and Democracy* in 1942.[3]

Schumpeter noted that every industry advances on technological progress—whether farming, manufacturing, power, transportation, or other—and organizational innovation. The old ways are destroyed incessantly and new ways are given life. Economists, he wrote—and this should apply to business executives, as well—have traditionally focused on price and quality when thinking about competition, but such variables give an incomplete picture. On this, he wrote: "In capitalist reality, as distinguished from its textbook picture, it is not that kind of competition which counts, but the competition from the new commodity, the new technology, the new source of supply, the new type of organization . . . competition which commands a decisive cost or quality advantage and which strikes not at the margins of the profits and the outputs of the existing firms but at their foundations and their very lives."

Now, more than sixty-five years after Schumpeter wrote those words, we find ourselves in this same situation. Competition over price is competition in commodities. Such competition is adequate but not acceptable. Some new thing, which we cannot yet see, will come along and make our commodity passé—and then we must compete with this intruder. It is the automobile to the buggy-whip makers, and file sharing and YouTube to the music labels. It's Saleforce.com to Oracle and IBM. It is entire economies—China and India to the United States and the European Union.

Management guru Peter Drucker noted that Schumpeter was much less known than John Maynard Keynes, his contemporary, and yet predicted that his ideals would influence business and management thinking into the twenty-first century. Drucker wrote: "The innovator is the true subject of economics. Entrepreneurs that move resources from old and obsolescent to new and more productive employments are the very essence of economics and certainly of a modern economy. Innovation makes obsolete yesterday's capital earnings and capital investment."[4]

Transformation Is a Process, Not a Destination

Transformation is not a singular event. A one-time makeover will not cut it. Growth through innovation must become part of the enterprise's soul. Successful, sustained enterprises are those that are continually transforming themselves, or have segmented themselves to enable overlapping transformative initiatives that grow their revenues and insulate their core business from economic disruptions. This requires new organizational structures, the creation and sharing of new kinds of information, and new decision-making processes. Only in this way can growth through innovation become repeatable.

The Continuing Transformation of General Electric

A master of transformation is General Electric. The company, founded by Thomas Edison, one of the greatest inventors in history, understood from its beginnings that continual invention and reinvention of a business was a necessity for success and viability. GE is credited with creating the electric society we live in today. It was the source of the incandescent light bulb, which necessitated the creation of a power generation and distribution system, which in turn led to the application of electrically powered devices ranging from toasters to fans to industrial machinery. And long before Henry Ford perfected his gas-powered Model T, Edison envisioned electric cars that drew their power from high-capacity batteries.

Despite recent stumbles, GE remains one of the most diversified and dynamic enterprises in the world. The company generates more than $156 billion annually from an array of businesses ranging from electrical generation equipment to appliances, locomotives to jet engines, and plastics to medical diagnostic equipment. Over the decades, GE has continued to reinvent itself by entering new businesses and decommissioning or selling off old businesses. In recent years, GE has deemphasized or sold off businesses—such as insurance and private equity investment—to raise capital or to focus on emerging businesses that have greater potential. In the company's 2007 annual report, CEO and chairman Jeffery Immelt wrote[5]:

> Management and the board spend a significant amount of time defining what makes a great GE business. We invest in leadership businesses that reflect the essential themes . . . and leverage our key capabilities: brand, technology, content development, globalization, people and financial strength.
>
> We like businesses where good management results in

superior financial results. We like broadly diversified businesses with multiple ways to grow. We believe that our process skills create a competitive advantage. We like businesses
where we can "retool" our strategies to capture new opportunities for profitable growth.

Over the last decade, GE has poured money into research and development, enhancing its research center in New York, and adding new
technology centers in Germany and China. These centers are churning
out a stream of new technologies. Management developed a list of 100
"imagination breakthroughs"—ideas that might generate $100 million
in sales over three years. Immelt took these ideas under his wing, protecting them from budget slashers and other forces within the current
businesses. One example is a hybrid locomotive. Immelt personally
picked the project manager and checks in on the project once a month.
He wants the number of such imagination breakthroughs to grow and
to come from all parts of the company. To be sure, GE has suffered
through the recession and took some serious hits from losses in its financing arm, GE Capital. But Immelt expects that these new products
and services will have higher margins. This makes sense, as they will not
have been subjected to copycatting and commoditization.

Moreover, they will be "new value," new contributions to the marketplace. A merger or acquisition expands the firm's size, but does not
create anything new in the world. And the "new" is where competition
occurs—new opportunities to please existing customers and attract new
ones, new opportunities to participate in marketplace shifts and even
lead them.

The Ongoing Transformation of LEGO Group

Sometimes, this transformative process is precisely what's needed to
rescue even some of the best-known companies from sliding into oblivion. Take the case of the LEGO Group, a toy company with a simple
product that has allowed children for generations to experiment with
creative building blocks. By the time Jorgen Vig Knudstorp took the
reins as chief executive in 2004, LEGO was bleeding more than $300
million annually. An attempt to reverse the slide by introducing a complementary children's clothing line failed. Facing the unthinkable pros-
pect of selling the family-owned business to a larger conglomerate,
Knudstorp and LEGO decided to embrace the new world order and

change their business model rather than running away from its challenges.

For years, LEGO has enjoyed a licensee relationship with Lucas Films, adapting the wildly popular *Star Wars* characters and models to the LEGO universe. Knudstorp expanded licensee relationships with children's brands as well, including SpongeBob SquarePants, Indiana Jones, Speed Racer, and Batman. When Mindstorm hacked LEGO's robotics products and released better versions, the company resisted suing and instead endorsed the superior product, which led to increased sales for both companies.

In an interview with the BTM Institute, Knudstorp explained:

> Yes, we're creating a new business model. The LEGO Group grew out of a carpenter's store. Plastic revolutionized toys in the twentieth century. Digital breakthroughs will do the same for the twenty-first century. We won't stop manufacturing plastic bricks. By 2015, about 20 percent of our total business will come from digital products. Today, two of the ten best-selling video games include our LEGO-branded *Star Wars* games. Connectivity has had a major effect on how today's children live. Some six-year-olds have cell phones. Teenagers like to use their cell phones to send text messages to each other. Eventually wireless broadband will be everywhere. A computer will replace the television. For all of these reasons, the LEGO Group needs to be in the digital space.[6]

More recently, LEGO adopted new management and manufacturing processes. It has trimmed its workforce from 10,000 to 3,000. It is outsourcing more of its manufacturing to third-party partners and has optimized its supply chain to ensure that raw materials are reaching factories at the right time and in the right quantities. LEGO's ongoing transformation has resulted in returning the company to profitability, securing its future, and ensuring its family ownership for years to come.

Transformation is the single idea that unifies governance, investment, and agility. It is a mindset, a strategy, and a set of tactics. It is a continuous, enterprise-wide process that keeps the organization tuned to opportunities and threats in its environment.

The Financial Impact of the Transformation Triangle

Business Agility, Sustained Innovation, and Operational Excellence are the strategic positions that make up the transformation triangle. Managers considering these transformative positions need to understand the contours of outperformance. How does the performance of a strategic position, through its convergence patterns, compare with other strategic positions? Which position will yield the greatest level of performance?

Organizations with a high degree of maturity in BTM management practices outperform their industry peers as measured by a range of financial metrics, including revenue growth, profitability, stock price predictability, and capital efficiency. We have tracked this performance correlation to convergence in the *Business Technology Convergence Index I* and *II*. Financial performance was calculated using publicly available financial information for the companies in each index as of December 2009, except for the long-term financial performance measures, which used data from 2005—2009, inclusively. The five-year performance, as noted in Figure 7–1, shows how enterprises that leverage the Transformation Triangle to achieve convergence in business and technology management have a higher performance curve across these key metrics.

The first and most revealing observation is that convergence-level maturity drives the highest levels of financial performance, demonstrating the advantage of a hybrid position comprised of all three strategic postures. With a few exceptions, the financial performance of organizations with convergence-level BTM maturity scored higher than any single strategic position in the Transformation Triangle in both the one-year and five-year findings. The only exceptions are revenue growth, for both the one- and five-year views, and EPS growth over the five-year view. Revenue growth outperformance, in both the one- and five-year findings, is the lowest performing of all the financial measures, no doubt reflecting the economic contraction of the recession. Similarly, EPS growth outperformance for 2009 averaged 6.25 percent across all strategic positions (including BTM maturity), but from the five-year view, the average dropped to 3.1 percent.

The assessment revealed in the BTM Convergence Index supports the notion that adopting more than one strategic position can produce superior financial performance. Recall that each strategic position represents a convergence pattern, which is a subset of the BTM Framework.

FIGURE 7–1 BTM CONVERGENCE PATTERN FINANCIAL IMPACT, FIVE-YEAR VIEW.

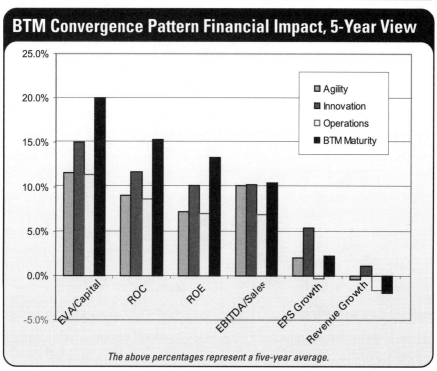

© BTM Corporation.

Convergence-level maturity drives the highest levels of financial performance, demonstrating the advantage of a hybrid posture comprised of Business Agility, Sustained Innovation, and Operational Excellence.

By definition, therefore, firms with a high BTM maturity level exhibit characteristics of all three Transformation Triangle strategic positions.

There are marked differences among the three strategic positions as well; there is, in fact, a clear order of performance preference that is consistently found in both the short-term (one-year) and long-term (five-year) positions: Sustained Innovation, then Business Agility, and finally, Operational Excellence.

The outperformance of the Sustained Innovation position over the other two is clearly demonstrated in every category. Only BTM maturity performs higher, suggesting that Sustained Innovation, while a winning strategy, can produce even higher levels of performance when combined with Business Agility or Operational Excellence. Organizations without a strategic focus on Sustained Innovation should quickly adopt one, and those organizations already pursuing a Sustained Innovation position have several alternative—and complementary—paths to improved performance. The choice will depend on the organization's market position, strategic imperatives, and approach to management performance.

The Business Agility position holds the performance middle ground in the Transformation Triangle. In the one-year view, Business Agility performance ranks markedly lower than Sustained Innovation in every performance category. Compared to Operational Excellence, Business Agility scores outperformed in four performance categories, ceding to Operational Excellence in the other two categories. Business Agility has better capital efficiency, higher margins, and lower EPS growth.

In the five-year view, the performance differences are less dramatic among all three of the Transformation Triangle positions. Business Agility still occupies the middle ground, with Sustained Innovation showing consistently higher performance—though the spread between the highest and lowest positions was less than three percentage points. When compared to Operational Excellence, Business Agility performance was about equal for most measures (five out of six), and no more than three percentage points on the remaining measures.

Organizations currently pursuing a Business Agility position that are seeking to improve performance have several alternatives to consider. Choosing among them will require a more detailed examination of BTM maturity, strategic focus, market position, and cultural flexibility.

Operational Excellence is a winning approach, demonstrating clear outperformance when compared to industry peers. However, when compared with the other Transformation Triangle positions, Operational Excellence—with a few notable exceptions—occupies the bottom layer of the performance spectrum, showing only a 7 percent to 11 percent average outperformance advantage, as compared to a 15 percent to 17 percent advantage for a full hybrid position—or full BTM maturity.

The one-year view found Operational Excellence at the bottom of every performance category except for margin, where it occupies the middle ground. A close examination shows that Operational Excellence and Business Agility have nearly equal performance on capital efficiency, and that Operational Excellence is a clear winner in EPS growth and in lower stock price volatility. It does not, however, measure up to the superior margin performance of Business Agility, which is nearly equal to that of Sustained Innovation.

The five-year view, similar to the observations made above for Business Agility, is relatively inconclusive. Operational Excellence perform-ance is nearly indistinguishable from Business Agility in capital efficiency and growth. And, just like the one-year view, it is the lowest performing position of the Transformation Triangle for margin, though it only lags the leaders by a few percentage points.

Organizations pursuing an Operational Excellence position face a dilemma: continued pursuit will result in outperformance of industry peers, but will cede a performance advantage to competitors pursuing either of the other Transformation Triangle positions, not to mention those competitors sufficiently advanced to pursue a hybrid position.

The Takeaway: Turning Ideas into Action

To be successful in today's business climate, most enterprises need to transform themselves on a regular basis. Although they need vision and goals to drive that transformation, companies also must address short-term objectives and develop new business processes.

The Transformation Triangle is the mechanism through which en-terprises put themselves into the motion of continuous innovation and reinvention. Business Agility, Sustained Innovation, and Operational Ex-cellence—the three sides of the triangle—are designed to guide enter-prise management through the process and provide measures for performance.

In the next three chapters, we will go into greater detail on what each of the three areas of the Transformation Triangle means in practice. For now, enterprises looking to engage a transformative process should prepare themselves by considering the following seven steps:

Step 1: *Establish* the business purpose of each investment. Is it to enable growth, maintain, or manage risk?

Step 2: *Determine* whether the metrics you use have changed along with modifications in business processes and technology.

Step 3: *Agree* upon metrics that show how your organization creates agility, sense-and-respond capabilities, and digital options. This will ulti-mately lead to metrics that accurately measure business value.

Step 4: *Understand* the business environment and how the firm adjusts its strategy to changes in the environment. This often requires real-time adjustments in operations, placing greater onus upon business technology executives to have a well-oiled system to gather information and present business alternatives.

Step 5: *Leverage* management capabilities such as Approval and Prioritization and Consolidation and Standardization to manage and define the requirements needed in support of a high-information-orientation culture.

Step 6: *Translate* the business strategy into tactical plans for which information and communication technologies can be deployed. It is increasingly the role of the business technology executives to make this connection. Executives must take the lead in communicating areas where business technology can add value. Employees must be made aware of how these opportunities relate to their jobs.

Step 7: *Instill* in employees the behaviors and values that will lead to the best use of information for customer, supplier, and partner relationships.

CHAPTER 8

Creating Business Agility

O NE AUGUST MORNING IN 2010, America awoke to shocking news from the Far East. No, North Korea hadn't invaded its democratic southern brothers. No, an undersea earthquake hadn't caused another deadly tsunami. No, Toyota's cars hadn't suffered another major defect resulting in a massive recall. No, the news was far more disturbing on an economic and psychological level: China had officially passed Japan in quarterly gross domestic product. Its growth numbers were so strong that by the end of the year, its economy on the global stage would be second only to the United States.

Since the Tiananmen Square uprising in 1989, the Chinese communist government had adopted a policy of limited capitalism. It allowed for privatization of businesses, foreign investment in economic development, profit-based production of goods, and global trade with the rest of the world. The result has been nothing short of stupendous, far exceeding any output of the series of disastrous five-year plans under Mao. The country's GDP has grown at a rate above 10 percent annually for the last twenty years. Today, it's not just the world's second largest economy with a total output of nearly $5 trillion annually, but the world's largest exporter of goods and the second largest importer, surpassed only by the United States.

Making this news especially disturbing to Americans is its air of inevitability. Previous estimates had China surpassing the United States in economic power in 2050. On its current growth curve, however, China will become the world's largest economy as early as 2030. The seemingly irreversible trend has prompted many economists to begin predicting the demise of America's economic stature, preparing the American public to resign itself to a "once-was" status that European powers Great Britain and France have already gone through.

But is China's economic eclipse of the United States inevitable? Can the trend be reversed? The American and Chinese economies are no different from any business. They compete. They innovate. They need growth to remain viable. They are able to respond to competitive threats, take advantage of new opportunities, and create new wealth. And just like any enterprise, an economy requires agility, which is precisely what the United States is attempting to undertake in light of the shifting global balance of economic power. The U.S. government and private sector are pumping billions of dollars into genetic engineering, health sciences, green energy, and next-generation information technology. The conventional wisdom is that advanced sciences will create new industries that will keep America at the forefront of economic prowess.

The modern economy—local, domestic, and global—operates in a state of accelerating change, driven by increasing and changing competition. This is due in part to easier market entry created by advances in technology and communications infrastructure, restructuring of product sourcing arrangements, the growing availability and changing costs of global labor pools, the continuous restructuring of capital markets, and, as noted above, the emergence of new economic powers.

One of the greatest challenges that business leaders and, by extension, their enterprises face is the ability to quickly respond to this constantly accelerating market change and to act as the catalyst of organizational adaptation.

As we discussed in Chapter 7, agility is part of the Transformation Triangle, the paths through which enterprises recognize and manage change amid economic strife, market uncertainty, and competitive challenges. Executives can take a set of strategic postures individually or in concert, depending on the actions most appropriate for a company's market position, core competencies, and strategic imperatives. That choice is one of the most important decisions a management team can make. Advanced businesses focus on hybrid patterns—being both innovative and agile at once, for example—that allow them to influence and drive business model evolution to reach strategic goals and imperatives.

Strategic postures are developed from convergence patterns, meaning that each posture relies on a select set of management behaviors and constructs. Business agility, sustained innovation, and operational excellence represent a particular convergence pattern.

Agility, by definition, is an enterprise's response to change and challenges driven by macro- and microeconomic conditions. In this chapter, we'll dig deep into what agility really means to an enterprise, the benefits derived from it, and how agility can be achieved and maintained to gain competitive advantages and, ultimately, creative and disruptive evolution.

Agility Is the Essential Competitive Element

Agile organizations possess the processes and structures, or what we call "intangible assets," that give them situational awareness into the macroeconomics and the competitive and operational trends inside and outside their four walls. They also have the management and technology mechanisms needed to act on that knowledge rapidly. In other words, Business Agility requires business/technology convergence—the art of managing business and technology as one.

In a recent research study conducted by BTM Corporation and IBM, published as the *BTM Business Agility Index*[1] in 2010, publicly traded U.S. companies were examined across multiple industry groups, using a range of financial measures—including value, performance, growth, margin, capital efficiency, and stock price volatility—to measure the financial effect of business agility against a maturity scale (see Table 8–1). This maturity scale was adapted from the BTM Maturity model to measure Business Agility maturity, described in Chapter 2.

This research confirms the economic value and financial performance advantages of companies that practice Business Agility. The overall results show that companies with highly mature business agility characteristics—the Business Agility leaders—exhibited superior financial performance:

- 13 percent to 38 percent performance advantage in capital efficiency and value.
- 10 percent to 15 percent performance advantage in margin.
- Up to 5 percent performance advantage in revenue and earnings growth.
- Up to one-third less stock price volatility compared to nonagile publicly traded organizations.

TABLE 8–1 BUSINESS AGILITY INDEX MATURITY LEVELS.

Maturity Level	Characteristics	Agility Effect
1	Chaotic, ad hoc, or individual heroics; islands of structure may exist, but are not connected and do not communicate with each other.	Little or no agility.
2	Repeatable and operationally capable, supported by high-level documentation.	Emergent agility. Inconsistent, sporadically effective.
3	Fully defined, supported by detailed documentation, consistently repeatable, with little overlap or conflict.	Threshold of agility. Slow and inconsistent response.
4	Disciplined and consistent management characterized by quantitative performance measurement and analysis.	Agile and responsive.
5	Continuous optimization, characterized by proactive and periodic management or operational improvements.	Fully agile and adaptable. A market influencer and leader.

Moreover, the study showed that the agility performance advantage was sustainable; these numbers reflect both the one-year view as well as a five-year view.

Business leaders often use the term "agility" to describe their business plans and strategic initiatives, but it is often little more than a word—and a fervent wish. Thriving under constant market pressure requires business leaders to identify, understand, and respond in real time to change and disruption. Companies must find new ways to compete by streamlining business processes to eliminate redundancy and costly exceptions, while creating higher value. Despite the fact that the cost of doing business continues to rise, agile companies are mastering cost containment by increasing their ability to respond and adapt to frequently changing market conditions.

On the other hand, we don't have to look far for enterprises that have stumbled or disappeared because they lost their agility. General Motors continues crawling its way back to life after suffering a catastrophic collapse resulting from years of inertia and stodgy missteps while foreign competitors invested and innovated. Sun Microsystems, once the superstar of Silicon Valley, was sold to software giant Oracle at a near fire sale price because it had become too fragmented in its products and failed to capture the imperative position among customers. And *Newsweek*, one of the more venerable weekly news and analysis magazines of the last century, was sold for $1.00 after having its value position eroded by new, Internet-based media.

Could these businesses have reinvented themselves to stave off disaster and collapse? Absolutely. It would have required rethinking their business models, making strategic investments in new technologies and markets, and taking a risk on immature ventures. Precipitating this change is situational awareness, or the ability to recognize change, opportunities, and competitive threats. But it takes more than recognition to act upon these changes. It takes agility and a willingness to respond. GM is a perfect example. For nearly forty years, it saw the future of automobile manufacturing and consumption unfolding around it, but it failed to implement long-term strategies that would avoid quality declines, market share erosion and, ultimately, corporate viability. GM mistook several short-term spurts of success—sport utility vehicles, minivans, and utility vehicles—as the catalyst for change. That caused them to abandon or compromise the vision of real change agents, such as the EV1 electric car and the innovative Saturn car line.

Conversely, GM nemesis Toyota correctly read the economic tea leaves. As a Japanese company, it designed and built cars that were smaller for the confined, resource-strapped nation. Fuel efficiency was always foremost among its goals, so its cars were in a perfect position to capitalize on the gas crises of the 1970s. While American carmakers kept trying to recapture their former glory with muscle cars and large sedans by borrowing some manufacturing techniques from their Japanese counterparts, Toyota plowed its profits into research and development to create the next generation of transportation. In 1997, it launched the hybrid Prius—a car that operated on both gasoline and electricity stored in a battery. Today, the Prius is the world's best-selling hybrid and the catalyst for alternative-powered vehicles. It was agility that enabled Toyota to outthink and outmatch its American rivals.

Change isn't permanent; it's continuous. The fortunes of enterprises rise and fall on how well they navigate change. Given such high stakes, it's not surprising that terms like agility, resilience, adaptability, and innovation reverberate off the walls in boardrooms and executive suites. But it also seems clear in this cacophony that there are as many definitions of these terms as there are people using them. Some people see agility as a matter of technology, which is at the heart of business processes and models today, and it's true that approaches such as Service Oriented Architecture (SOA) can introduce a flexibility into an enterprise's infrastructure that allows the business to be nimble. Others use a broad and somewhat vague definition: agility is about the speed and ease of response to market changes. Yet a third definition is results oriented: agility is the ability to consistently perform above market average in terms of revenues, growth, profitability, or some other comparative metric.

All of this can lead to confusion for anyone seeking to move beyond talking about agility and actually implementing it. Michael Schrage, a senior adviser to the Massachusetts Institute of Technology's Security Studies Program, once quipped that agility means "never having to say you're sorry." He shared the following perspectives from various CIOs on how they define agility:[2]

- Greater agility demands greater centralization.
- Agility demands greater decentralization and delegation.
- Agility means ever-exquisite technology responsiveness to business needs.
- Agile business should inspire and enable greater business-unit agility.

We define agility as the ability to see and seize opportunities in the marketplace. Resilience is the flip side of the same coin: the ability to react to unexpected changes. Agility is proactive; resilience is reactive. The distinction is important: A company can have one but not the other, for example, a lean and mean company might be able to enter a new market quickly, but it may lack the abundance of resources needed to weather a major setback such as the bankruptcy of a key supplier. A company that has Business Agility needs both of these characteristics.

Ultimately, the evidence of agility is that an organization survives and has the ability to move quickly to introduce new products, revamp business processes, and create new business models and the evidence of resilience is that the organization bounces back when unanticipated events occur leaving behind damage.

Definitions are important, and we have dwelt on them at some length because one of the biggest issues corporations face today is the inability of its various groups to talk to each other and collaborate on strategy and its implementation. Terms like agility can have different meanings for a marketing manager and a programmer. A common vocabulary is a good starting point for any business endeavor.

Agility Introduces New Challenges

Agility is a new paradigm for the production and distribution of services and products. It achieves economies of scope rather than economies of scale. To be agile, organizations must serve ever-smaller niche markets and individual customers without the high cost traditionally associated with customization. Being agile requires sense-and-respond capabilities that are shaped by designing and managing business processes and technology enablers together. Three requirements express the challenges managers face:

1. **Sense-and-respond capability.** To respond to changes in their environment, organizations must facilitate learning from various processes. This learning must operate at different levels and within different areas of the firm and should be based on recurrent sense-and-respond cycles.[3] Business technology can facilitate these learning processes by supporting: (a) collection, distribution, analysis and interpretation of data associated with business processes, and (b) generation of response alternatives, decisions on appropriate courses of action, and orchestration of selected responses.

2. **Improvement and innovation emphasis.** Business agility is more than just improvements in the current operating state or aiming toward higher aspirations of performance through innovation. Even in mediocre organizations, improvements happen over time. What is critical to enterprises operating in dynamic environments is the speed of improvement and innovation. The speed of these two elements working in concert is what we call business agility. Opportunistic organizations emphasize improvements, but often fail to foster innovations. They follow best practices, listen to the customer, and are good at improving current capabilities. Innovative organizations, by contrast, are focused on innovating processes through new technologies, services, and strategies. They generate "next" practices but often have a limited focus on fine-

tuning current operations. Fragile firms lack both the ability to identify and explore opportunities as well as the ability to innovate. When market pressures are high and the environment is turbulent, an agile firm is ideal since it combines improvement and innovation initiatives (see figure 8–1) to constantly reposition itself.

3. **Distributed and coordinated authority.** Agile organizations must adopt radically different forms of governance and translate their mission and objectives into information that can easily be interpreted by constituents.[4] These firms must replace traditional command and control approaches with mechanisms that facilitate coordination within and across locales. These mechanisms must provide individuals, groups, and units with the autonomy to improvise and act on local knowledge, while orchestrating coherent behavior across the firm. Also, processes ("who or what does what to what and with what") must be supplemented with personal accountability ("who owes what to whom and by when").

Regardless of where the journey toward agility begins, a crucial issue rapidly emerges: aligning the processes of business networks and the information service architecture that supports them.

In the previous section, we talked about how Toyota used agility to its advantage to predict market conditions and develop products that captured the customers' imagination. Toyota is an agile company, but even it has missteps, and one of the biggest in its history came in early 2010 when its cars began experiencing acceleration and braking problems that resulted in numerous accidents. In the best-selling Prius, a design flaw in the gas pedal caused a braking and uncontrolled acceleration issue. The fix was simply the application of a small shim that literally cost pennies. What Toyota failed to understand was the public mood. Toyota's cars were held in high regard for their value, quality, and style, but that was before General Motors was on its deathbed. As GM and other U.S. automakers struggled for survival, the American public and government initially jumped on the opportunity to eviscerate Toyota over a defect. Toyota's lack of situational awareness caused it to play into the negative public sentiment by responding slowly to the concerns and evolving controversy.

The Anatomy of Business Agility

To understand how business and technology together can become integral at the strategic level, it is helpful to briefly review the basics of

FIGURE 8–1 RESPONSE-ABILITY STATES.

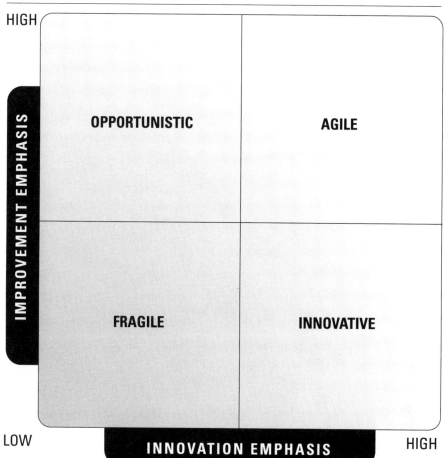

This figure is based on the concepts developed by Rick Dove in *Response Ability: The Language, Structure, and Culture of the Agile Enterprise.*

All businesses typically engage in the improvement of operations and the innovation of processes and products, simultaneously.[5] The level of emphases on these two activities will determine an enterprise's ability to respond to changes in their competitive landscape. Speed is a factor, and the combined level of emphasis on operational improvement and innovation is a reflection of speed. BTM calls this "business agility."

strategy. An organization fabricates a strategic vision and assembles the competencies enabling it to occupy a niche within a product market. Typically, this is done through competencies in cost leadership, product/service leadership, and/or customer leadership in a product market.[6]

If an organization is alone in a product market niche, this extraordinarily favorable situation typically does not last long as competitors respond to the above-average returns. It is crucial, then, to both establish a profitable strategic position and to be able to sustain it. With today's globalized—and, hence, increasingly competitive—marketplaces, this is more difficult than ever.

Business strategists discover profitable opportunities—new market spaces or gaps in existing market spaces—by considering:

1. Signals regarding product/service, customer, technology, socio-economic, and cultural trends.

2. Competitors' current and future strategic positions.

3. The organization's internal competencies.

4. The competencies it might gain through access to partners.

An organization's initial position in the product market must then be regularly augmented such that it continues to offer a value proposition beyond those provided by competitors. Business and technology together play a critical role in establishing a strategic position or in sustaining it once established; failing to understand these roles across each of an organization's product markets can—and often does—lead to inappropriate levels of business and technology investment. By giving visibility to the particulars of an organization's business strategy and the technology resources deployed to achieve it, the BTM Framework allows firms to gain that understanding.

As an example, the BTM capability of Strategic Sourcing and Vendor Management recognizes this, and defines the approach for creating and managing these relationships. This includes identifying areas of strategic opportunity for outsourcing, co-development, and vendor selection. By each strategic partner nurturing its distinctive competencies to world-class levels and by tightly coordinating partner activities, these networks of cooperating enterprises can continuously improve their value propositions or engage radically transformed or newly created product markets.

By being agile, an organization is able to sense and respond to competitors' strategic moves within existing product markets, as well as sense and respond to environmental signals arising from shifts in customer desires or in new technologies.

Organizations demonstrate strategic agility in four major ways:

1. They continuously scan their environment to identify both threats to existing positions and opportunities to forge new positions.

2. They regularly engage in strategic experiments. That is, they implement small-scale strategic initiatives to challenge internal or external work environments to gain experience with emerging technologies, work practices, product or service concepts, customer segments, or product markets.

3. They devise adaptive business architectures so that their competitive assets (as well as those of partners) can be realigned quickly—shutting down activities, commencing new activities, or shifting resources among activities.

4. They learn to radically renew the competencies that characterize their competitive nature.

Processes for Agility

To enable agility, process improvement and innovation initiatives must span a firm's business network, which includes its customers, suppliers, and the regulatory environment. In large measure no longer siloed, technological developments have enabled business networks to coordinate predictable activities. For instance, many companies share their forecasts and plans with suppliers and distributors to extract network-wide efficiencies. Going further, some firms, such as retailers, have relinquished their decision rights on when and how much to replenish to their suppliers, assuming that this creates even greater efficiencies for all concerned.

While efficiencies can be extracted through the coordination of predictable activities across a business network, such processes impose significant constraints on the sensing of and responding to unpredictable events.[7] Simply put, these disciplined business networks perform well in a predictable world but are not robust in an uncertain world. Agility requires the dynamic configuration of processes across a business network based on changes in customer requirements. This shift toward real-time business networks requires five key enablers:

1. **Managers must focus on process enablement of customer requirements.** Agility requires that customer requests be sensed and interpreted so they can be negotiated and translated into specifications of production and final outputs.

2. **Managers must ensure process enablement of business network intelligence.** Business network intelligence requires the aggregation of disparate information, and the filtering and distribution of this information to points of relevance. Processes must be established to not only share information between two partners but to aggregate information across the network and create intelligence for agile behavior. It is critical to avoid overloading nodes in the network with information. This requires the constraints of governance arrangements. It is also critical to safeguard sensitive information from inappropriate access or use.

3. **Managers must emphasize partnering agility.** Agile partnering requires that firms initiate, reconfigure, or sever ties with others. Both core and noncore activities can be distributed across business partners. While core activities are typically distributed only to long-term, trusted partners, noncore activities are typically distributed across long-term partners that excel in commodity provisioning or, alternatively, across spot markets. Both the nature of the partnership and the type of activities should shape process requirements for partner interactions. Processes supporting the exchange of limited information must be tailored for spot market interactions, while processes supporting exchange of private and idiosyncratic information will be required for long-term stability.

4. **Managers must focus on process enablement of activity allocation and coordination across the business network.** The distribution of activities for real-time configuration of products and services requires visibility of contracted resources and capacities, and service levels associated with these types of activities that can be completed and maintained as needed. The coordination of these distributed activities requires a rule-based architecture for the enforcement of their interdependencies. The rules depend on the granularity with which activities are traced. Granular tracking and high levels of awareness provide superior control capabilities in that exceptions can be detected, alerts cascaded, and corrective actions initiated.

5. **Managers must emphasize process enablement of relationship governance.** This requires negotiation of outcomes and approaches to achieve them, and learning for continuous improvement. Both business and process models can facilitate negotiation of contracts, including service level agreements. These models can be used to establish a shared understanding of approaches and outcomes, including incentives under different conditions. Once negotiated, service level goals must be monitored against performance.

Technologies for Agility

Deploying and managing technology is often critical in establishing business agility. Understanding the four classes of technology investments—transaction focused, decision focused, intellectual capital focused, and relationship focused—helps in recognizing how technology contributes to business agility. The different classes of technology allow the corporation to better exploit strategic resources, and to better explore strategic alternatives and options

1. *Transaction-focused investments* facilitate exploitation by handling business transactions (both within an enterprise and with external parties) faster and more reliably (fewer errors or steps), thereby increasing productivity and responsiveness as well as lowering costs. Transaction-focused investments facilitate exploration by increasing both the number of potential parties with whom transactions can be executed and the potential types of transactions that can be handled, as well as by increasing the visibility of transactional events across the extended enterprise. This last point has become extremely important today as most firms find themselves having to expose data about key business events—orders, deliveries, low inventory levels—to customers or suppliers and likewise expecting their strategic partners to do the same. With increased information visibility across supply chains and value nets, business models and value propositions that were unimaginable only a few years ago have become the norm.

2. *Decision-focused investments* facilitate exploitation by enabling decision automation through the embedding of decision rules within software as well as by providing employees with enhanced information and proven decision filters for decision situations that

are not automated. Decisions are made faster, more reliably, and more completely, thus increasing decision quality and responsiveness as well as employee productivity. This lowers costs and better aligns products and/or services with customer requirements. Decision-focused investments facilitate exploration by enabling decision authority to be distributed more widely, increasing the number of perspectives brought to bear on a decision, and allowing more discretion to employees closest to a decision. Emerging opportunities are more likely to be recognized, interpreted from a variety of perspectives, and acted on.

3. *Intellectual capital–focused investments* facilitate exploitation by codifying, archiving, making accessible, embedding in processes and decision schemas, and transferring across the enterprise the knowledge that has been acquired and created. This use of knowledge regarding its product markets, as well as the assets and activities needed to enhance strategic positions in them, produces deeper, more consistent thought, purpose, and ability across the enterprise. Intellectual capital–focused investment facilitates exploration by extending an enterprise's "intelligence at the edge." It does this by enhancing sensing and interpretation, increasing the number and variety of accessible external sources of knowledge, increasing enterprise-wide visibility into what is happening at its edges, and enabling specialized knowledge sources to be easily established, promoted, and accessed.

4. *Relationship-focused investments* facilitate exploitation by tightening relationships across an enterprise, as well as with its trusted partners. Within an enterprise, it provides collaborative work environments in which the insight of all employees involved in fashioning and maintaining a strategic position can be brought to bear without regard for time, location, or positions. Externally, it creates resilient links with partners that enable the enterprise's ability to work with them and understand them better. Relationship-focused investments facilitate exploration by broadening relationships across an enterprise and with partners and allowing them to be easily formed or disbanded. As a consequence, a breadth of assets, skills, and competencies become available to identify, assess, and act on opportunities. Just as important, those associated with underperforming positions can be reassigned or eliminated.

To illustrate the many and varied roles served by technology investments, consider the action initiated by office furniture company Herman Miller in the late 1990s to stake a strategic position in an underserved market—that of offering small businesses no-frills, quality furnishings delivered quickly at a reasonable price.[8] In accomplishing this strategic initiative, Miller established a new operating unit, Herman Miller SQA ("Simple, Quick, and Affordable"), and introduced a flurry of innovations that have since migrated into the parent company:

○ Local dealers are provided with innovative 3-D visualizing tools and product configurations that are used in consulting with customers about a potential order—furniture, design styles, fabrics, wood finishes, space layout, etc. [*Decision-, intellectual capital-, and relationship-focused business technology investments*]

○ Once the dealer and customer have reached agreement on an order, the software creates an order list with all parts and the final price. [*Decision- and transaction-focused investments*]

○ As soon as an order is accepted it is sent via the Internet to a Miller SQA manufacturing facility, where it enters production and logistics scheduling systems. Within two hours, the dealer and customer receive confirmation of delivery and installation dates. [*Decision-, relationship-, and transaction-focused investments*]

○ And, Miller SQA's supply net transparently links its many suppliers to its operations, streamlining purchasing, inventory, and production processes. Here, the 500 suppliers are provided visibility into the data in Miller SQA's systems and are expected to automatically send more materials when needed. [*Decision-, relationship-, intellectual capital-, and transaction-focused investments*]

By applying business strategy and technology exceptionally well in both exploitative and exploratory ways, Miller SQA reduced an industry order cycle of about fourteen weeks to about two weeks, and in the process redefined what was required for competitive success in this product market niche.

At first glance, the Herman Miller example belies the notion that technology assets are, for the most part, commodities. However, with a deeper look, it becomes clear that success was achieved from more than technology investment alone. True success came from aligning these assets with firm-specific structure and content, embedding these within business architectures enabling business strategies to unfold, and providing careful management of these assets through a well-honed set of business technology management capabilities. In this way, these "commodities" can be transformed into value-adding assets.

The Journey Toward Agility

Building an agile enterprise is a journey that includes creation of a "management playbook" to coordinate myriad activities, functions, models, and operations. The playbook for each enterprise is unique, reflecting its management capabilities, business architecture, operational practices, and cultural norms. However, there are underlying foundational principles that, together, construct templates that can accelerate playbook development, communication, and execution.

Bringing a management playbook to life requires a number of key steps, each of which is supported by activities specific to an organization's capabilities, current state, and agility objectives. To create an effective playbook, an organization must:

- Validate and communicate its business technology strategy to all stakeholders.
- Establish a mechanism for rapid, continuous business model development.
- Manage its investments from both strategic and tactical perspectives.
- Identify and mitigate risk.
- Optimize and manage partner relationships.

The management playbook should also contain other elements, including the organization model, a description of agile business architectures and processes, key operational and performance information and measures, and automation tools and requirements. The management playbook must be communicated to the key executives and managers responsible for its execution. And, most importantly, progress must be tracked, investments made, risks managed, and lessons learned. Business Agility is not simple or straightforward, but as demonstrated by our research, a most worthwhile endeavor.

Our research demonstrates that agile companies have a dominant short-term performance advantage of 20 percent and a long-term advantage of 12 percent; they also have lower stock price volatility (23 percent short term and 29 percent long term) than their industry peers. Looking beyond the averages, individual measures of performance reinforced the agility dominance: leader firms outperformed their peers in every measure. From a short-term perspective, the range was from 0.2 percent (revenue growth) to 37.6 percent (EVA/capital); long-term, the range was from a low of 1.1 percent (revenue growth) to 29 percent (volatility reduction).

This research reveals the key role business agility plays in economic performance. Achieving agility is not exclusive to organizations of a certain size by revenue or industry sector, but is available to all companies. Further, this research specifies the behaviors and constructs that drive agility, as described throughout this chapter. Those behaviors and constructs are defined as a repeatable management practice that can be implemented utilizing the BTM Framework.

An organization that has the ability to successfully negotiate its path through the ever-shifting competitive landscape has developed the talent to continuously transform itself as opportunities and threats appear. This organization maintains three characteristics:

1. *Ongoing assessment* of activities, eliminating those that don't serve the core business strategy.

2. *Continual refinement* of activities for greater efficiency and productivity.

3. *Redirection of resources* to new products, processes, and business models.

Building an agile organization is not easy. Change must become a part of an enterprise's fabric. Bringing in a persuasive leader might help the transformation, but it is the change management skills they bring to the table that will help make the journey a successful one. More crucial to that success, however, is the need to incorporate new ways of doing business into the company's management systems and business processes. This means new organizational structures, the creation and sharing of new types of information, and establishment of new decision-making processes.

The Takeaway: Turning Ideas into Action

Investing in business technology should begin with an organization's strategic position. However, these positions are often crafted without a clear understanding of the current state of an organization's business technology, as well as its potential to influence other decisions that need to be made. Since business technology is so critical in establishing or sustaining a strategic position in its overall successful execution, not understanding its roles across a firm's product markets can lead to inappropriate levels of investment—which in turn can result in failure. To avoid that outcome, the following steps assist in ensuring your business strategy matches your technology investments:

Step 1: *Review* your firm's strategic position, as well as your business strategy and technology strategy formulation activities. Are marketplace and competitive analyses part of these activities? Is the role of business technology prominent in these analyses? Is strategic experimentation used to better understand the roles served by business technology investment in acquiring and sustaining favorable market positions?

Step 2: *Determine* how technology and business technology investments are handled in your firm's strategic planning and budgeting activities. To what extent do investment levels across operating units reflect the role that business technology actually serves in enabling strategic positions? To what extent do investment levels across staff or support units reflect the role that business technology actually serves in enabling these units to accomplish their mission? Are the baselines for such analyses founded on historical grounds, industry benchmarks, or carefully selected (strategically and operationally comparable) peer groups?

Step 3: *Assess* the existence and maturity of BTM capabilities across the enterprise. Which BTM capabilities, given the role that business technology serves in enabling your firm's strategic posture, need to be maintained at world-class levels? Has sufficient investment in BTM capabilities occurred at an enterprise level and within each business unit?

Step 4: *Answer* these questions: Is your business strategy and strategic position well communicated and understood across the organization? Are your organization's business strategies reflective of exploitative strategic actions, exploratory strategic actions, or both? What roles do your business technology investments play in enabling these strategic actions?

Step 5: *Develop,* after these questions are understood, an appropriate mix of the various kinds of business technology to advance your firm's strategic agenda. Technology thus becomes a significant tool for the CEO and the board from a business standpoint as opposed to a line item in next year's budget.

CHAPTER 9

Sustained Innovation: The Science of Constantly Moving Forward

DEEP IN THE HEART OF TEXAS is a cult of eccentrics and fanatics known simply as "the Lunatic Fringe." They comb through the ranks of engineers, entrepreneurs, and innovators in search of the next great idea; the next solution to complex problems; the next evolutionary step in technology development. At least that's their *modus operandi*. Their true mission is much simpler: Keeping their patron—Texas Instruments (TI)—on the cutting edge of technology and market.

The Lunatic Fringe, the topic of a *Fortune* magazine feature,[1] isn't a conventional R&D project or department. It isn't even a formal organization within the corporate structure. It's more of a construct of people and philosophical thinking that—by design—break conventional wisdom to think outside the box and come up with innovations. They imagine things that today are only conceptual or, in some cases, science fiction. This loosely affiliated group of engineers, technology tinkerers, and deep thinkers are responsible for producing power- and processing-efficient analog chips that enable devices ranging from Apple iPods to medical scanners. The first rule of the Lunatic Fringe: The company benefits financially when smart people are allowed to pursue projects for the joy of the technical challenge and, ultimately, achievement of their accomplishments.

Texas Instruments created the first analog circuits and, subsequently, the first transistor radio. It leveraged its technical prowess to build one of the first mega high-tech electronics companies. It provided the circuitry that powered many consumer and industrial products, as well as developed and marketed a spate of goods ranging from handheld calculators and digital watches to children's toys and defense systems. At the dawn of the personal computing era, it was among the companies marketing desktop computers and peripherals. Through the 1970s, TI was a true powerhouse and bigger than many of the tech icons of the modern era (adjusted for inflation).

Surprisingly, the Lunatic Fringe is a relatively modern invention at Texas Instruments, and not a construct made by design but rather by necessity. As the company grew larger and more successful, it became bloated and complacent. As the digital revolution started taking hold in the 1980s, TI was stodgy and arrogant. While rising rivals such as Intel were creating new markets, introverted Texas Instruments was jealously living on its past accomplishments. It held on to unprofitable units such as defense components, personal computers, and memory chips out of misguided desires to preserve its legacy businesses. Worse, it was cold to the suggestions and requests of its biggest customers, and completely ignored smaller companies and entrepreneurs. Its insular and isolationist attitude was pushing Texas Instruments into irrelevancy. Radical thinking was required to pull the company out of its Lone Star–sized malaise.

A combination of scaling back underperforming business units, a shaking off of corporate arrogance, embracing the Lunatic Fringe, and luck in market dynamics saved TI from sliding into oblivion. The presumption that the world would go completely digital, it turns out, was greatly exaggerated. As more mobile electronic devices come on the market, the greater the demand for high-performance analog chips to power them. And the job of the Lunatic Fringe is to find those new uses, opportunities, and ventures to propel TI's growth.

The Lunatic Fringe is just one example of how enterprises embrace sustained innovation for their advancement and viability. Any company can develop a new product. Companies can even innovate ideas into action. But it takes a truly concerted effort—a result of converged management—to develop, implement, and foster a program of repeatable, continuous processes that result in the creation of new ideas, technologies, and products. Through convergence, enterprises harness the creative talents of its employees, business partners, and customers to break conventional thinking and advance the state of the art.[2]

Where agility, as we discussed in Chapter 8, is the ability to recognize opportunities and execute new ideas, sustained innovation is the process through which agility energy is channeled toward operational excellence (which we'll discuss in Chapter 10). In this chapter, we will review the importance of innovation to the enterprise, examine how sustained innovation differs from ideation, and explore how enterprises build and maintain a sustained innovation engine through management convergence.

The Anatomy of Sustained Innovation

In 2003, the stalwart business magazine *The Economist* declared, "Innovation is now recognized as the single most important ingredient in any modern economy." Innovation is more than just new ideas and invention. It's a means for describing the maturation of existing products, the creation of new products, and the response to shifting economic conditions. If an enterprise simply stands pat on its processes and products, it runs the risk of becoming obsolete. Worse, the absence of innovation means that an enterprise will lack any product for when its current output reaches market saturation.

Innovation as a destination isn't enough. Even if a company creates a new product or technology, failure to capitalize on that innovation to create new and diverse offerings opens fissures for competitors to exploit. That's precisely what happened at Texas Instruments—failure to continuously innovate led to a decline in revenues, market share, profitability, and stature. Consider what would have happened if Toyota had stopped investing in research and development. The Prius remains the best-selling hybrid vehicle, but it's no longer in a class by itself. Every major carmaker now has a hybrid vehicle. Staying ahead of the competition means that Toyota needs to capitalize on its first-mover advantage to create a new market where it has no peer, and it's now investing in the development of fully electric vehicles and alternative fuel sources as the next stage of transportation. This is the stuff of Sustained Innovation.

What do we mean by "sustained innovation"? In the BTM context, Sustained Innovation is the state attained by an organization in which it is capable of innovating in all aspects of its business—management, divisions, operations, customers, and suppliers. It requires a seamless, structured management approach that begins with board- and CEO-level leadership and connects all the way through technology investment and implementation. Above all, Sustained Innovation is a journey, not a destination—meaning that the enterprise doesn't stop innovating after attaining one goal; it's in a continual process of reinvention, invention, and discovery.

As we noted in our discussion of TI's Lunatic Fringe, Sustained Innovation is powered by people who come together to share ideas, compare observations, and brainstorm solutions to complex problems. Enterprises with a strong focus on innovation share three common principles that act as the glue binding people together in productive collaboration. They are:

1. *Converged disciplines:* Ideas aren't isolated; they're celebrated in groups that enable the entire organization to act as one entity. Of particular importance is the convergence of business and technology management to ensure that no one unit or division is missing the opportunity to capitalize on new ideas and possibilities.

2. *Cross-boundary collaboration:* No enterprise operates in a vacuum. Every manager, employee, and contractor potentially has a piece of the puzzle to create a new breakthrough business opportunity. Suppliers, partners, distributors, and customers are an equally valuable source of information and ideas.

3. *Innovative business structure:* Not every organization can empower an unstructured development culture like the Lunatic Fringe; most require structure that *compels* convergence of disciplines, management, and operational units.

To bring these principles to life, Sustained Innovation enterprises focus on three distinct, intimately related practices that require business/technology convergence to perform at a high level of maturity.

Cascaded Lifecycle

Like most companies with an innovation focus, enterprises employ an innovation lifecycle that begins with invention. Unlike their peers, however, innovative enterprises extend the lifecycle to include market success, scale, and prominence. Such lifecycles enable and encourage an innovation cascade, wherein one lifecycle can spawn another, linking and building each lifecycle (see Figure 9–1) that is congruent to and coherent with the enterprise's values and mission.[3]

Digital Business Models

Enterprises are not content to invent new products and bring them profitably to market. To attain lasting viability, they must examine new and sometimes disruptive business models. Digital business models are nonrivalrous.[4] Unlike land, labor, and capital, their use by one organization or individual does not preclude its use by another.

Sustained Innovation enterprises leverage business technology convergence across the innovation lifecycle to create cross-disciplinary management practices that allow professionals to innovate sustainable business models.

Cultural Diversity

Innovation is a holistic human endeavor that requires both left-brained (analytical) and right-brained (creative) talents. Innovative enterprises

FIGURE 9–1 CASCADED INNOVATION LIFECYCLE.

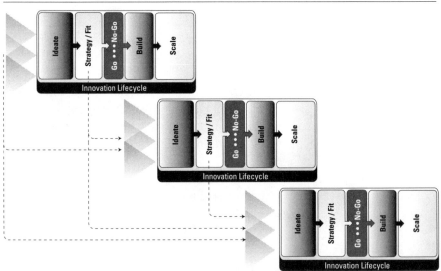

© BTM Corporation.

Cascaded innovation lifecycles not only depend on converging business and technology management, they must embrace process and people horizontally across silos in order to maintain a continuous flow of innovation.

build a culture that embraces both approaches to thinking, executing, and communicating. More than for either of the other two strategic postures in the Transformation Triangle, Sustained Innovation requires the left brain and the right brain to work together. Sustained Innovation enterprises approach this collaboration challenge by defining personas that individuals adopt as the lifecycle unfolds. Some personas are analytical, some are creative, and others are a combination. Not all innovation teams require all personas, and individuals can function in several personas,[5] or change them as the process unfolds.

◑ *Learning personas* keep an enterprise from being too internally focused and caught in their comfort zone. Learners need to be sufficiently humble to question their worldview and remain open to new insights every day.

◑ *Organizing personas* serve to move the innovation lifecycle forward. Even the best ideas must continuously compete for attention, resources, and time. These champions are skilled at navigating processes, politics, and red tape to bring an innovation to market.

◑ *Building personas* are the connections between the learning and organizing personas; they apply insights from the learning personas and channel the empowerment from the organizing personas to make innovation happen. Builders are often highly visible and close to the heart of the innovation action.

Enterprises must drive innovation on two levels: product and business model. Products must evolve with market dynamics and customer needs and desires. Consequently, business models must change or evolve as innovation creates or changes products. We can see this dynamic unfolding today with the evolution of cloud computing. Virtualization technology and the availability of affordable, persistent high-bandwidth Internet connectivity are enabling the delivery of many information technology software and infrastructure products as a service. This shift in the delivery and consumption of technology is not only forcing many technology companies to change the way they develop their products, but also their business model. Technology is no longer a one-time purchase or an annual support contract, but rather as a service like a power or water utility. It's a dramatic departure in the way technology companies charge for services and recognize revenue.

To sustain product and business innovation, enterprises must build a flexible culture that can attract and empower a wide variety of talent. It is all too easy for organizations to fall into the "analysis trap" and focus on left-brain skills like process, measurement, and execution. Sustained Innovation enterprises embrace right-brained skills—creativity, imagination, analogy, and empathy. Unlike most organizations that separate these individuals into silos (such as marketing versus engineering), innovative enterprises build teams that morph as new processes and ideas unfold. This results in the creation of focus during ideation and analytical emphasis as market growth accelerates.

All three of the core Sustained Innovation practices—converged disciplines, cross-boundary collaboration, and innovative business structure—require the convergence of business and technology management. Establishing and institutionalizing a coherent, Sustained Innovation capability requires all stakeholders to understand how the innovation process works and the role they play in it. They must understand and accept that they must collaborate with other stakeholders, whether they are colleagues, customers, or partners. And they must embrace the concept of continual building and rethinking of ideas through constructive—and sometimes adversarial—dialogue. The magic of the TI's Lunatic Fringe isn't based on everyone being in total agreement (and they certainly are not), but rather on different disciplines and domains sharing and—oftentimes—criticizing ideas. The result of this open process is praise and criticism producing a better net product.

Technology's Strategic Role in Sustained Innovation

Convergence of business and technology management is *the* capability that differentiates innovative enterprises from their underperforming and stagnant peers. Convergence enables the following three practices that drive the innovation lifecycle, business model innovation, and cultural flexibility that underpin Sustained Innovation:

1. Unification of the strategic top management with the tactical implementation levels of the organization.

2. Collaboration within the organization and across its boundaries with outside partners to identify and assess new opportunities.

3. Processes that tie business technology investment to business strategy and capture the strategic opportunities created by business technologies.

BTM's research reveals that fewer than one in five corporations have adopted governance structures that deliver these capabilities. Companies have typically focused on governance rights for isolated, high-level business technology decisions. Their attention has been on which of three organizational designs would be most appropriate: centralized, decentralized, or federated. In a centralized design, most key business technology decisions are made by the technology function. In a decentralized design, the business units make most decisions, with the technology function in an advisory role. The federated design combines elements of both by dividing authority for specific decisions to either the business units or the respective technology function, as appropriate.

These enterprises have discovered that converging the management of business and technology allows them to create a sophisticated organizing logic to encourage innovation, strategic experiments, and calculated risk taking. The creative energy and productive benefit of Sustained Innovation doesn't come from the converged management, but networks of cross-disciplined individuals. Enterprises that have fostered and mastered this approach typically form one of three types of innovation networks.[6]

1. *Visioning networks* foster collaboration on a strategic vision about the role of technology in the function and objectives of the business. One way to establish a visioning network is to have the CIO as a formal member of the top management team. Other ways include the establishment of a Business Technology Management Council and a Business Technology Investment Board. Boards of directors should also consider establishing their own technology oversight committees.

2. *Innovation networks* foster collaboration in conceptualizing and implementing technology applications. These applications are often aimed at enhancing the enterprise's agility and innovation in customer relationships, manufacturing, product development, supply chain management, or enterprise control and governance systems. One mechanism that promotes innovation networks is corporate and divisional project-approval committees. Whereas

visioning networks shape overall enterprise perspectives, innovation networks focus on specific innovations and strategic applications.

3. *External networks* establish and foster relationships with external partners and customers. Their purpose is to enable collaboration between internal and external parties when designing and managing multisourcing arrangements, joint ventures, or strategic alliances. These external sourcing networks help companies improve their capabilities and business thinking about innovative uses of technology. To be effective, attention must be emphasized in key organizational units that deal with the technical architecture and infrastructure or the management of technology investments.

These "networks" are the bodies that collect innovative ideas, evaluate them, and pursue the most promising. Selecting the structure and who will participate in them will vary from enterprise to enterprise. Some enterprises will want to designate individuals or create subcommittees in these groups to focus strictly on innovation. Other enterprises will impose mandates within their existing management hierarchy to facilitate the function of these networks. The commonality of any of these efforts is the fostering of intra-domain collaboration and systemic innovation.

Each of these networks standing alone adds value, and technology is a critical factor in their success. However, the key to achieving Sustained Innovation is the linkage of capabilities that results in an ideal use of technology in pursuit of business goals. As opposed to disruptive innovation—a one-time innovative idea that results in a new product, but has no perceivable encore—Sustained Innovation is not ad hoc. It requires a governance and decision management structure that supports each activity stage of the lifecycle using a framework that fosters business technology collaboration. The key BTM Capabilities that enable such repeatability are Strategic and Tactical Governance, Approval and Prioritization, and Strategic Planning and Budgeting (as discussed in Chapter 2). Collectively these capabilities serve to establish a decision-making construct that protects and supports fledgling innovations and guides them through to commercialization and market success.

Designing and operating organizations capable of Sustained Innovation not only requires a cascaded lifecycle, digital business models, and cultural diversity, it also demands a system constructed around the following core principles[7]:

⌒ **Listen.** Listen broadly for ideas through visioning, innovation, and external networks; listen to the customer; listen to the front lines in your organization.

⌒ **Understand.** Understand who your actual and potential customers are, what they want and need, what they will need, and why those needs have not yet been met.

⌒ **Organize.** Organize the innovation team to include those with a stake in the innovation, organize the innovation program, and organize the resources and investments needed to address the problem.

⌒ **Create.** Create an environment and capability for innovation by giving the team the ability to fail; create many alternative solutions by leveraging the cascaded innovation lifecycle.

⌒ **Experiment.** Experiment and learn from failure; conduct many experiments in parallel; use prototyping and other iterative, feedback-driven techniques.

⌒ **Listen again.** Listen again to the customer to help them imagine; use prototypes to elicit feedback; listen to customer acceptance/buying criteria; listen to what could go wrong, but don't let the devil's advocate take control.

⌒ **Design.** Design the concepts to address customer-centric values, such as cost, intuitive use, ease of change, and sense of enhancement.

⌒ **Implement.** Implement the final go/no-go decision; consolidate or eliminate competing alternatives to a manageable number; send concepts back for reinvention, retesting, or redesign; implement the second stage of the innovation lifecycle—manifestation.

The best way to approach Sustained Innovation is through the creation of a management playbook—a codification of the enterprise's innovation principles. This playbook coordinates the myriad activities, functions, models, and operations that comprise the innovation lifecycle, digital business models, and cultural diversity and often includes descriptions of the organization model, operating business architectures and processes, operational and performance information and measures, and automation tools and requirements. The playbook for each enterprise is unique, reflecting its management capabilities, business architecture, operational practices, and cultural norms. This unique playbook acts as the "Innovation Bible," a document that provides strategic direction to all team members on the purpose of their participation and the role they play.

All of this may seem counterintuitive. After all, how does anyone impose creativity? Isn't innovation often the result of accidental invention? History is replete with examples of technological breakthroughs that are a byproduct of some mistake or fluke. Penicillin and Viagra, microwave ovens and Teflon, Velcro and stainless steel—all commonplace products—weren't the result of some elaborate groupthink innovation system; they were the result of accidental discoveries or individual observations that resulted in the creation of a new product. Post-It notes, masking tape, and the Google search engine were all the result of individual or isolated creativity. True enough—but these examples are more isolated than you may think.

Sustained, systemic innovation produces far more breakthroughs than garage inventors do. The Dyson vacuum cleaner, Dean Kamen's Segway personal transporter, and the Apple iPhone are all considered great innovative breakthroughs, but they were developed and perfected by teams, not individuals. The true test of sustained innovation isn't the invention itself, but the net benefit produced by the innovation for the business. Converged organizations with Sustained Innovation constructs perform far better than those that innovate in vacuums or not at all. This benefit is demonstrated in the results published in *BTM Sustained Innovation Index*, which we'll review in the next section.

Calculating the Innovation Benefit

To underscore the importance of Sustained Innovation, we return to Apple—widely considered an innovation powerhouse, but it wasn't always that way. In the mid-1990s, Apple was languishing. Founder Steve Jobs was sent packing into exile, and the company was directionless without his leadership. Sure, he was arrogant and controlling, but he had vision. Seemingly on its last leg, Apple brought Jobs back to the C-suite in 1997 as a Hail Mary move to keep the company alive. It even borrowed $150 million from archrival Microsoft to keep the lights on. Jobs did a lot of things to revive Apple—limited third-party clones of their computers and tightened spending—but the single most important change was innovation and the empowerment of the organization to think outside the box.

In the mid-1990s, Apple was a personal computer company that competed against myriad other manufacturers that operated machines with the Microsoft Windows operating system. For all of its features and functionality, Windows was still somewhat difficult for novice PC users. Apple started down its road to revitalization by launching the iMac, an all-in-one machine that included a computer and monitor in the same casing. It was affordable, reliable, and easy to use—it was perfect for the novice home user. What came next, though, were successive waves of business and technology innovations.

Apple didn't invent the portable MP3 player. That honor goes to Saehan Information Systems, which introduced the MPman in 1998. Apple didn't invent the online music distribution service either, but it did buy SoundJam MP in 2000 and rebranded it "iTunes." It married the two technologies and business models to create the most powerful and disruptive waves of change in entertainment history. From that moment, Apple has leveraged sustained and cascading innovation to create numerous versions of iPod music players, smart phones, tablet computers, and myriad peripherals. So successful has this sustained innovation been that Apple is now the most valuable technology company in the world by market capitalization.

Apple is just one example of the benefits of sustained innovation. Various research studies we have conducted between 2005 and 2009 found that enterprises with an emphasis on innovation often perform better financially and are better able to weather economic change than more stagnant, insular organizations. Of the three legs of the Transformation Triangle, Sustained Innovation in a stand-alone implementation often produces more tangible benefits to an enterprise than either Business Agility or Operational Excellence. Only hybrid strategies, such as Sustained Innovation–Business Agility or Sustained Innovation–Operational Excellence, have financial results superior to a Sustained Innovation strategic posture.

The financial benefit of Sustained Innovation is measurable across many of the common fiscal metrics used by businesses. In capital efficiency, enterprises see better performance in return on capital and return on expenditures. In margins, enterprises recognize higher sales rates and EBITDA. In revenue and earnings, enterprises see higher revenue growth and better EPS. And in volatility, enterprises have more predictable and stable stock prices and shareholder value.

Innovation sounds good in theory, but needs objective data to prove the rule. BTM developed the *Sustained Innovation Index* with publicly available financial information for the companies. For each company in the Index, financial measures were calculated and compared with the performance achieved by their industry group; then, outperformance was calculated as the unweighted difference (industry performance less individual company performance).[8] The industry comparison serves to normalize the results and to reduce the number of factors that could otherwise account for performance differences. The Sustained Innovation posture proved to be a consistent source of financial outperformance. in both the one-year as well as the five-year data analyzed. Both views were impacted by the great recession of 2007–2009. EPS growth, however, remained robust, as did margin and capital efficiency. Stock price volatility (beta) was very stable, indicating that the market viewed the Sustained Innovation leaders as stable, high-performing companies even during a recession.

These figures are not limited to any one area within the enterprise; they reflect enterprise-wide returns, and therefore reflect the performance of the entire enterprise. Taken together, they tell the story that these leaders have discovered and implemented a business approach that allows them to drive continuous improvements in innovation—and to create higher levels of economic value than their industry peers.

BTM Corporation's research demonstrates that Sustained Innovation companies have a dominant short-term and long-term performance advantage over their industry peers of 9 percent; they also have lower stock price volatility (26 percent short term and 40 percent long term). Looking beyond the averages, individual measures of performance reinforced the Sustained Innovation dominance: Enterprises that have embraced and fostered Sustained Innovation outperformed their peers in every category. From a short-term perspective, the outperformance range was from a low of 0.2 percent (revenue growth) to 13.6 percent (EVA/capital). Long term, the range was from a low of 1.1 percent (revenue growth) to 15.0 percent (EVA/capital). Looking beyond revenue growth, the outperformance of the Sustained Innovation stance lifts the average short-term outperformance to 10.7 percent from 9 percent, and the long-term outperformance to 10.5 percent from 9 percent.

The *BTM Operational Excellence Index* report, which we'll discuss in Chapter 10, revealed the critical role Sustained Innovation holds in economic benefits. Achieving such excellence is not exclusive to companies of a certain size by revenue or industry sector; it is available to all companies. Furthermore, the Index specifies the behaviors and constructs that drive Sustained Innovation as a repeatable management practice that can be implemented in any company. In other words, Sustained Innovation is an essential ingredient for success in companies ranging from the Fortune 500 to Main Street shops.

Enterprises do not have to be Sustained Innovation leaders to reap the economic benefits of this process. Even enterprises with less mature and structured Sustained Innovation models had strikingly high financial gains. Regardless of an enterprise's current level of business and technology management maturity, the process of adopting and nurturing convergence that includes Sustained Innovation has substantial financial rewards. BTM's research shows that each stage of advancement carries greater degrees of efficiency, viability, and financial benefit.

Building a Sustained Innovation organization is not easy. Cascaded innovation lifecycles, digital business models, and cultural diversity must become a part of an enterprise's fabric. Crucial to success is a relentless focus on continuous improvement at all levels of the organization. Managing business and technology together opens up greater areas of the organization to the advantages of Sustained Innovation. Finding those advantages—and maintaining them over time—requires dedication and focus. But with focus and effort comes greater rewards than were expended on implementing and sustaining the innovation process.

The Takeaway: Turning Ideas into Action

Discipline and innovation are not opposites, but complements. Establishing an innovation culture consumes a great deal of organizational energy in overcoming the forces of inertia and entropy. But once an idea has been successfully commercialized, respected champions emerge to drive new sources of the energy, creativity, discipline, and resources that sustain and grow an enduring culture of innovation. Successful companies manage innovation from concept to commercialization so that good ideas not only get created, but also find their way into the products and services portfolio. A culture of innovation is characterized by teams that can sense and respond to customers and evaluate what works and what does not work free of the organizational inertia—or friction—that is the enemy of change and its partner, innovation.

A successful culture of innovation requires an organization to master the art and science of managing business and technology together, as described by the following five-step approach:

Step 1: *Improve* strategic planning, business leadership, and management capability to support relentless execution.

Step 2: *Encourage* creative thinking and creative problem solving that can support rapid idea generation and diffusion across the enterprise.

Step 3: *Drive* rapid development of new and improved products, processes, or services that cultivate customer intimacy and build service dependency.

Step 4: *Enable* higher productivity, performance, and growth through collaboration and the capture and adoption of new learning practices.

Step 5: *Develop* new business models that aid in the differentiation of an organization's core offerings from that of its competitors.

CHAPTER 10

Driving Operational Excellence

R IVALRIES MAKE MARKETPLACES INTERESTING, and there are many to take note of. All of sports is dominated by the Red Sox–Yankees' rivalry, considered the granddaddy of all feuds. Toyota and General Motors have battled for top honors in the car industry. Boeing and Airbus compete for preeminence in the air. Coca-Cola and Pepsi are locked in a competitive struggle that will likely last as long as people consume soft drinks. And the Energizer Bunny continues to try to thump copper-top battery rival Duracell for the right to power portable electronics. In the computer world, though, no rivalry tops that of Apple and Microsoft.

We've referenced Apple and Microsoft quite a bit in this book, mostly because few companies can beat their collective innovations, successes, and missteps—especially considering that both companies are roughly the same age and have accomplished their respective success faster than most companies in history. This chapter could be written about their overall operational efficiency (or periods when these companies lacked it). However, we're going to indulge for a few paragraphs in the source of this famous and continuing rivalry: operating systems.

The early computers didn't have operating systems, per se. They were simply massive machines that ran commands given to them by individual programs or what would become known as software. The advent of personal computers meant these machines could run multiple applications and perform simultaneous tasks on a desktop as opposed to only through a server. To do this required a system that managed tasks. That management layer became known as operating systems. Microsoft found its first success in MicroSoft Disk Operating System, better known as MS-DOS. In the early 1980s, MS-DOS provided the features and functionality needed for the nascent personal computer marketplace. Rather than relying on the embedded binary language in the PC, MS-DOS provided the underlying set of instructions that made it possible for PC users to run various applications and interface with peripherals, such as monitors, tape drives, storage discs, and printers.

The problem with MS-DOS was that it was a command line–driven system, which meant that novice users had to memorize or reference complex codes to get their machines to perform the simplest of tasks. Command-line interfaces were a tremendous inhibitor to adoption. Microsoft's answer to that problem was Windows, a graphical user interface (GUI) that also enabled multitasking. Windows wasn't perfect when it was introduced in 1985; in fact, it didn't attain commercial success until 1992 when the fourth iteration hit the market. Microsoft gradually evolved Windows into a rich graphical and functional platform that powers more than 90 percent of the computers in the world today.

Windows wasn't the first GUI operating system. Apple had actually beaten Microsoft to market with the release of Macintosh in 1984. Apple's system, which was a commercial success out of the gate, used icons and menus to guide users to tasks they wanted to perform. Navigation was suddenly easy. Apple initially agreed to license parts of its GUI to Microsoft for the development of Windows. When Microsoft incorporated more features in Windows 2.0 (released at the end of 1997) that conflicted or looked too much like Macintosh, Apple immediately filed a lawsuit claiming copyright infringement. In effect, Apple was asserting that Microsoft stole the "look and feel" of its GUI. And when a third party joined the battle, that's when things got interesting.

Photocopier and document management giant Xerox filed suit not against Microsoft but Apple. Xerox claimed Apple had improperly appropriated the GUI concepts, technology specifications, and the all-important "look and feel" from *its* computer system. Yes, the GUI was first developed and fielded by Xerox as "The Alto," a personal computer developed in the 1970s by the company's Palo Alto Research Center, better known as PARC. It had all the characteristics of both Apple's and Microsoft's GUI—a graphical display of folders and applications, multitasking operating environment, drag-and-drop functionality of the icons, and tasks initiated by a "pointer" controlled by a physical device known as a "mouse."

After nearly six years in court, Apple lost nearly every claim it made against Microsoft. Xerox had its entire case thrown out because, as the courts stated, it lacked validity to make infringement claims against Apple. Many observers at the time noted that the court's decision against Xerox was more a reflection of the company having waited too long to initiate legal action. Failure to execute or move to protect intellectual property became the dig against Xerox and, more specifically, its research and development arm, PARC. And PARC is the example of the consequences of failed operational excellence.

Why did we go into such lengthy detail about an Apple-Microsoft lawsuit if we intended to talk about PARC? Because the lawsuit was the epitome of how PARC became known as an innovation center that its parent, Xerox, failed to capitalize upon. PARC is where the GUI and first viable personal computer was made. It's where the computer mouse was perfected. It's where an alternate version of the Internet—PARC Universal Packet—was born. And it generated many other innovations that never made it to market or failed to reach commercial success, at least under Xerox.

To be fair, PARC—now an independent technology research and development corporation—did produce many innovations and technical advancements for Xerox's printing and document management products. It's the failures that we're focusing on, since they show how an enterprise can recognize the need for agility (Chapter 8) and create a sustained innovation (Chapter 9) engine to keep it ahead of competition and the market, but still fail to reap the benefits of its efforts. True success requires all three legs of the Transformation Triangle, the concept we introduced in Chapter 7. The capitalization of Business Agility and Sustained Innovation is the process we call "Operational Excellence."

Operational Excellence is the ability to drive continuous improvement throughout an organization by focusing on the needs of the customer, empowering employees, and optimizing existing activities in the process. In this chapter, we'll delve into Operational Excellence in practical terms and financial benefit. More importantly, we'll show how technology is the tool through which business managers build infrastructure and processes for facilitating Operational Excellence that meets short- and long-term business objectives.

The Anatomy of Operational Excellence

Operational Excellence provides managers with a sustainable advantage by giving them the ability to continuously improve an organization's decision, investment, and asset performance; its service delivery; and its human resources capabilities. Operationally excellent enterprises possess the processes and structures—or what we at BTM call "intangible assets"—that give them the visibility, control, tools, and management practices necessary to drive greater operational effectiveness and efficiency. In other words, Operational Excellence requires convergence— the art and science of managing technology as one.

Operational Excellence had its genesis in manufacturing dating back to the pre–Industrial Revolution. In 1776 Adam Smith, one of the first people to describe manufacturing processes, attempted to illustrate the division of labor in his now-famous example of a pin factory. As Smith so aptly noted, the assignment of different roles and responsibilities across an enterprise enables scale, lowers costs, and leads to greater operational efficiencies. Smith had no idea how prescient his concepts were. His basic concepts haven't changed much over the last two centuries even as manufacturing and management techniques have evolved. Enterprises have added objective data-driven analytics to their operational excellence processes. Management teams use techniques such as Six Sigma, Total Quality Management, and BTM to streamline their processes, achieve scalability, and maintain quality.

But Operational Excellence is an easily distorted term. Business managers often use it to describe their philosophy and strategic initiatives. Sadly, it is often little more than a set of objectives and accompanying performance metrics. Delivering continuous improvement in the marketplace among competitors and customers requires enterprises to identify, understand, and create the capabilities, behaviors, and focuses necessary for repeatable, continuous, and measurable operational improvement. Recognizing that change is ever-present, operationally excellent companies relentlessly build their capability to tailor their business processes, architectures, standards, partnerships, and human resources to continuously improve value for their customers.

Enterprises that achieve Operational Excellence establish formal definitions and standards for their business processes, link them with their strategic imperatives, and empower individuals to act in an independent but coordinated fashion to improve the work within their span of authority. Being operationally excellent requires a focus on management capabilities to develop and promulgate standards, to coordinate decision making, to optimize service delivery, and to manage the workforce. Orchestrating these capabilities—especially in the rapid execution cycles required by management—requires a unification of the business and technology management disciplines. In other words, converged management must become institutionalized and part of an enterprise's culture (see Figure 10–1), organized around the following three core characteristics:

FIGURE 10–1 OPERATIONAL EXCELLENCE DYNAMICS.

© BTM Corporation.

The combined elements of Operational Excellence build on the standardized work and visible performance measurements that drive continuous improvement, necessary for achieving ever-greater improvements in efficiency and effectiveness.

Standardized Work Companies must define standardized component work processes and services that comprise the company's value activities. These definitions must be dynamic and visible through the value chain that connects an individual activity or service to the end customer. These standards must be constructed around the concepts of workforce management—including internal as well as external resources and suppliers. Finally, a networked governance model combined with a repeatable and consistent decision-making capability is necessary to bring the excellent operation to life. Standardization is the force that enables various pieces of the workforce to execute independently, but in a coordinated manner.

Measured Performance Operational Excellence relies on a foundational capability to measure outcomes and business value—from an end-to-end view and within each standardized work process or service component. This requires two distinct but related classes of information: operational and performance. Operational information is the symbiotic partner of work processes and services, defining the activities and services that combine to deliver value to the customer. Performance information quantifies the results of the work in business value terms to which the customer can directly relate. Operationally excellent companies have a standardized set of architectural constructs that enable performance information to be defined, measured, and disseminated along the value flow, where it is consumed by the process, decision maker, or service provider directly responsible for its performance or primarily affected by its performance.

Local Execution Local execution requires distributed and coordinated authority. Operationally excellent enterprises must adopt flexible and distributed forms of governance and translate their mission and objectives into easily interpreted information. These firms must replace traditional command-and-control approaches with mechanisms that facilitate coordination within and across locales. These mechanisms must provide individuals, groups, and units with the autonomy to improvise and act on local knowledge, while orchestrating coherent behavior across the enterprise. Processes—the assignment of tasks and responsibilities—must be supplemented with personal accountability.

These three core characteristics provide the mechanisms through which an enterprise is able to monitor performance and make adjustments to maintain optimal productivity and capitalization on agility and innovation activities. Recognition of abnormal and suboptimal workflows and productivity is critical, particularly in transitional enterprises trying to leverage their legacy business and revenue streams to the maximum potential while investing in new opportunities that will drive the next stage of their evolution. Regardless of whether an enterprise is managing an existing and well-established work process or developing a new product or operation, ensuring steady and efficient operations is essential to the organization's overall fiscal health.

Operationally excellent companies distinguish themselves through the establishment of standardized workflows, well-defined performance measures (metrics), and local execution (meaning giving authority to execute at the point closest to the work being performed). The combination of these factors not only gives an enterprise greater insight into their operational performance efficiency, but a greater ability to effectuate corrective actions and initiate organizational change management.

Standardizing work requires a Technology Architecture and associated Business Technology Standards—both of which are key elements of a Strategic Enterprise Architecture (as introduced in Chapter 2). SEA includes a business architecture as well as a technology architecture that together provide the capabilities necessary to design the enterprise from business, process, application, data, and infrastructure perspectives. As an example, a Service Oriented Architecture (SOA) describes how services interact via a loosely coupled, message-based communication model. Services can be comprised of coarse or fine-grained components, encapsulated business functions within existing application suites, or actions taken by human operators. At the highest level, service orchestration is the operational realization of process descriptions.

Performance measurement provides visibility. Standardized work activities have performance metrics and measures that broadcast their current status through the value chain, including the governing management teams.

Local execution—or giving management teams the authority and autonomy to act quickly to resolve defects and drive improvements—then provides the enterprise with operational agility. Local autonomy combined with enterprise-level coordination requires a delicate balance; too much autonomy creates chaos and destroys coordination, while too much coordination can lead to a hierarchical—and rigid—command and control system. The balance is preserved by standards, which allow each autonomous work unit to operate without constantly obtaining authority or approval from a superior work unit, and visibility, which informs local decision making and creates the critical negative feedback necessary to create a stable end-to-end system.

From a systems perspective, Operational Excellence is characterized by structured components, each responding to its local environment, that together form a more comprehensive and capable system that, in turn, responds to its environment. System integrity is thereby maintained at both the local work unit level as well as at the overall value chain level.

Designing and operating operationally excellent organizations not only requires a well-designed system, visibility, and local autonomy, it also demands a system constructed around the following core principles:

- ○ **Lean value chain**—designing and constructing a converged business and technology architecture that leads to efficient processes.

- ○ **Value chain flow**—organizing the value chain to ensure that local processes and autonomous work units fit together without restricting—hopefully, enhancing—the flow of value.

- ○ **Visualization**—optimizing the degree of external visibility and manageability of each process in the value chain.

- ○ **Standardization**—creating standards that define the expected normal flow through the value stream, including the performance metrics—in customer-centric business terms—that measure the normal "operating range" of the value flow.

- ○ **Identification of abnormal and/or suboptimal flow**—enabling the rapid and accurate identification of a value flow outside the normal operating range, along with sufficient information to enable root cause traceability.

- ○ **Predefined response**—developing and deploying predefined responses to abnormal operating conditions, both at the local work unit level as well as at the enterprise level.

- ○ **Feedback**—gathering performance information along the value chain, and ensuring that it is consumed locally as well as at the enterprise level.

- ○ **Local autonomy**—maximizing the ability of the local manager of a work unit within the value chain to operate without constraints, with the prime directive of maximizing the local as well as enterprise operating metrics.

Underpants Gnomes and the Excellence Journey

One of the finest satires of poor business planning comes from none other than *South Park*, the animated foul-mouth comedy series set in the high plains of suburban Denver.[1] Created by Trey Parker and Matt Stone, the show mocks and satirizes a full range of social, political, sexual, and religious issues through the prepubescent, bathroom humor–obsessed characters of Kyle, Stan, Kenny, and Cartman (the loudmouth of the group). In one of its takeoffs on business, the South Park boys learned about corporate operations and profits from "underpants gnomes." (Trust us, this is worth reading if you haven't seen or don't recall the episode.)

Struggling to complete a school assignment about business and profit, the boys are constantly distracted by a classmate, Tweak, an over-caffeinated son of a coffee shop owner. Tweak complains about gnomes sneaking into his room at night to steal his underwear. The boys dismiss Tweak's wild story, only later to discover the underpants gnomes are real and, surprisingly, they know about business. In fact, their stealing of little boys' underpants is an enterprise activity.

Desperate to understand the inner workings of a corporation and how they make money, the boys ask the underpants gnomes for help. The gnomes are only too happy to reveal their secrets—a three-part plan:

- Phase 1: Collect underpants.
- Phase 2:
- Phase 3: Profit.

The South Park boys don't get it and probe further. Gnomes working on a giant pile of pilfered underwear go back and forth about how Step 1 is collecting underpants and Step 3 is profit, but can never be pinned down about Step 2. And, of course, Step 2 is execution—what they do with the underpants to add value to some customer, which then leads to revenue and profit. What Parker and Stone tapped into in the episode is something business leaders encounter everyday: ideas that, without a sound business plan, are merely ideas.

Parker and Stone know much about this problem, since they have broken the conventional rules about animation production to create *South Park*. While popular animated series such as *The Simpsons* and *Family Guy* take months to produce a single show, each episode of

South Park is written and produced in one week. More amazing, Parker and Stone—who remain the creative geniuses behind the show—often don't start conceptualizing the content for the next show until after the last installment airs.

That kind of a schedule for a labor-intensive product such as animation can be stressful, but it matches their business model: make the product as fresh and relevant as possible. Authenticity trumps all else in this model. And it works. *South Park* is not only a huge moneymaker, but also a critically acclaimed production.

Just as the underpants gnomes revel in their vacant business model, entrepreneurs and enterprise executives alike love to indulge in the pleasant diversion known as explaining their business model. It was the diversion of the dot-com era, the fodder for venture capitalist pitches and foosball tournament chatter. Everyone was drawing models on napkins, and no one was executing. It's the fun part of business, but in reality it's the most serious of all the matters before us: creating and implementing a business model successfully is real work.

In essence, the technology-driven transformation of today's business environment puts a premium on the model we adopt. Not only are entirely new business models possible, they are *necessary* for survival. And they must be designed so that they can morph into something new on the fly when the environment changes. The *South Park* magic is that Parker and Stone can create shows as events happen, while animation rivals must trail popular culture. The magic of companies such as Google and Apple is that their business models are flexible and adaptable enough to change with evolving economic conditions.

This is what makes up the BTM functional area of Strategic Enterprise Architecture (SEA), which includes the capabilities necessary to design the enterprise from business, process, application, data, and infrastructure perspectives. It consists of the Business Architecture (business strategies, operating models, and processes) and Technology Architecture (applications, data, and infrastructure) scenarios.

Modeling the Operational Blueprint

Every structure in the world—from a single-family residential home in Hartford to the International Commerce Centre in Hong Kong—starts with a set of plans and instructions known as blueprints. No one would start constructing a new building with the roof first—not just because it's illogical, but because the blueprints would instruct the contractor to begin with the foundation and build up.

A building is an apt analogy for the blueprints behind an SEA, since no structure or strategic architecture is built by just one person. A series of specialists from concrete pourers to carpenters to plumbers to electricians collaborate and cooperate in building even the simplest of structures. The same principle holds true for the enterprise executive, who should use an SEA as a blueprint to marshal domain experts—each of whom will have a different idea on how to build and execute operational blueprints with various options and scenarios—onto the same page, the same blueprint.

Enterprise executives shouldn't underestimate the work involved in producing a comprehensive SEA and supporting portfolios. Building an SEA and portfolios are difficult endeavors, but only with this knowledge can decision makers really understand what's going on and what needs to be done in their organizations.

With this knowledge, enterprise executives can begin to lay out scenarios of the future. They can select the best scenario based on evidence and information, and not hunch or desire.

To arrive at the ideal scenario, enterprise executives need to use predictive modeling, a method for visualizing the end goal before beginning costly—and often irreversible—strategy implementation. In the broadest sense, a model is a virtual representation of a real thing. Modelers can preview a solution and address design flaws before they manifest themselves in implementation.

Modeling is not a new concept. In fact, everyone does it without thinking. Recall the invention of the spreadsheet? Before the personal computer revolution, Wall Street analysts performed complex spreadsheet calculations by hand using only a simple calculator. This process was completely inflexible, prone to mistakes, and thoroughly mindnumbing. To make changes to a model (whether to vary inputs or correct mistakes), analysts had to rework the entire thing, a process that—needless to say—was inefficient.

In 1978, Harvard Business School student Dan Bricklin recognized an opportunity to automate this tedious process using software and the rapidly maturing PC. He introduced the VisiCalc spreadsheet to the market, and almost overnight transformed how financial analysts worked. The obvious advantage to Bricklin's innovation was efficiency. Complex models that once took hours to update can now be modified with a few keystrokes.

Not surprisingly, spreadsheets like VisiCalc became the de facto standard for financial modeling, and frustrated business school students and financial analysts quickly put the new technology to use. The demand for spreadsheets was so overwhelming, in fact, that they are frequently credited with creating the initial boom market for business PCs.

But the real revolution that the spreadsheet kicked off wasn't just about efficiency and automation. By unburdening analysts from the heavy lifting of manual calculations, spreadsheets lowered the marginal costs of evaluating new scenarios from thousands of dollars to near zero. This in turn encouraged experimentation and creativity, and the same employee who once spent days perfecting a single model could suddenly produce several alternatives in a single afternoon.

Spreadsheets kicked off an industry-wide movement toward experimentation that revolutionized how analysts—and the financial services industry—worked. By allowing workers to easily create and analyze the impact of multiple scenarios, spreadsheets and predictive modeling encouraged a culture of rapid prototyping and innovation, or impact analysis, that is as applicable today for converging business and technology as it is for the financial world.

Effective scenarios and modeling must be accompanied by impact analyses, which enable decision makers to alter factors, create multiple output scenarios, evaluate the end-to-end impact of each scenario, and eventually select and implement the optimal solution. This stands in direct opposition to conventional, linear problem-solving techniques, where decision makers analyze subproblems at each logical step along the way, and then assume that the overall impact of their individual choices will lead to the best solution.

As with modeling in general, impact analysis can be used to address a broad range of activities. For example, it is often used in supply chain planning for advanced data-driven calculations that optimize a particular function (such as inventory costs) given unique inputs and constraints (such as market demand, logistical restrictions, and manufacturing capabilities).

In the above examples, individuals vary inputs, rules translate these inputs to outputs, and team members compare the impact of multiple scenarios to choose the solution that best fits their needs. For impact analysis to work, the scenario being modeled should conform to three guidelines:

1. **Easily identified inputs, rules, and outputs.** Impact analysis requires defined sets of inputs that are linked to outputs using prede-

fined rules. These inputs and outputs are often quantitative (as in our supply chain optimization problem), but they can also be qualitative (such as our PC configuration options). To produce good results, these criteria—and the rules that link them—must accurately reflect the real-world problem.

2. **Multiple configuration options and decision factors.** Problems that contain only a few inputs and outputs aren't suited to impact analysis because the effect of altering inputs is often obvious. When the outputs are less intuitive, impact analysis helps decision makers identify good solutions.

3. **Low-design, high-implementation cost.** Scenarios that are inexpensive to design but difficult to implement are ideally suited to impact analysis. It's unrealistic to contract a builder to construct five houses so that you can then choose the one you like the most. It's entirely possible, however, to commission an architect to draft five blueprints. A person can compare plans, choose a favorite, and give it to the contractor. This is where the synergy between modeling and impact analysis really comes into play. Predictive modeling is a powerful tool for lowering design costs, and as such it is a crucial driver for impact analysis.

Disconnects between business, process, and technology are often introduced when individual decisions have unforeseen effects on the blueprint as a whole. Enterprises tend to decompose the problem several times and decide a course of action that probably was suggested in the initial round of analysis.

A couple of obstacles need resolution before a company can get started with modeling and impact analysis. The most obvious is the common perception that the time it takes to develop a model during the design stage is better spent on implementation. This is due, in part, to previous experiences with models that were frighteningly inaccessible to all but the most die-hard experts. Since nonspecialists (a group that frequently includes managers and other authority figures) couldn't experience their value firsthand, they assumed that the models were a waste of time.

The simple solution to this concern is to make the modeling environment friendly enough for a broad range of people to pick it up and experiment according to their own level of comfort. A good example to point back to here is a financial model whose inner workings may be exceedingly complex but whose overall purpose is clearly communicated to a nontechnical audience.

In extreme cases, modeling can be a waste of time. This happens when people get stuck in an endless design loop; by continuously tweaking the model in the quest for a perfect solution, they never get around to actually implementing what they're working on. The way to counter this trap is by linking a system of real-time monitoring to metrics, goals, and objectives that are established at the beginning of the project. This implies a link to both project and performance management that is crucial to any type of modeling.

The other obstacle that stands in the way of modeling and impact analysis is "white space"—the gaps that exist between multiple models and between models and the real world. These gaps are the usual culprits in cases where modeling hasn't been successful. Typically, the tools that are available to technology employees to model the business, processes, and technology are disjointed, and so they tend to exacerbate rather than overcome the white space problem.

Most tools are geared either to a particular task (process modeling, object modeling, or knowledge management) or to broad horizontal activities (word processing, drawing, or spreadsheets). A consequence of these disjointed offerings is that companies tend to use multiple tools and environments to develop their models. When changes are made in one environment (say a process diagram) they aren't automatically propagated (into a requirements document, say, or business strategy memo). Without integrated tools, decision makers must proactively disseminate modeling data to maintain alignment.

Once the current business model is understood, enterprise executives can begin to create the business scenario models that form the basis for end-to-end impact analysis. Each scenario represents an alternative for accomplishing the firm's goals. The structured and visual nature of models makes it easy for the team to compare these scenarios and eventually combine the best of each—and that equates to what's best for operational efficiency.

Key Steps in the Operational Excellence Journey

It's important to recognize, though, that building an operationally excellent enterprise is a journey that includes a management playbook to coordinate the myriad activities, functions, models, and operations that comprise the organizational value chain. The key steps in the Operational Excellence journey are:

Develop Technology Architecture and Standards What enables Parker and Stone to produce an animated TV show in a week is a set of repeatable processes. These processes leverage tailored technologies and business decision making that produce optimal intended product outcomes.

Define Value Chains As we've discussed previously in this book, a value chain consists of the managers, departments, partners, and customers that oversee or influence processes and productivity systems. Understanding the composition and scope of these value chains is essential for measuring operational performance and to effectuate change.

Measure Value Flows and Performance Measuring performance may seem self-evident, but many enterprises mistake this task as a point-in-time or a one-time event. In operationally excellent organizations, performance is measured throughout the process chain—not just the outcome—and is an ongoing effort. This measuring enables an enterprise to make adjustments that enhance operational excellence.

Visualize Abnormal or Suboptimal Performance This step directly relates to the measurement of performance in that it requires managers to recognize when operational performance lags or suffers from unusual variations in activities. Understanding and recognizing deviations enables the enterprises to take corrective action that ensures consistency in performance and outcomes.

Define Response Mechanisms The enterprise should have predefined operational responses when either overall performance lags or processes suffer potentially serious deviations. Anticipating and planning for worst-case and minor scenarios will enable the quick-response and corrective actions that will put an enterprise back on track. These predefined responses include defining roles and responsibilities for divisions, departments, managers, and individuals. And these responses should include metrics for ensuring corrective actions return a process to a known good baseline.

Facilitate Balanced Enablement Enterprises need to empower their people to take action in the absence of orders. At the same time, enterprises don't want local managers to deviate too far from the corporate policy or plan, since such localized changes could trigger a cascading effect across enterprise operations that throw off processes and productivity. Enterprises need to establish parameters for local managers and corporate operations to ensure that individuals have the ability to act in the company's best interest, while also undertaking an escalation process for seeking higher authority for changes and adjustments.

It should go without saying that the management playbook must be communicated to the key executives and managers responsible for its execution. And, most importantly, progress must be tracked, investments made, risks managed, and lessons learned. Can we say that this is how it works at *South Park*'s studios? Not really, since Parker and Stone are truly unconventional souls who invest tremendous amounts of personal capital and sweat equity into their product. What we can say is that enterprises seeking to replicate the *South Park* model on a large scale must follow these steps and constructs if they have any hope of achieving a financial return on their excellent operation.

The Process to Continual Return on Investment

If Business Agility is the ability to make rapid adjustments to change and Sustained Innovation is the ability to stay ahead of the competition and market dynamics, then Operational Excellence is the epitome of fiscal discipline, maximizing the use of resources and the assurance of revenue sustainability and, ultimately, profitability. There is no sense in converging business and technology management, establishing strategic enterprise architectures, and imposing heavy governance over business operations if none of it produces an incremental return to the business. By incremental, we mean that operationally excellent enterprises, by definition, have higher revenue and profit yields than their mediocre peers.

Before getting into the financial benefits of Operational Excellence, let's start by defining what a fiscal byproduct of this discipline is *not*. It's been said time and again that businesses cannot cut their way to success—and cutting costs isn't the primary driver of Operational Excellence. Many businesses—particularly during the great recession of 2008–2009—did just that; they cut costs to satisfy Wall Street analysts and investors. While this made shareholders happy by producing a profit, the reported profits came at the expense of future growth since these cost-cutting enterprises slashed through talent and operational capacity.

A perfect example of how slash-and-burn cost cutting can come back to haunt management is found at Hewlett-Packard. In August 2010, HP shocked the technology world and financial markets when it inextricably ousted CEO Mark Hurd for the relatively minor offense of fudging expense reports. The firing (he actually resigned under duress) came as a result of a sexual harassment claim by an HP contractor. The charge was dismissed, but the board of directors was displeased with the way Hurd handled the situation. While the industry praised Hurd—a numbers cruncher and fiscal control zealot—people inside HP complained that his cuts had ripped out the company's soul and impaired its operational ability. Worse, these cuts—which many managers and staffers deemed arbitrary—were causing talent to leave in droves. Hurd's conduct in the sexual harassment probe was the icing on the cake for the board, and they used it as the excuse to take out the chief executive who was going too far in cost cutting.

That's the danger in cost cutting. Operational Excellence is more about efficiency and performance than the elimination of redundant activities and streamlining. By definition, an operationally excellent organization is already streamlined and optimized for maximum productivity and the optimal level of expense. Note we said "optimal," not "lowest," since lowest doesn't always equal best. Consider the contrast of two retailing companies—Walmart and Costco. Walmart is known for its low wages and is often criticized for not providing benefits to its employees; it's even been sued for age and gender discrimination. Walmart's defense for its policies is that it's a means to an end—low wages contributes to low operational costs, and that keeps prices low and profits high. In contrast, Costco pays comparatively generous wages and extends health care benefits to its employees. While Costco is several orders of magnitude smaller than Walmart, it's more profitable on a dollar-to-dollar comparison and has a significantly lower employee turnover rate.

While viewing performance from a human capital perspective as the prior example illustrates is one possible metric, when we wanted to quantify the true financial benefits of operational excellence, we created the BTM Operational Excellence Index to examine the output of enterprises that have established and are working toward the principles we've outlined in this chapter. We used publicly available financial information for the companies in the Index as of December 2009, except for the long-term financial performance measures, which used data from 2005—2009, inclusively.

Our research reveals several advantages in operationally excellent enterprises.[2] The level of industry peer outperformance is most striking in the capital efficiency and value, margin, and volatility measures. Long-term impact was higher for capital efficiency and value and beta (56 percent and 83 percent, respectively), while revenue and earnings growth and margin showed a superior long-term performance advantage (growth more than doubled, and margin showed a 17 percent advantage).

A comprehensive understanding of the financial impact of Operational Excellence is based on the following set of financial performance measures:

- ◑ Capital efficiency and value measures were chosen to highlight management capabilities on the efficient use of resources.
- ◑ Margins to highlight cost control and pricing power, especially in a changing (and challenging) market.
- ◑ Revenue and earnings growth to demonstrate consistent performance over time.
- ◑ Stock price beta to examine the effect of Operational Excellence on stock price volatility.

For each company in the Index, financial measures were calculated and compared with the performance achieved by their industry group; then, outperformance was calculated as the unweighted difference (industry performance less individual company performance). The industry comparison serves to normalize the results and to reduce the number of factors that could otherwise account for performance differences. (The organizations included in these financial measures are only those publicly traded in the United States, and therefore have audited financial results available. While there are private companies and public sector entities in the database, their results were not reflected in this paper.)

Operational Excellence leaders focus on three core practices, each of which requires business and technology convergence in order to perform at a high level of maturity.

1. **Value flows**—the activity streams, consisting of business processes and services that comprise value networks that define stakeholder relationships, especially those with the customer.

2. **Stakeholder visualization**—the individual and collective perspectives of the members of a value chain, showing the value activity as well as its relationship to the customer.

3. **Participatory optimization**—the activities of the value chain members, each proactively working to improve local processes and services in order to deliver increasing value to the customer.

Operationally excellent enterprises have rigorously defined standards that establish the primary activities of every stakeholder in a value flow—chains of activities or services—and then empower those stakeholders to continuously improve their portion of the flow. To be effective, each stakeholder must have the visibility into their local neighborhood of the flow, and the authority to act within that neighborhood to make improvements. Each improvement flows downstream to the customer, who experiences the collective value improvements that originated all along the value flow. It's critical that these improvements be coherent, that is, additive; otherwise the customer experience will be chaotic with no value-add.

All three of the above core practices for Operational Excellence require that the management of business and technology be converged. Establishing—and then maintaining—coherent optimization activities requires that each stakeholder knows what to do, is able to see the outcome, and has the ability to act in concert with other stakeholders.

Empirically speaking, the BTM Operational Excellence Index proves that the establishment of these core values, processes, and mechanisms produce a lasting and sustainable financial gain for the enacting enterprises. When combined with the disciplines in business agility and sustained innovation, Operational Excellence positions the enterprise for accelerated growth and greater resiliency to marketplace dynamics.

The Takeaway: Turning Ideas into Action

To manage most business operations, enterprises must cultivate a culture of risk management that is vigilant in its pursuit and disciplined in its execution.[3] Today's businesses are learning hard lessons about operational risk: BP Deepwater Horizon, naked credit default swaps, and more than $63 billion in failed U.S. technology projects are but a few of the high-profile cases that demonstrate the perils of failed risk management and poor operational execution. Each of these disasters caused billions of dollars in value destruction, yet each of them happened on the watch of competent risk managers who appeared to do their jobs properly. Each had compliance systems, regulators, and oversight mechanisms expressly designed to mitigate risk. So what went wrong?

In two words: systemic failure. Systemic operational risk originates in the complex interactions among the components that constitute a system. Either individual component can function flawlessly while the overall system experiences a massive failure, or the system functions as an impact multiplier, magnifying the impact of a single component failure.

Managing systemic risk requires a culture of operational risk management that extends beyond the individual components to the edges, seams, and overall system behavior. Mature risk cultures are characterized by a set of essential management practices that ensure that the risk framework of the enterprise functions at a consistently high level. These include the following:

Step 1: *Identify the risks*. Operational risk identification is the process of identifying sources of risk from all directions, internal and external. Risk identification is an inherently creative process, and as such, it requires the collaboration of diverse minds and different perspectives that represent all constituencies.

Step 2: *Establish a control system*. Risk mitigation is an analytical process that devises a control system to mitigate each identified risk. Control systems range widely. They can be designed to respond to a risk event, to reengineer the process to eliminate or transfer the risk, or to detect the risk early, before it can cause significant damage.

Step 3: *Test, test, and test again*. Control systems require compliance to be effective, and testing simulates risk events and the control-system response. Test results are fed back into improved and more effective control systems; they also serve to identify new sources of risk, each of which requires a corresponding control system.

As our knowledge economy expands and global interconnections increase, complexity grows exponentially. Business leaders and operating managers must proactively manage complexity by constructing control systems that not only function in complex environments, but also adapt and evolve along with them.

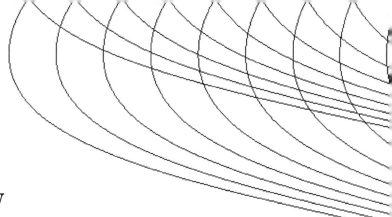

PART IV

Let the Journey Begin

CHAPTER 11

Becoming a Better Business Technology Leader

O VERHAULING AND IMPLEMENTING a totally new management system may seem daunting and risky to managers. The last thing an executive wants is disruption to an existing, productive, and profitable business without empirical and experiential evidence that the new system will yield greater returns on investment, long-term viability, and security against economic disturbances. It's a fair position, since enterprise leaders are compensated on the performance of their business, and changes to management structure put the business and its security—and their jobs—at risk.

Up to this point in the book we've discussed management structures, roles, and responsibility and measurements of performance in the converged enterprise achieved through the BTM Framework. The underlying, critical element of achieving and maintaining convergence in the modern enterprise is nothing less than individual leadership. It takes leaders with perseverance and courage to build and implement the BTM constructs and to spur compliance with the tenets of the converged enterprise, as well as the wherewithal to articulate and follow through on an adaptable vision that produces a higher outcome than ordinary management paradigms.

Any management construct requires leadership; business technology management is no exception. BTM has no ending. It is a continual evolution and revolution of concepts and opportunities that reflect contemporary and future business operations and objectives. Many of its tenets can be applied at any level of an organization with limited scope; but such implementation has limited benefits. The truest and greatest BTM value comes from an enterprise-wise adoption, and responsibility for initiating that process resides in the executive suite and boardroom. The ultimate success, however, is dependent on the compliance of line managers acting upon the BTM framework in their localized operations. In other words, BTM is about individuals. In this chapter, we will show how individual managers within enterprises initiated the convergence process and instilled the BTM Framework within their organizations to stimulate change and generate improved performance.

The Many Faces of Convergence

Convergence has many faces. The framework of Business Technology Management does not prescribe any one particular look and feel. It begins with a comprehensive self-examination by an enterprise that leads to a unique, customized roadmap. An underlying theme is the need for an enterprise to discover, document, and execute its purpose for being. Only in this way can it stand out in its marketplace. Only in this way can it perform as a leader in its industry. And this can only be accomplished by executives taking the BTM lead within an organization.

As is often the case, leadership is not something that can be assigned or enforced. It's a learned art cultivated through study, apprenticeship, and emulation. Individual managers are the sum of their experiences, and often draw upon their past engagements and roles to find solutions to contemporary problems. Over the years, experience shapes the behaviors of individuals, often limiting their flexibility to change and new direction. And, of course, executives and line workers are motivated and respond to change based on their level of compensation and overall job security. The first step visionaries take in transforming their organization's management approach is an introspective look at their company, their peers, and themselves. Such transformative managers often ask questions like:

○ Do I agree with management's perspectives on business and technology management? If not, how would I do it differently?

❍ Is my organization likely to accept a new, different kind of leadership and structure?

❍ What special training would be of benefit to me? What training do peers and managers require to adopt the new structure?

❍ What assets and information are available to create a foundation for transformation and convergence?

❍ What new authority would I need to implement convergence?

❍ Where does that authority currently reside?

❍ What can I do right now to advance the convergence agenda?

❍ What steps can be taken to organically convert peers to the convergence philosophy?

The last question is where Kent Thiry began his convergence journey as CEO and chairman of DaVita, one of the largest outpatient kidney dialysis treatment center networks in the United States.[1] While largely successful at delivering life-sustaining care to thousands of patients, Thiry recognized that his company could benefit from a different kind of thinking and approach to innovation and operations. The problem he recognized was nothing less than the conventional segregation of management into expertise domains.

Thiry restructured DaVita management into cross-functional teams. No longer would executive, clinical, operations, finance, information technology, and compliance teams operate in isolation. They were brought together to provide insights and perspectives to the development of programs, patient care, and technology development and implementation. Rather than having a traditional hierarchical organization chart, DaVita has a roster of personnel that lists positions, their areas of responsibility, and to whom they are responsible. Even Thiry is listed, along with the people to whom he must answer.

The cross-functional approach took root at DaVita in 2008 with the development and adoption of "Chairside Snappy," a software application that assists doctors and nurses in keeping abreast of their patients' treatment. The project team included representatives from all of the core constituencies. Thiry admits that corralling these various bureaucratic entities posed some challenges. But once they found consensus, they collectively set aside their respective agendas to focus on the task of implementing Chairside Snappy and the determination of their goals for the project.[2] How did Thiry create consensus and find common ground?

"We created what we called 'the Cheddar Process,' based on Dr. Spencer Johnson's best-selling book and video *Who Moved My Cheese?* To understand the seismic change this application would make at our centers, we had everyone involved read the book and watch the video."[3]

What Thiry's experience demonstrates is that sometimes it's the simplest things that spark the BTM process into life. Moreover, the process of finding common ground often plants the seeds that germinate into ideas within organizations and individuals, respectively, that become the convergence of business and technology into more dynamic products that generate greater returns on investment in capital, resources, and people.

In subsequent examples, we will use the experience of individual executives to illustrate how they discovered the power of convergence and brought managerial conversion to their organizations. These examples are not intended to recommend any particular approach to implementing and achieving BTM, but rather to demonstrate what others have done to stimulate ideas.

More Than a Seat at the Table

A recurring topic among technology leaders is "getting a seat at the table." The table, of course, being the executive team or the boardroom. Technologists have long recognized that their success is oftentimes contingent on having a voice in the business deliberations and decisions. But even having a seat at the table is only a first step. Being present doesn't mean that the technologist will be listened to—much less understood—and certainly doesn't mean that technology will be integrated and deployed effectively with the business goals in mind.

What's really needed is the breaking down of silos that isolate technology and business management perspectives and decision making. Technologists need to learn to drop the jargon and forego the flashy features of their gadgets and software. They need to speak of technology in business terms—efficiencies created, benefits in meeting business objectives, and maximum potential return on investment. This does not absolve business managers of their responsibility to study technology in order to understand its potential and limitations. Just as technologists are expected to speak intelligently about business, business managers must also speak at least on a foundational level about technology they wish to use. In other words, both management structures must cross

their respective chasms so they can have meaningful dialogue that results in real progress.

This is precisely the journey that Aurelia Boyer undertook. As chief
information officer of NewYork-Presbyterian Hospital, she is responsible
for building and maintaining systems that ensure the care and safety of
the facility's patients.[4] This includes everything from diagnostic equipment to medical recordkeeping to accounting and compliance systems.
The hospital's management team believes that patients should have access to their medical records and be full participants in the health care
process. This means that Boyer must maintain systems that provide full
accessibility to physicians, clinicians, and patients, respectively.

As Americans have learned through the health care reform debates
over the last several years, achieving this level of transparency isn't easy.
Legacy health records and medical delivery systems were never designed
for transparency and portability. Actually, they were designed precisely
with the opposite intent. The result has been a collective system that
isolates information from the people who need it to make faster, better
decisions. This chaos literally costs Americans billions of dollars annually in bloated health care expenses.

Boyer, a registered nurse, helped bring NewYork-Presbyterian out
of the dark ages of patient information management through the adoption of electronic medical records. The system the hospital developed
gives patients control over what personal information goes on the chart,
who sees it, and what decisions are ultimately made. It's a revolutionary
concept of giving patients control over the dissemination of their data
and expediting decision making. NewYork-Presbyterian is on the leading
edge of change, and every day it demonstrates the benefits of technology
by way of:

◑ Reduced patient errors through electronic physician order entry.

◑ The elimination of transcription errors.

◑ Reduced pharmacy errors because all prescriptions are sent elec-
tronically.

◑ Reduced dosing errors in pediatrics, where dosing is calculated by
weight and age.

Fewer patient errors means lower costs. Administratively, the same
data is used to measure and manage the hospital's delivery of services.

These things are possible because the hospital has invested in technology that follows a seven-year plan. More importantly, its management of technology is converged with its management of health care.

One sign of a converged company is that the same people make both the business and technology decisions for the organization. They have an understanding of their organization's business mission and an appreciation for the technologies that enable it.

At NewYork-Presbyterian, CEO Herbert Pardes, a physician, is intensely involved in technology decisions. Both the CEO and COO agree that a robust business/technology infrastructure provides the required underpinning for getting health care to where it needs to go on these quality measures and efficiencies. To this end, their executives have the widely held view that technology is one of their most critical initiatives.

Boyer's background in nursing gave her certain advantages. In addition to being a nurse, she held many different administrative roles in a hospital. Together, that experience helped her to understand workflow and how the patients move, and, thereby why the management dashboard needs to look the way it does. She was able to better discern what constitutes helpful data and what doesn't.[5]

The situation at NewYork-Presbyterian is still somewhat rare but no longer unknown. The line between business and technology has blurred and has even disappeared at many leading companies. The split between business and technology may have been normal in the early days, but it is unnecessary and even harmful today.

Management, Musical Chairs–Style

As we learned from NewYork-Presbyterian, enterprises need representation from different operational segments in the technology evaluation and decision-making process to gain insights from different perspectives. But what about creating structures that provide executives with direct exposure to technology and business issues? What about making a business manager responsible for technology decisions and a technologist responsible for business operations? This isn't some topsy-turvy, harebrained scheme. It's actually how some organizations operate, believing—and we concur—that it provides their management teams with a better understanding of and empathy for their team's function.

Businesses that engage in alternating leadership gain deeper understanding of the power and potential of technology for meeting objectives by providing nontechnologists with direct exposure to technology in a nonconventional construct. Through this exchange of responsibilities, business managers often learn how technology is a strategic instrument rather than a tactical tool. Likewise, technology managers gain deeper understanding of how the business views technology and how it can better influence the adoption and application of new systems.

Alternating responsibilities for business and technology management means that the application of technology and the responsibility for that technology's role in meeting business objectives within an enterprise is no longer someone else's problem. The changes required to get a company in fighting shape are the responsibility of every leader, no matter what his or her function or level may be. This is precisely how it works at Eastern Mountain Sports (EMS), a $200 million manufacturer and retailer of sports clothing and equipment, with seventy-five retail stores in eleven East Coast states.

As former CIO Jeffery Neville explained in an interview with the BTM Institute:

> We frequently go through the organization systematically using a number of process improvement opportunities. We might use the organizational upheaval created by an application change to modify behaviors, to alter the culture, and to redefine processes. We might also go in the other direction, and do bottom-up requirements and then deliver on those requirements. We try to use both techniques wherever possible.
>
> For example, we changed the way we delivered products and our Eastern Mountain Sports brand to customers by addressing our product lifecycle management processes (PLM). These changes meant looking at the culture and the behaviors of the cross-functional organization required to bring, say, a Techwick shirt from design to store delivery or placement on our Web site. We chose to use a systems implementation project to put in a PLM system. We used that as a tool to drive those changes around the processes that we wanted to achieve.[6]

Note that Neville didn't wear "two hats," removing his business hat and putting on his technology hat and vice versa. Rather, he wore one hat, his business technology hat. When technology takes the lead and invokes change, it's seen as part of a larger undertaking involving changes in processes, behaviors, and culture. Many technology projects have failed because they were developed and executed in a vacuum—they were created by technologists separated from the people and real-world environments in which the tools would be used. At EMS, changing the technology, the processes, and the people are seen as one undertaking. All are designed, and redesigned, as a single entity.

Optimizing Technology Investment Management

Technology investments that matter follow the money. We'll never know for sure how many hundreds of millions of dollars have been squandered on ill-conceived and poorly executed technology initiatives in corporations and government agencies over the years. The headline-making blunder is one thing. The new technology declared a success because it's in place, but not used or used poorly because of a disconnect between its designers and the users is another. The implementation costs may hurt, but the lost-opportunity costs can mean death to an organization.

As organizations' use of BTM capabilities mature, their perspective on technology investments changes. Investments are judged less in isolation and more as integral parts of business strategy. At leading companies, technology investments are proposed and advocated by business executives, who assume responsibility for their success during development, implementation, and operations.

Managers in converged enterprises—or those trending toward convergence—often review technology investment spending to ensure it's optimized based on business goals and objectives, and review the benefits from prior investments to ensure they were worth the effort and expense. Moreover, these leaders will seek clarity on whether technology benefited from cross-functional team collaboration and whether the various constituencies within the organization benefited from the technology.

Optimizing technology investment was the chief mission of Gary Masada, the former CIO of Chevron and former president of Chevron Information Technology Company, Chevron's in-house business technology provider. He moved Chevron toward more centralization in its technology through a convergence framework. His goal: creating the maximum benefit from technology at the lowest possible expense.

As Masada detailed in an interview with the BTM Institute, "Many times when you are in a decentralized model, you start thinking you should make decisions about everything. You end up with things that don't fit together, but you aren't thinking of the big picture, and not looking at interconnectivity. You minimize the value of the investments."[7]

But the benefits of finding the right mix between centralization and decentralization are much larger, he says:

> One of the ideas I had was that if you lived in a decentralized world with only regional governance, you ended up with a system that was both ineffective and inefficient. Investment dollars need to be aligned with the major strategies of the corporation, but when we checked, we found that many of the technology investments were based on good ideas rather than a sound strategy.
>
> The first thing that we did was to align the major technology investments with the major strategy of the corporation and each of the operating companies. We tested them against the strategy by identifying the gap. We then put the technology investments on the roadmap to fill the gaps that existed. Not only did it align with the business, but it was also an effective strategy check for the business.[8]

The changes in the company that resulted were widespread. First, executives previously isolated from technology gained a greater understanding of the benefits derived from technology projects. Second, business units understood the magnitude of the technology investments they were making and truly supported them.

"They often heard about projects," Masada said, "but didn't really understand how significant it was and the impact that it would have on their business." He went on, "The dialogue that now takes place enables them to have a deeper understanding of how their investments in technology are going to provide benefits to the business. In the end, it actually led to almost every business [within Chevron] increasing their respective technology budgets because for the first time there was a clear understanding of what they could expect in return of their investment."[9]

The fruits of Masada's convergence efforts are self-evident: To date, his programs have saved Chevron $200 million.

Redefining Business Strategy with Technology

All too often technology initiatives that look great on paper fail because in the real world, people aren't perfect. End users don't use what they are given. Or they constantly change their minds about what they want. Technologists get enamored with the newest gizmos and there's no process for evaluating the business impact of their enthusiasms. Business managers don't understand a new technology fully or have no ownership of its success. The best-laid plans of mice and technologists need to account for the vagaries of very human organizations.

The BTM Framework sets forth a number of management capabilities that first crystallize the company's stance in the marketplace and then equip it to succeed. Determining its value discipline—for example, customer intimacy, operational excellence, or product leadership—and its value type—stability or agility—will lead the enterprise to the appropriate enabling technology.

Dr. Richard Salluzzo is a double board-certified physician and the former CEO of Wellmont Health System, a thirteen-hospital system with 7,000 employees and facilities in Tennessee and Kentucky. He discovered the need to change the application of technology after changing his organization's objectives to focus on customer service. More significantly, he discovered that people approached technology differently when the mission objectives changed.

"By concentrating on customer service excellence, we increased our patient volume, and in turn our revenues. I used tools to measure and to benchmark the quality of our services against other hospitals in the U.S. Our emergency department went from 60,000 visits annually to 92,000 annually," Dr. Salluzzo said in an interview with the BTM Institute. "ER patients saw a doctor within forty minutes. We had a 90 percent or better score for our ER customer service."[10]

Dr. Salluzzo doubled the company's revenues and made it profitable. He explains:

> We track metrics on everything we do. That is one of our cardinal principles and part of our business strategy. We strive to get reasonable benchmarks wherever possible. For

> example, we try to answer every call light within thirty seconds. We look at the number of falls. We put in room service so patients can order food from 6 a.m. to midnight. This process has empowered our staff to speak with patients and to manage their diet as part of a team with a clinical nutritionist. Our price per meal decreased from $1.80 to $1.60 with room service. Room service has taken a lot of work off nurses. We now provide better meals at a lower cost and with less waste.[11]

Technology enables all of this, of course. The important lesson here, however, is that technology alone accomplishes little. The real value comes in how people work.

"I'm all for technology automation," Salluzzo says. "Many doctors and administrators view business technology as a panacea. If you automate a bad pharmacy process, for example, then you'll have a hard time correcting it. We decided to clean up many of our processes before we automated them. We couldn't manage our finances without technology. Here it creates process in and of itself."[12]

Planning and budgeting technology investments successfully requires a careful analysis of the "real world" of people and processes. At Wellmont, caring for a patient can have as many 250 processes. A simple overlay of new technology would be counterproductive, as Salluzzo points out.

"Like most hospitals, we find it impossible to self-report medication errors with any type of reliability. Moving quickly to bar coding medications, a drug prevention cycle, and a physician order entry system made a lot of sense. These things become their own processes. Technology needs to be an enabling and an agile thought process in people's minds."[13]

The Who, What, and Where of BTM

In previous chapters, we've written about Strategic Enterprise Architecture (SEA), a seemingly complex and daunting capability of the BTM Framework. SEA is overwhelming to many business executives because it requires a reassignment of managerial responsibilities. In reality, though, SEA really boils down to the answers of three basic questions:

Where are we now? Where do we want to be? And how are we going to get there?

These are the questions that Kent Thiry asked when he became CEO and chairman of DaVita in 1999. As we discussed earlier in this chapter, Thiry used a converged management approach to create more efficient and profitable delivery of outpatient kidney dialysis services. What we didn't explain is why he initiated this process. Simply put: DaVita, a company with $1.4 billion in annual revenue, was in trouble. Over the years it had made too many acquisitions, causing operating costs to soar and valuable resources to dwindle. Meanwhile, the company's 12,000 employees lacked basic technology, such as telephone extensions.

Thiry recognized that DaVita needed more than just streamlining. It needed a redefinition of its strategic intent and organizational objectives. It needed to focus on objectives rather than to reflect on past accomplishments. "We ruthlessly try to figure out what are the three or four things that will unambiguously and dramatically change for the better if we do this," Thiry explained:

> Those items might be clinical, operational, financial, or strategic. Our goal is to develop a very vivid "show-me" picture of the way things would work better. For example, you might walk me through how this new application would work in one of our centers. We try to simulate exactly how decisions will be made differently, and exactly how new pieces of technology will benefit patients. This process helps to distinguish incremental benefits from real breakthrough benefits. Once we agree on the simulation, we lock and load on the cost and key benefits, and then work together with rigor to drive the whole process towards getting them."[14]

This is a form of predictive modeling, a process enabled by an SEA. An SEA marries a business architecture with a technology architecture. Its words and diagrams should be intelligible to every decision maker, not just to the specialists with their incomprehensible jargon.

An SEA will not only state the overall mission and business design of the firm, it will also show all of the processes, from supplier to customer, and everything in between. It will show the technology that drives the process at each step along the way. It will also specify standard technologies, interfaces, business technology processes, and other essential items that ensure the company runs optimally. This is how redundancies, bottlenecks, underuse of technology assets, and missing information can be spotted.

How has it worked at DaVita? Today, it is a $5.2 billion company, and it is well positioned to become the nation's number one provider of kidney dialysis centers. DaVita's 32,200 employees, who work in 1,400 locations across forty-three states, treat about 110,000 patients a year. It's a dramatic change from the state Thiry found when he arrived.

Governing the Converged Organization

Obviously a converged enterprise governs itself differently. It will use permanent and ad hoc groups and committees to function in a new way. Technology and business leaders must identify where technology decisions are made within their organizations and who is making them, the processes for how business and technology managers collaborate in decision making, and the processes for identifying and weeding out redundancies. Above all, they must identify or create the process for ensuring that technology decisions and investments reflect the overall enterprise strategy.

Identifying and optimizing the technology governance process was the job given Michael Paravicini in 2003 when he joined Zurich Financial Services as chief information technology officer. This was no trivial task. He had to figure out how a highly decentralized, locally based staff of 7,700 professionals, including thirty CIOs, could better respond to the company's global needs. His initial action was to create new connections between business and technology management.

"We created an important liaison role between technology and the business. Our key account executives serve a dual function: They act in similar ways to that of local CIOs, who are responsible for end-to-end delivery of all technology services for a particular business. Their other duties include business analysis and business change management. Our goal is to have these people become part of the local executive team. For each business segment, we have one key account executive. If the business is large, then we'll have an account executive for each line of business," Paravicini told the BTM Institute.[15]

Next, Paravicini examined Zurich's investments at different levels from several perspectives. He then turned to outsourcing and centralization to build flexibility into the organization, and uses a multilayer governance scheme to ensure that all functions are involved in decisions regarding technology, and to eliminate waste and redundancy.

> We have a three-tier governance organization. All projects must first go through the respective local governance council, which includes business technology, business, and finance. These local councils agree on the priorities, timing, and schedules for these projects. Once the projects have been approved, they go to the Chief Information Technology Office (CITO) approval panel, which looks at them from an architectural and finance perspective. Specifically, this panel looks to see if anyone has done a similar project, and if so, is it possible to share some of these capabilities. After this panel approves the projects, they move to the project approval panel (PAP). It's the group finance committee of the operations council that is chaired by a group CFO, the COO, and myself. We review these projects and make a final decision.[16]

These groups will go by different names, but converged companies have offices and committees at multiple levels in which all functions and units collaboratively set the technology course. The leading practitioners of convergence recognize that it is all about the process. It would be foolish to think that in a time of hyperchange one management plan would be written in stone.

"We'd like to bring more strategic views to the table rather than just looking at the business plan and figuring out how we can support it through the business technology strategy plan," Paravicini goes on to say. "We should be able to give input and to feed propositions into the business plan based on emerging technologies and trends, and the implications to the business. We also went very quickly from a low degree to a high degree of offshoring and outsourcing. I'm very happy where we are, but we're by no means a mature company in a multi-vendor environment."[17]

As Paravicini demonstrated at Zurich, governance is more than just a check on policy compliance. Governance is an essential part of ensuring that technology is serving the needs of the business, that managers are collaborating on adoption decisions, and that investments are returning value to the enterprise objectives. Convergence through the BTM Framework is simply impossible without accountability through cross-functional governance.

The Final Takeaway: Are You Ready?

Do you have the right stuff for convergence management? What is the right stuff? In many ways BTM is simply good management. BTM Corporation's research consistently finds that companies that manage their business and technology holistically manage *everything* well.

Most organizations already have certain tools available for implementing the BTM framework—technology assets, funding, intelligence through data and metrics, and seasoned professionals. And you—a business leader—have in place some of the necessities like decision-making processes and collaborative groups. Although these will change and assume new roles and responsibilities, you are not starting from zero. The path has been marked ahead of you.

The following are some of the critical steps you and your organization will need to take:

Step 1: *Bring senior management on board.* Make sure senior management values the impact technology has on your business to ensure you have their full support of the initiative.

Step 2: *Work from a roadmap.* Be thorough and thoughtful. Let your management know how you wish to proceed, how long it will take, and what it will feel like at each milestone.

Step 3: *Don't stop with process or with organizational bodies.* Nothing will doom a program faster than to create operational handbooks and to put into place newly created boards and committees if they lack reliable information, authority, and usable technology.

Step 4: *Put first things first.* Focus initially on the acknowledged point of greatest pain—whether that's governance and investment management, or strategy execution, or any other area—and work to show value as soon as possible in terms those business professionals will appreciate. You will need to continue to make your supporters happy they have backed you—particularly in the beginning—and you will need to have ready answers for your critics.

Step 5: *Don't throw out the baby with your enterprise's bathwater.* Find ways of doing things that are within the boundaries of your business model. Increasing maturity doesn't mean discarding and replacing everything that makes your company what it is; rather, it means improving and sharpening what is in place and extending your strengths to become and remain a leader in your industry.

Step 6: *It's okay to start small.* Recognize that you can work on relatively isolated topics at the beginning of the journey, but that—as you move closer to convergence—your focus must broaden to all areas within Business Technology Management, to ensure that they all will arrive at the same location at the same time. Fortunately, with the work that has gone before, your program will have enjoyed successes, and it will have won over detractors. Converged behaviors become a way of life in converged enterprises.

These are the hallmarks of the converged organizations. By applying their lessons and interpreting them through the lens of your own business, your organization as well can realize the benefits of being a converged enterprise.

Maturing in convergence management is a big job, and it takes time. We have learned, however, that a payback can begin almost immediately, given the huge disconnect in so many firms.

Doing nothing is not an option. The changes sweeping over corporations and other organizations will not stop because they make us uncomfortable. Your organization is already experiencing the strain of these changes—globalization, speed, new competitors coming out of nowhere, existing competitors unpredictably changing the playing field. The only way to win is to get out ahead of these changes, to manage them in your favor. You can't do that today unless your business and technology are united as one.

Somebody has to make that happen. It may very well be you.

For Further Information

Online Supplementary Materials

One of the first steps you should take as you begin your journey toward convergence is learning where you stand today. As a supplement to the book, we have created a dedicated website that provides our readers with complimentary, online self-assessments focused on the key areas needed for effective business technology convergence. These assessments, along with other related materials available on the site, will help you organize necessary "next steps." These supporting resources focus on areas relevant to convergence, such as Governance, Strategy and Planning, Strategic Investment Management, Strategic Enterprise Architecture, Business Agility, Sustained Innovation, and Operational Excellence. To learn more, visit: www.thepowerofconvergence.com.

More from the Author

To review a full collection of writings published by Faisal Hoque, including articles, research reports, and blogs, as well as a library of audio and video clips, visit: www.faisalhoque.com.

The BTM Institute

The BTM Institute, founded by BTM Corporation in 2003, is the only global research think tank exclusively focused on the convergence of business and technology. Through various research and educational initiatives, publications, books, and knowledge exchanges, its goal remains to continuously advance the knowledge of Business Technology Management (BTM). To learn more, visit www.btminstitute.org.

Notes

Introduction

1. Faisal Hoque, *e-Enterprise: Business Models, Architecture, and Components* (Cambridge, UK: Cambridge University Press, 2000).
2. Faisal Hoque, *The Alignment Effect* (Upper Saddle River, NJ: Financial Times Press, 2002).
3. Faisal Hoque, Vallabh Sambamurthy, Robert Zmud, Tom Trainer, Carl Wilson, *Winning the 3-Legged Race* (Upper Saddle River, NJ: Financial Times Press, 2006).
4. *Business Technology Convergence Index*, A BTM Research Report (Stamford, CT: BTM Corporation, 2007); http://www.btmcorporation.com/regis tration/convergenceindex.aspx.
5. *Business Technology Convergence Index II,* A BTM Research Report (Stamford, CT: BTM Corporation, 2009); http://www.btmcorporation.com/regis tration/convergenceindex.aspx.

Chapter 1

1. Doug Bartholomew, "PLM: Boeing's Dream, Airbus' Nightmare," *Baseline* magazine, February 2007; http://www.purdue.edu/discoverypark/PLM/SME/ plmboeing.pdf.
2. Walsh, Lawrence M., "Symantec's Midnight at the Oasis," *Baseline* magazine, March 2008; http://www.baselinemag.com/c/a/Enterprise-Apps/Syman tecs-Midnight-at-the-Oasis/.
3. Ellen Messmer, "Compuware to Acquire Covisint B2B Exchange," *Network*

World, February 5, 2004; http://www.networkworld.com/news/2004/0205 covisint.html.

4. Kobe, Gerry, "Covisint Is Dying," *Automotive Industries*, December 2002; http://findarticles.com/p/articles/mi_m3012/is_12_182/ai_96553922/.

5. Songini, Marc L., "Ford Kills 'Everest' Procurement Software System," *ComputerWorld*, August 18, 2004; http://www.computerworld.com/s/article/ 95335/Ford_kills_Everest_procurement_software_system.

6. Ibid.

7. J. Nicholas Hoover, "FBI Director Reports on Delayed Sentinel System," *InformationWeek Government*, April 16, 2010; http://www.informationweek .com/news/government/enterprise-apps/showArticle.jhtml?articleID = 2244 00547&cid = nl_IW_daily_2010–09–16_h.

8. Goldstein, Harry, "Who Killed the Virtual Case File?" *IEEE Spectrum*, September 2005; http://spectrum.ieee.org/computing/software/who-killed-the -virtual-case-file.

9. Ibid.

Chapter 2

1. Board Briefing on IT Governance, 2nd Edition, The IT Governance Institute® and the Information Systems Audit and Control Association (ISACG)® 2003; http://www.isaca.org/Knowledge-Center/Research/Docu ments/BoardBriefing/26904eBoard_Briefing_final.pdf

Chapter 3

1. Kiley, David, "The New Heat on Ford," *BusinessWeek*, June 4, 2007; http:// www.businessweek.com/magazine/content/07_23/b4037036.htm.

2. Fortune 500, May 2010; http://money.cnn.com/magazines/fortune/fortune 500/2010/full_list/.

3. http://www.btmcorporation.com/Registration/convergenceindex.aspx.

4. http://www.btmcorporation.com/Registration/convergenceindex.aspx.

5. Vinton Cerf, "A Brief History of the Internet," The Internet Society (ISOC); http://www.isoc.org/internet/history/cerf.shtml.

6. The 0.5 revenue growth was net of the effect of two outliers in the pharmaceutical and electronics sectors, who undertook major acquisitions just prior to the start of the downturn. The combined effect of these outliers shifts revenue growth down by 2 percent, yielding a revenue growth of negative 1.5 percent for the convergence leaders.

Chapter 4

1. *Fortune*, May 3, 2010; http://money.cnn.com/magazines/fortune/fortune 500/2010/full_list.

2. Thomas H. Davenport and Jeanne G. Harris, *Competing on Analytics* (Cambridge, MA: Harvard Business School Press, 2007).

3. Netflix Prize, www.netflixprize.com.

4. Karen Breslau and Daniel McGinn, "Just the Ticket," *Newsweek*, September 26, 2005; http://www.mail-archive.com/medianews@twiar.org/msg04906.html.

5. Carl J. Schramm, *The Entrepreneurial Imperative* (New York: HarperBusiness, 2006), pages 1–2.

Chapter 5

1. National Research Council and Committee on Innovations in Computing and Communications: Lessons from History, *Funding a Revolution: Government Support for Computing Research* (Washington, D.C.: National Academies Press, 1999); http://www.nap.edu/openbook.php?record_id = 63 23&page = R1#.

2. BTM Corporation interview with Lester Diamond, former Assistant Director of the GAO, *IT Management Issues*, GAO, May 2005.

3. Eric Zeman, "Little Computer Makes a Big Impact" *Mobile Enterprise Magazine*, December 1, 2005.

4. United States Government Accountability Office (GAO), Report to Congressional Requesters, *CHIEF INFORMATION OFFICERS: Responsibilities and Information and Technology Governance at Leading Private-Sector Companies*, September 2005; http://library.ahima.org/xpedio/groups/public/doc uments/government/bok1_028283.pdf.

5. Dr. Patricia Diamond Fletcher, "Creating the Front Door to Government: A Case Study of the FirstGov Portal," *Library Trends* 52, no. 2 (Fall 2003), pages 268–281; http://www.ideals.illinois.edu/bitstream/handle/2142/8522/librarytrendsv52i2g_opt.pdf.jsessionid = E7EA3E4E6BE53919F88AD52C 937C1172?sequence;eq1.

6. Ibid., page 274.

7. Ibid., page 276.

8. Jeanne W. Ross and Cynthia M. Beath, "Beyond the Business Case: New Approaches to IT Investment," *MIT Sloan Management Review* 43, no. 2 (Winter 2002), pages 51–59; http://sloanreview.mit.edu/the-magazine/arti cles/2002/winter/4325/beyond-the-business-case-new-approaches-to-it-in vestment/.

Chapter 6

1. U.S. Small Business Administration; www.sba.gov/advo/stats/sbfaq.pdf.

2. U.S. Census Bureau and Kaufman Foundation; http://www.kauffman.org/newsroom/business-dynamic-statistics.aspx.

3. U.S. Small Business Administration; www.sba.gov/advo/stats/sbfaq.pdf.

4. Dave Hitz, *How to Castrate a Bull: Unexpected Lessons on Risk, Growth and Success in Business* (San Francisco: Jossey-Bass, 2009).
5. U.S. Census Bureau, 2010.
6. Thomas L. Friedman, *The World Is Flat* (New York: Farrar, Straus and Giroux, 2005), page 200.
7. See Chapter 5, "The Takeaway: Turning Ideas into Action."
8. Tom Steinert-Thelkeld, "Growth Spurt: Endo Pharmaceuticals," *Baseline* magazine, May 2003; http://www.baselinemag.com/c/a/Projects-Enterprise-Planning/Growth-Spurt-Endo-Pharmaceuticals/.

Chapter 7

1. "History of Saab"; http://www.swedecar.com/saab_history.htm.
2. General Motors and Investors AB bought a 50 percent stake in Saab in 1989 for $600 million that included an option to buy the remaining shares within a decade. In 2000, GM paid $125 million to make Saab a wholly owned subsidiary. Under GM ownership, Saab suffered declining sales like other GM brands. Under bankruptcy and reorganization pressure, GM sold Saab to Dutch sports car maker Spyker in February 2010.
3. Joseph A. Schumpeter, *Capitalism, Socialism and Democracy* (New York: Harper, 1975 [orig. pub. 1942]), pages 82–85.
4. Peter F. Drucker, "Modern Prophets: Schumpeter or Keynes?" *Forbes*, May 23, 1983, pages 124–128; http://www.druckersociety.at/index.php/peter-druck
erhome/texts/modern-prophets-schumpeter-or-keynes.
5. General Electric (GE) 2007 Annual Report; http://www.ge.com/ar2007/pdf/ge_ar2007_full_book.pdf.
6. Interview with Jorgen Vig Knudstrop, "Lego Group CEO Talks About Transforming This Toy Company One Brick at a Time," BTM Institute Executive Insights Series, 2008.

Chapter 8

1. *BTM Business Agility Index*, A BTM Research Report (Stamford, CT: BTM Corporation, 2010); http://www.btmcorporation.com/Registration/btmbusinessagilityindex.aspx.
2. Michael Schrage, "The Struggle to Define Agility," *CIO* magazine, August 15, 2004; http://www.cio.com.au/article/185655/struggle_define_agility/.
3. Stephen H. Haeckel, *Adaptive Enterprise: Creating and Leading Sense-and-Respond Organizations*. (Boston: Harvard Business School Press, 1999).
4. Haeckel, *Adaptive Enterprise*.
5. Rick Dove, *Response Ability: The Language, Structure, and Culture of the Agile Enterprise* (New York: Wiley, 2001).
6. Michael Treacy and Fred Wiersema, *The Discipline of Market Leaders:*

Choose Your Customers, Narrow Your Focus, Dominate Your Market (Reading, Mass.: Addison-Wesley, 1995).

7. Hau L. Lee, "The Triple-A-Supply Chain," *Harvard Business Review*, October 2004, pages 102–112; http://cours2.fsa.ulaval.ca/cours/gsf-60808/AAA_SupplyChain.pdf.

8. C. K. Prahalad and Venkat Ramaswamy, *The Future of Competition* (Boston: Harvard Business School Press, 2004); David Rocks, "Reinventing Herman Miller," *BusinessWeek E. Biz*, April 3, 2000.

Chapter 9

1. Peter Lewis, "Texas Instruments' Lunatic Fringe," *Fortune*, November 14, 2006; http://money.cnn.com/magazines/fortune/fortune_archive/2006/09/04/8384732/in dex.htm.

2. Faisal Hoque and Terry Kirkpatrick, *Sustained Innovation* (Stamford, CT: BTM Press, 2007).

3. *BTM Sustained Innovation Index*, A BTM Research Report (Stamford, CT: BTM Corporation, 2010); http://www.btmcorporation.com/Registration/btm sustainedinnovationind ex.aspx.

4. Arnold Kling and Nick Schultz, *From Poverty to Prosperity* (New York: Encounter Books, 2009).

5. Tom Kelley and Jonathan Littman, *The Ten Faces of Innovation* (New York: Doubleday, 2005).

6. Hoque et al., *Winning the 3-Legged Race*, chapter 5.

7. David Pollard, A Prescription for Business Innovation, 2004 http://blogs.salon.com/0002007/stories/2003/02/17/aPrescriptionForBusinessInnova tion.html.

8. Companies with outlying financials were excluded from the index to reduce the impact of unusual or one-time financial events on the overall index. Corrections were also applied to minimize the effect of under- or overrepresentation of industry groups.

Chapter 10

1. South Park Studios, "Underpants Gnomes," 1998.

2. *BTM Operational Excellence Index*, A BTM Research Report (Stamford, CT: BTM Corporation, 2010); http://www.btmcorporation.com/Registration/btmoperation alexcellence.aspx.

3. Jeffrey Bruckner, "Systemic Risk Poses Big Threats," *Baseline*, July 2010; http://www.baselinemag.com/c/a/IT-Management/Systemic-Risk-Poses-Big-Threats-512852/.

Chapter 11

1. Elizabeth Ferrarini, "DaVita CEO Talks About Giving New Life to a Healthcare Provider," BTM Institute, November 2008.

2. Ibid.
3. Ibid.
4. Ferrarini, "CIO of New York City's Largest Hospital Talks About How IT Improves the Quality of Patient Care," BTM Institute, July 2008.
5. Ibid.
6. Ferrarini, "Eastern Mountain Sports CIO Jeffrey Neville Talks About the Convergence Across the Enterprise," BTM Institute, May 2008.
7. Ferrarini, "Chevron CIO Talks About the Challenges of Getting the Right Investment Mix," BTM Institute, April 2008.
8. Ibid.
9. Ibid.
10. Ferrarini, "Physician and CEO Dr. Richard Salluzzo Talks About Transforming Two Healthcare Facilities," BTM Institute, February 2008.
11. Ibid.
12. Ibid.
13. Ibid.
14. Ferrarini, "DaVita CEO Talks About Giving New Life to a Healthcare Provider," BTM Institute, November 2008.
15. Ferrarini, Elizabeth M., "Zurich Financial CIO Michael Paravicini Talks About Bringing Technology and Business Closer," BTM Institute, June 2008.
16. Ibid.
17. Ibid.

Index

About the Author and Contributors

FAISAL HOQUE is the founder and chief executive officer of BTM Corporation, a management solutions provider that leads the industry in the convergence of business and technology management with unique products and solutions that innovate new business models, enhance financial performance, and improve operational efficiency. For his commitment to the convergence of business and technology, *CIO Quarterly* magazine designated him "Mr. Convergence." In May 2008, the editors of Ziff-Davis Enterprise listed him in their "Top 100 Most Influential People in Technology" for helping organizations transform into "whole-brained enterprises."

A native of Bangladesh, Mr. Hoque came to the United States at the age of seventeen and immediately began working toward achieving the dreams that drove him to move here. He built his first commercial business technology product at the age of nineteen while studying at the University of Minnesota, and went on to hold management positions in Pitney Bowes and then Dun and Bradstreet. In 1994, General Electric (GE) recruited him, then one of its youngest technology executives, to launch a comprehensive business-to-business electronic commerce spin-off. As a serial entrepreneur, he founded two other award-winning companies prior to the BTM Corporation and is an early pioneer of reusable software application components.

His founding of BTM Corporation in 1999 turned into a convergence crusade. Along the way, Hoque has written five management books, established a nonprofit institute—The BTM Institute—and become a leading authority on the effective interaction between business and technology.

Two of his previous books, *Sustained Innovation* and *Winning the 3-Legged Race*, were included in *CIO Insight*'s feature "Five Insightful Transformation Books," while *Sustained Innovation* also ranked in *CIO Insight* magazine's "Editor's Picks: The 10 Best Business Books of 2007." A regular contributor to *Baseline* magazine and *CIO Update*, his articles have also been featured in publications such as *BusinessWeek*, *The Economist*, *Forbes*, *Wall Street Journal*, and *CIO* magazine.

For more information about Faisal Hoque, please visit: www.faisal hoque.com.

About the Contributors

Lawrence M. Walsh is an award-winning journalist, editor, and technology advisor. He has written for and edited such market-leading publications as *Information Security*, *VARBusiness,* and *Baseline* magazines; several newspapers, including the *Boston Globe*, *Brockton Enterprise*, and *MetroWest Daily News*; and organizations, including the American Society of Business Publication Editors, the New England Newspaper Association, the New England Press Association, and the Massachusetts Press Association. Walsh is the founder of The 2112 Group, a technology channel advisory firm. He currently writes the technology business blog "Channelnomics" and freelances for publications such as *Newsmax*.

Diana L. Mirakaj is responsible for leading global marketing and corporate development at BTM Corporation. As chief marketing officer, she focuses on corporate messaging, market branding, and the distribution of content through various media channels. Prior to joining BTM Corporation in 2004, Ms. Mirakaj held roles within UBS Investment Bank in International Equity Capital Markets, and then the Corporate Client Services Group. Her background provides a unique perspective in translating the connection between business strategy and the value of technology.

Jeffrey Bruckner is responsible for leading knowledge and framework architecture at BTM Corporation. As chief knowledge officer, he brings more than thirty years of experience spanning management consulting, methodology research and development, process and decision modeling, technology operations, outsourcing development, software engineering, and human capital management. In an effort to create methods for maximizing the value of the interaction between business and technology, he developed the Information Technology Decision Framework and the Decision Dialog model.